The Critical Study of Non-Religion

Bloomsbury Advances in Religious Studies

Series Editors: Bettina E. Schmidt, Steven Sutcliffe and Will Sweetman
Founding Editors: James Cox and Peggy Morgan

Bloomsbury Advances in Religious Studies publishes cutting-edge research in the Study of Religion/s. The series draws on anthropological, ethnographical, historical, sociological and textual methods amongst others. Topics are diverse, but each publication integrates theoretical analysis with empirical data. The series aims to refresh the interdisciplinary agenda in new evidence-based studies of 'religion'.

The Critical Study of Non-Religion

Discourse, Identification and Locality

Christopher R. Cotter

BLOOMSBURY ACADEMIC

LONDON • NEW YORK • OXFORD • NEW DELHI • SYDNEY

BLOOMSBURY ACADEMIC
Bloomsbury Publishing Plc
50 Bedford Square, London, WC1B 3DP, UK
1385 Broadway, New York, NY 10018, USA

BLOOMSBURY, BLOOMSBURY ACADEMIC and the Diana logo are
trademarks of Bloomsbury Publishing Plc

First published in Great Britain 2020

A catalogue record for this book is available from the British Library.

A catalog record for this book is available from the Library of Congress.

ISBN: HB: 978-1-3500-9524-3
         ePDF: 978-1-3500-9525-0
        eBook: 978-1-3500-9526-7

Bloomsbury Advances in Religious Studies

Typeset by Integra Software Services Pvt. Ltd.

To find out more about our authors and books visit www.bloomsbury.com
and sign up for our newsletters.

For Saoirse, whose imminent arrival pushed me
to finally finish this book.

Contents

List of illustrations

Figures

Tables

Acknowledgements

This book could never have come to fruition without the generous support of the Arts and Humanities Research Council during my doctoral study at Lancaster University, and the Leverhulme Trust in my current position at the University of Edinburgh.

Thanks are due to all who helped with my empirical research, particularly the Southside Heritage Group, Southside Community Centre, the Museum of Edinburgh, the University of Edinburgh's Scottish Studies library and, most importantly, all those Southsiders who gave of their time and themselves.

Thanks to all at Lancaster University and to the continued support and friendship from colleagues at the British Association for the Study of Religions, the Nonreligion and Secularity Research Network, the Religious Studies Project and Culture on the Edge. Thanks to Martin Stringer and Linda Woodhead for their thorough examination of my doctoral dissertation, to Steve Sutcliffe for his supervision of my pre-doctoral degrees and current mentoring at Edinburgh, to Carole Cusack for the unofficial mentoring and opportunities, and to the anonymous peer reviewers and all at Bloomsbury. Thanks also to, in alphabetical order, Naomi Appleton, Stephen Bullivant, Tommy Coleman, Ryan Cragun, James Eglinton, Lois Lee, Eoin O'Mahony, Russell McCutcheon, David Robertson, Johannes Quack, Ethan Quillen, Liam Sutherland, Teemu Taira, Jonathan Tuckett and Kevin Whitesides – I owe you all a drink. And to the most important colleague of all, Kim Knott – I couldn't have asked for a better doctoral supervisor, and I couldn't have done this without you. Thank you, Kim.

Finally, a huge thank you to those in my life outside academia – through singing, acting, politics and the vicissitudes of life – for their grounding, support and enthusiasm, and for making this all worthwhile. Thanks to Bob, Lindsey, Geoff, Ben and Kate for proofreading help – and to Lindsey once more for doing it all again! To Mum, Dad, Lindsey, Keith and Sarah-Lou, whose support and belief go far beyond family. And to Saoirse for making this happen.

Introduction

Non-religion, non-religions, non-religious

'So, what is it that you do, Chris?'

This is a fraught question for anyone at the best of times. It's a question I try my best not to ask others. Or, when I do ask, I try and remove the risk of defining someone by their work or their potential worth in terms of capital – social, economic, cultural or otherwise – by asking, 'What do you like to do?', 'What do you do in your spare time?' or 'Tell me a bit about yourself: who is <X>?' Not perfect questions, by any means, but should my conversation partners then wish to define themselves in terms of their economic activity – through passion or habit – that is their choice. And oftentimes this leads to a more interesting conversation for everyone involved, if only for the sheer novelty of briefly stepping outside of our habitual opening gambits.

However, for those of us who are positioned within the academic field of Religious Studies, the question 'what do you do' comes with additional, field-specific anxieties. The admission that one is a Religious Studies scholar tends to produce – in my experience – one of three responses: the assumption that you are training for Christian ministry, a question about whether you are 'religious' or bafflement as to why someone might study something so esoteric with such seemingly limited economic prospects. Depending on my mood, on whether I feel like getting into a lengthy conversation or on whether I feel like using the conversation as a data-gathering exercise, I may deflect the question with a stock response of 'an academic', 'a lecturer at the university', 'a social scientist', 'a sociologist' or the like. Sometimes the word 'religion' will creep into my response, heavily caveated with qualifiers: 'I'm a sociologist of religion', 'I study/teach the critical social science of religion', 'I work on the comparative study of religion' and so on. You have to pick your battles, and sometimes a social interaction just doesn't call for a lengthy digression on how people don't tend to ask criminologists if they are criminals or medical students if they are ill, nor on how the myths, rituals, values, morals, philosophies, lifestyles, practices, politics, truth claims, cultural artefacts and more that we tend to associate with 'religion' – and the very political acts of deeming something 'religion' or not – are far from esoteric and have had, and continue to have, major ramifications that affect our day-to-day lives.

Given that my empirical research over the past decade has focused mainly upon 'non-religion' in various forms, my response to this question is made both easier and harder. Easier because I get to sidestep some potential stock responses by identifying myself as 'the Atheism Guy' in the Religious Studies department or by semi-seriously pointing to 'all that stuff that you would assume goes on in a Religious Studies department' and claiming that I do the boundary work by studying 'everything else'. Harder because of a prevalent assumption that I must be engaged in some sort of 'know thy enemy' mission – particularly given that I have spent most of my academic career in a School of Divinity[1] – and also because, as if 'religion' wasn't esoteric enough, how might I even begin to define what counts as a legitimate object of my study?

These personal struggles are woven throughout this book and are part and parcel of what makes the critical study of non-religion such a fascinating area of research. This book constitutes what I consider to be the first serious and substantial attempt to engage with a constituency so often excluded from the purview of Religious Studies whilst taking full account of the devastating critiques that have been levelled at the ideological underpinnings of Religious Studies over the past twenty to thirty years. This book concerns borders and boundaries, politics and identity politics, disciplinary struggles, personal stories, the practice of research, why any of this should matter and more. But before I go any further, and before the reader is lulled into thinking that my own story is what is solely at focus here, let us take a detour through three brief stories, which each provide multiple entry points into what's in store in the chapters that follow.

* * *

Keith – a cheerful, down-to-earth guy in his late forties, with a keen interest in football – is a native of Edinburgh, Scotland. More precisely, he is a *Southsider*. He has lived and worked in Edinburgh's Southside for almost his entire life – 'I moved away, but I've always come back' – and managed a pub in the area for many years. Keith claims to have never been 'big on religion'.

Keith's wife is Catholic, and thus he imagines he'd 'probably be more at church now... with her and her family', yet the 'long-winded' nature of the services hasn't inspired him to 'change my religion and become a Catholic'. As he gets older, he finds himself increasingly attending funerals,

> which is weird. I'm getting to know hymns a lot better. But, me … growing up … I was never. I wasn't … my mother and father weren't religious either, so … we were never a religious family and … not that I had any, I never had a faith, but … when I lost my mum and dad to cancer … that just sorta put [an end to it], coz they weren't, I mean, they were a good age but then I just sorta … any interest I had <pause> I probably lost … eh, when they died, aye. And, various other members of my family. … I've found <pause> that's probably the closest I've got to religion is being … is going to funerals … I just find … they always seem to use the same sermon, which doesn't … which never makes it feel, em, very personal … Which puts me off as well … Especially if they were young, and <long pause> I don't understand why, I don't … I still don't understand why people, some people have to die so young … when there's arseholes still alive, like you know what I mean? That's the bit I don't get … I don't think anybody could ever explain it to me, so …

* * *

Across the Atlantic in Canada[2] we meet Mohammed – a young man originally from Pakistan, who enjoys trail running in the woods and mountains around Vancouver's North Shore. He is 'definitely an atheist' but describes being 'born into Islam', with a father who was 'very religious' and 'strict'. His mother and sister's experience as women in this context apparently caused Mohammed to draw away from 'organized religion', which he found 'for the most part to be patriarchal, hegemonic, hierarchical'. Yet atheism is not the full picture for Mohammed:

> I admire Buddhism. I meditate every day. I go to the Buddhist temple for my lunch break. But I wouldn't call myself a Buddhist, I just like the Buddhist philosophy. I like being in the present moment, the concept of no self, how our ego is just something that we create. And we're all sort of like one.

He finds the Buddhist temple 'super nice and welcoming' but finds those at the mosque to be more judgemental – 'maybe it's the Pakistani culture'? At the same time, 'because I'm brown, and my first name is Mohammed, I'm still a victim of Islamophobia', and even though he acknowledges that he is Islamophobic himself, in an ideological sense, 'when someone is Islamophobic to me I find myself defending Islam'.

* * *

Back in Scotland, Niamh – a young, first-year student of Celtic studies at the University of Edinburgh – hails from the north of England. Her mother's side of the family is Irish Catholic, whilst her father's is Protestant. For Niamh, religion was 'always about family relationships and politics, basically. It was never about faith'. She acknowledges that she might appear 'contradictory', having enjoyed reading *The God Delusion* (Dawkins 2007) and regularly self-describing as an atheist but also finding herself in church when personal circumstances are causing anxiety. In her own words: 'I swing from not really knowing if there's a God or not, to being adamant there isn't, to finding myself praying when I hit rock bottom.' She stopped regularly attending religious services at the age of fourteen (having previously attended Catholic and Methodist services), is unsure how she feels about life after death, acknowledges that religion has 'done a lot of bad things in the world' and concludes, laughing: 'when I think about it I'm an atheist; when I'm in trouble I'm not.' Regardless of these 'contradictions' and 'fluctuations', if asked on a survey about her religion, she wouldn't claim to have none:

> You can't escape your childhood really and I still ... I would put myself as a Catholic mostly because I don't want to be associated with my Grandma ... and that sounds horrible, but ... I don't want to be like her in any way because she's ... done so much damage ... and so if I identify myself as something, I identify myself as a Catholic because of that.

* * *

I have long been a believer in the power of three. In this context, I'm not referring to the 'charmed ones' (although the invocation of Rose McGowan is never a bad thing) but to the power of three quotidian exemplars to open the door to a deeper theoretical discussion. For the scholar of religion, these brief introductions to Keith, Mohammed and Niamh should immediately provoke a whole raft of questions.

A first batch might include: Are these three individuals to be classified as non-religious or religious? What is the relationship between family and religious identity? Do traumatic experiences tend to push people towards religion or non-religion? What is the connection, if any, between religion and morality? Is religion a choice? Is this choice rational? What is the relationship between institutional and individual forms of religion? Is religion separable from culture? From ethnicity? Why might an individual give different answers to religion-related questions in different contexts? What does it mean to participate in or identify with religion for other-than-religious reasons? At what point does 'liking' a religion equate to being an adherent of that religion?

And in a second batch: What does the term 'religion' bring to these three narratives? Do we need to bring it in at all? When these individuals are classified as 'religious' or 'non-religious', who is doing the classification, what position are they speaking from, what purpose does the classification serve and who gains or loses through such a classification? Where do folk models of religion come from; that is where do people get the standards by which something is judged to be authentically 'religious' or not? Why might we assume consistency? How are these individuals' narratives relating to religion affected by their position in other interlocking systems of oppression and privilege such as sex, gender, class, race, income, health, age and more?

The first batch of questions are examples of the type of question that I brought with me when I began my journey in the study of religion as an undergraduate at the University of Edinburgh. Although I occasionally strayed from the path – taking worthwhile courses in New Testament, Islamic history, systematic theology, Hebrew Bible – I intuitively knew from the start that I wanted to position myself within Religious Studies, and not one of the other (as I saw them) narrower or more confessional subject areas on offer within the School of Divinity. Soon I was being introduced to the work of scholars such as Talal Asad, Timothy Fitzgerald, Bruce Lincoln, Luther Martin, Tomoko Masuzawa, Russell McCutcheon, Robert Segal and Donald Wiebe, and taking classes which cast an enthusiastic but critically engaged gaze at Islamic Eschatology and Art (with Christian Lange), the Sociology of Religion (with Carole Cusack), Phenomenology of Religion and African Indigenous Traditions (with James Cox) and New Age Spiritualities (with Steven Sutcliffe). These teachers were those with whom I found the most affinity, those who (to my mind) worked with interesting substantive case studies from across the globe and throughout history, but who saw these case studies not as ends in themselves but as contributing to a larger theoretical project which went far beyond the study of religion. The seeds for my interest in the second batch of questions – and, thus, in the *critical* study of religion – had been sown.

In the second year of my degree I was introduced to the late Jonathan Z. Smith – specifically his seminal 'Religion, Religions, Religious' (1998), to which I have paid homage in the title for this introductory chapter. Here, through a broad-ranging discussion of the colonial exploits of various European states, Smith argues:

> 'Religion' is not a native category. It is not a first person term of self-characterization. It is a category imposed from the outside on some aspect

of native culture. It is the other, in these instances colonialists, who are solely responsible for the content of the term. (1998: 269)

This is my first recollection of being won over to the idea that religion is a problematic and contested category which can be (and indeed is) strategically deployed in several distinct yet interrelated ways by individuals, groups and societies as they go about their daily lives. It is a word that is laden with power and hostage to its own very particular history. The concept 'is absent in the ancient world' (Nongbri 2013: 4) and finds its way to its contemporary 'common sense' usage through a complex etymological process, first through the Latin *religio* (worship practices, superstition, etc.) of the early decades of the first millennium, through to the development of the twin concepts *religiosus* and *saecularis* of the mediaeval period, which distinguished between clergy leading a monastic lifestyle and those pursuing their calling in the 'secular' world (Nongbri 2013: 5, 28–31; Asad 1993: 39). It has been argued that until the early Enlightenment period 'there was arguably no concept in the English language' either of 'a religion' or of 'secular neutrality', and that 'religion' was a term applied solely to 'Christian Truth' in contrast to others' 'barbaric superstitions' (Fitzgerald 2007a: 283). In the Enlightenment period, with the European 'discovery' of new worlds, and the attendant rise in colonial exploitation, the notion of 'religions' then began to take shape due to 'an explosion of data' (J. Z. Smith 1998: 275). This same period saw the rise in the concept of 'the secular' as a separable, public, 'neutral' space and the compartmentalization of religion into 'the private sphere, the realm of conscience, apart from the public sphere of the state' (Knott 2005: 66).

Thus, the contemporary term 'religion' is implicated in a particular historical trajectory, constructed along the lines of Protestant Christianity, and 'deeply implicated … in the discourses of modernity, especially … in technologies of power' (Jantzen 1998: 8). This argument forms the backbone of the aforementioned 'critical' study of religion, a distinctive position within contemporary academia, which is primarily concerned with 'the critical historical deconstruction of "religion" and related categories' (Fitzgerald 2015b: 303–4). The basic premise of this position is social constructionism, holding that 'there is no such thing that answers to the name "religion"', but only phenomena that 'we habitually label religious' for historically contingent reasons (Jong 2015: 20). With this book, I position myself firmly in this critical strand of the contemporary study of religion, whilst also retaining a keen interest in the sorts of empirical questions that I have rhetorically grouped together in my first batch above.

The critical study of non-religion

The first decades of the twenty-first century have seen a marked rise in the number of individuals choosing to not identify as religious across the (Western) world.

> In both the United States and Canada, for example, religious nones have steadily risen since the late 1980s and early 1990s: today, nearly one-fifth of Americans and a quarter of Canadians do not identify with any religion …These figures contrast those in 1985 when religious nones made up 7 percent of the American population and 11 percent of the Canadian population. Comparable trends are also evident in Western Europe … and Australia. … Representing historic highs in these countries, religious nones are expected to continue to grow for the foreseeable future. (Thiessen and Wilkins-Laflamme 2017: 64)

Debates continue to rage as to the significance of this apparent rise and what it might mean and the causal relationship between these apparent statistical 'facts' and the methodologies used to produce them. Nevertheless, the same decades have seen a related rise in academic studies of what it might mean to be other than religious, and a burgeoning body of substantive data from work in psychology, anthropology, sociology, history and other disciplines, mapping and theorizing the beliefs, practices, identifications, values and social contexts of 'non-religious' populations. In Chapter 1 I provide a synthesis of the key research in this area to date.

Given my brief introduction to the critical approach (more on this in Chapter 2), it is little surprise that scholars who label themselves as 'critical' tend to be broadly dismissive of studies of 'non-religion', viewing them as simply reproducing and perpetuating the attendant problems of the category 'religion', and as uncritically reifying and substantiating a category created for multiple-choice surveys. On the other hand, many of those scholars who are engaged in such studies seem quite uninterested in important questions surrounding category formation, classification, power, authority, essentialism, legitimation and so on. This is not to say that there is no quality substantive work being carried out; as we shall see in Chapter 1, this is far from the case. However, from a critical perspective, most of these studies are merely peppered with a few peripheral references to Talal Asad, with the main goal being to continue gathering, typologizing and theorizing data for a new field of study on 'the nones', 'non-religion', 'the secular' or whatever they choose to call it. In this book, I argue that both camps have a lot to learn from each other and that it is possible for rigorous empirical work to be conducted ostensibly under the religion/non-religion binary with the potential or explicit aim of contributing to the critical project. This book represents an original attempt at doing so – as both a manifesto and a first step in putting that manifesto into practice. Hence the title: *The Critical Study of Non-Religion*. But what of the subtitle?

Discourse, identification and locality

It is rhetorically useful for me to reflect on this book's subtitle – *Discourse, Identification and Locality* – via a further look at my own research trajectory. In 2008/2009, following a roundtable discussion in the School of Divinity upon the publication of David Fergusson's *Faith and Its Critics* (2009), I became interested in applying the theories, methods and insights of the discipline (as I then understood them) to the recent construction of 'New Atheism' (coined in Wolf 2006). While researching my undergraduate dissertation – which examined the narratives of four popular atheist authors in comparison with Enlightenment, Romantic and New Age themes (Cotter 2011a) – I became aware of a substantial gap in existing literature concerning religion's 'other', the 'non-religious', which did not easily fit within standard models in the academic study of religion. It turned out that my recognition of this gap was shared with many others around the same time, and I had the privilege to attend the inaugural conference of the Nonreligion and Secularity Research Network at Wolfson College, University of Oxford, on 11 December 2009. Through this network (of which I am currently co-director) I became socialized into an emerging scholarly community and quickly embraced some of the key questions that were motivating the field at the time, producing an analytic typology of the narratives of ostensibly non-religious Edinburgh students via my Master's dissertation (Cotter 2011b, again at the University of Edinburgh). In this dissertation, I adapted an earlier iteration of Lois Lee's oft-cited definition of non-religion as 'anything which is *primarily* defined by a relationship of difference to religion' (Lee 2012b: 131; emphasis in original). However, my own thoughts concerning how to best understand non-religion within Religious Studies have developed in my subsequent publications and doctoral thesis through a combination of three broad scholarly currents – both within and outside the study of the other-than-religious – and the coalescence of my 'identity' as a critical scholar of 'religion'.

The first of these currents concerns the 'discursive' study of religion. The specifics of this approach will be discussed in detail in Chapters 2 and 3, but for now, it suffices to state that discursive approaches are directly related to more formal forms of Discourse Analysis which have emerged, primarily from scholars within linguistics, over the past twenty years or so (Wodak and Meyer 2009: 2–3), although the origins of a discursive line of thought can be traced to the late 1960s/early 1970s (see van Dijk 2007). Acknowledging the constructed nature of religion and its implication in power structures such as law courts, 'the hegemonic discourse of the national media', 'parliamentary forums' and so on (Asad 2003: 12), recent years have seen some critical scholars 'move away from attempts at defining the term "religion"' (Quillen 2015a: 30) and instead utilize the analytical tools of Discourse Analysis to focus on 'the processes that make certain things … recognizably religious' (Bender 2012: 275) – in other words, on *discourse*. In retrospect, many of the key texts that had already played a key role in my scholarly development could be interpreted as incorporating discursive analysis (e.g. Fitzgerald 2000b, 2007a; Masuzawa 2005; McCutcheon 1997, 2007), but the years around the start of my doctoral study produced a critical mass of publications – particularly Garling (2013), Granholm (2013), Hjelm (2011), Moberg (2013), von Stuckrad (2003, 2010b, 2013a, b) and Taira (2013) – which provided the theoretical and methodological push for my nascent doctoral project.

I began to feel some discomfort concerning my Master's research and the way I had placed individuals into ideal-typical categories. None of the participants in this research were easy to classify into one of the five types I proposed – naturalistic, humanistic, familial, spiritual and philosophical – and all made statements which could be associated with other types. I shall return to this in greater detail in Chapter 2, but on revisiting this research with some chronological distance, and with the discussion above in mind, I realized that many of the difficulties associated with the generalizing classifications I had made could be overcome by reframing these types in terms of what my informants *said*, that is, in terms of discourse. Indeed, an embryonic version of this shift can already be detected in my move from speaking of types of non-religion to 'types of narrative' in a publication emerging from my Master's project (Cotter 2015). A shift in focus from the individual to the discourse they employ, from the person to what they say, and how they say it, allows the social reality of the individual to be incorporated analytically into the wider societal conversation of which they are inherently a part. Thus, my doctoral project began to take on the discursive thrust which characterizes much of this book, with the theoretical and methodological approach being outlined in detail in Chapters 2 and 3, and the empirical results infusing the remainder of the volume (particularly

Chapter 4). This thrust was helped enormously by being based at Lancaster University for my doctoral study – which, unknown to me at the time, was a global leader in Critical Discourse Analysis with Norman Fairclough, Ruth Wodak and others – and through interacting closely with Edinburgh-based colleagues David G. Robertson and Ethan G. Quillen, who were also embracing discursive approaches in their doctoral studies (Quillen 2015a, b; Robertson 2016).

The second current concerns a move away from the study of identities to the study of identification. The conceptualization of individuals as embodying a number of discrete, ideal-typical identities relating to religion, politics, gender, ethnicity and so on can be very valuable – indeed, sometimes absolutely necessary for macro-level, quantitatively focused analysis – but it fundamentally breaks down at the level of the individual where heterogeneity and contextuality abound. 'Religious, spiritual, secular, and non-religious identities are not stable, unitary formations' (Hoesly 2015: 9), but rather 'operational acts of identification' (Bayart 2005: 92). My engagement with this line of argument has been greatly facilitated by the research collaborative *Culture on the Edge*, which began in the Spring of 2012, with the aim of using 'social theory to offer more nuanced understandings of how those things that we commonly call "identities" are manufactured, managed, and continually reproduced'.[3] Following Jean-Francois Bayart's *The Illusion of Cultural Identity* (2005), this collaborative (of which I am now a part) proposes

> moving from studying identity as the presupposition of an inner sentiment that is somehow externalized in the public domain (i.e., the assumption that drives such common phrases as 'express yourself',) towards a method that, instead, analyzes discrete strategies of identification and the situationally-specific techniques that create a sense of authenticity, autonomy, and/or primordiality.[4]

Although most scholars who employ ideal types (myself at many times included) have never claimed that classifying individuals is a simple matter and have emphasized that there is a large amount of overlap between identities, it is almost invariably the case that their artificial and constructed nature becomes lost in translation, giving the false impression that individuals can be easily boxed off into one of a discrete number of identity silos.

With this critique in mind, I began to take my lead from Johannes Quack's 'relational approach' (2014) – a ground-up methodology which utilizes the notion of non-religion as 'a descriptive term for a certain group of understudied phenomena and not as an analytical term aiming to draw clear boundaries between religion and non-religion' (2014: 441). Non-religion, in this understanding, is not everything which is not religious. Neither does utilizing the term mean that one is defending 'any universal distinction between religion and non-religion' (2014: 441). Merely for analytical purposes these are understood as mutually exclusive categories; they do not cover the full range of extant phenomena. For Quack,

> 'Non-religion' is not to be understood as a something with thing-like existence, not as something that has clear definitions with primary and secondary features but as denoting various ways of relating to religion (whatever is understood to be religious in any specific case). (2014: 448)

And thus, the study of 'non-religious identities' becomes the study of various 'operational acts of identification' in a particular context, relative to particular contextual constructions of 'religion' – more on this in the chapters that follow (particularly 2, 3 and 4).

As should be clear from the above, my interest in the study of non-religion was developing away from grand theorizing and typologizing, towards a nuanced, critical, relational and discursive approach. This sits well with a third current in the academic study of religion, a body of work which aims to particularize our study by focusing upon specific localities, namely spaces, whether material or discursive, that are 'meaningful for those [actors] within it', are 'important for individual and group identity' and are 'practical working environment[s]', which are also amenable to academic study due to their size and relative internal coherence (Knott 1998: 283–4). One of the key advocates of such an approach is Kim Knott, whom I had sought out as my doctoral supervisor.

Again, more shall be said on this in the following chapters, but existing studies of religion in/and locality demonstrate enormous potential for both the 'expansion and subversion of the category "religion"' (T. Jenkins 1999: 12) and, by extension, 'non-religion' (see O'Mahony 2014). Space and locality have been theorized in a manner which makes them eminently compatible with the discursive current outlined above. Spaces are 'conceived (in language)' that is read, heard and uttered (Knott 2005: 17, 40) and, like discourses, are 'socially constituted' in a manner that is dynamic and 'full of power and symbolism', making them 'complex web[s] of relations of domination and subordination, of solidarity and co-operation' (N. Smith and Katz 1993: 155–6). Importantly, from a critical perspective, '[a]n examination of specific places (whether physical, social or discursive) … challenges the conception of "World Religions" as unities focused on discrete, systematic sets of traditions, and normative beliefs and practices' (Knott 2009: 159), and similarly affects conceptualizations of the non-religious. Localities are 'more than a mere context or backdrop' for the playing out of interactions between various actors (Knott 2009: 159), and although specific localities 'cannot be said to exhibit agency' by themselves, they affect 'agency in those who experience and participate' in them (Knott 2005: 129). The research that forms the empirical backbone of the arguments advanced in this book was conducted with a specific locality at focus – Edinburgh's Southside.

Finally, it is worth acknowledging a more unpleasant factor which contributed to the critical thrust of this book, and the specific approaches taken. A few months before my doctoral study was to commence, a senior colleague asked to see a copy of my research proposal. Upon sharing the two-page summary version with them, I received an e-mail arguing that my proposed project was completely unoriginal and that I had appropriated this scholar's work without acknowledgement, leaving them feeling surprised, saddened and personally let down. This is not the place to get into the specifics of these charges, which I still believe to be baseless and overblown. However, this power-play towards a fledgling academic who had not yet begun doctoral study has stuck with me to this day and had a profound effect on the direction my work has taken. Had this colleague responded with pride and interest in the common threads they found, this book might have been quite different. Indeed, I may have ended up much more firmly in the 'substantive' camp, with quite a different (and, I would now argue, worse) book to show for it. So, in a sense, I am grateful that this incident occurred. But, further – and more importantly – as seen in Acknowledgements, each of the strands that has been intentionally woven into the substance of this book has in large part been the result of supportive, collegial engagement in both the 'meat-world' (see Tuckett and Robertson 2014) and the virtual world. I am pleased with how things have turned out, and grateful to all those friends and colleagues who have been supportive conversation partners along the way. Hopefully, as readers, you will be too …

Summary of the book

In many senses, this book can be read as part textbook, part manifesto and part original empirical study. As mentioned above, I begin in Chapter 1 with a broad survey of current research on the non-religious, with a focus on the UK. I set critical issues aside in this chapter and instead build a case for the study of non-religion and present an up-to-date overview of the field focusing upon vocabulary, demographics and statistics, some key manifestations – New Atheism and Humanism – and some central issues emerging in contemporary scholarship. In Chapter 2 I then place critical issues front and centre by introducing the 'critical religion' approach and applying this to the body of research introduced in Chapter 1. After dispensing with the approaches I dub 'insubstantial', 'context-specific' and 'substantial' – whether through being too narrowly focused to prove useful at the level of theory and comparison, through an over-proliferation of terms or through ideological assumptions entangled with the category of 'religion'. I build a case for the discursive study of non-religion and outline the research agenda for the rest of the book, that is to take up Timothy Fitzgerald's call for the interrogation of the discourse that distinguishes between the religious and the non-religious, but also to go further and provide space for empirical work that goes beyond the 'merely' intellectual and discursive. Chapter 3 takes the theoretical arguments advanced thus far and addresses the task of operationalizing them in an empirical project. I outline what my discursive approach will look like in practice, argue for locality as a viable organizing rubric and introduce readers to my chosen field site – the Southside of Edinburgh – and the specific bodies of data and analytic techniques I embrace. These include seventy-one interview transcripts and sixty-two questionnaire responses, which were analysed using close reading and multi-level Discourse Analysis and triangulated with historical data sources and ethnographic observation. Chapters 4 to 7 then present the results of this empirical endeavour.

Chapter 4 maps the religion-related field of discourse in Edinburgh's Southside, demonstrating that it encompasses a wide variety of discourses with specific entanglements. Through in-depth discussion of discourses on multiculturalism, moderation, meaning, morality and more, certain discourses are shown to be effectively 'a-religious' in that they can be 'described and analysed without any reference to religious phenomena' (Quack 2014: 446), whilst others cannot be described without recourse to contextual constructions of religion (and non-religion). The chapter demonstrates the importance of looking beyond the surface of discourses and tempers the temptation to reify the religion-related field, focusing attention instead on the nature and implications of its entanglements with other fields of discourse.

In Chapter 5 I argue for setting aside the particularities of the religion-related 'identities' of individuals and communities, viewing them rather as 'operational acts of identification' (Bayart 2005). Through these 'relational' (Quack 2014) and 'situational' (Stringer 2008) acts of identification, social actors make use of discursive resources to contextually position themselves and others in relation to religion. Some of these contextual acts result in the positioning of phenomena as 'non-religious'. In other cases, the non-religious is implicit in the subject position of particular actors. In all cases, religion-related categories act in dialectical interplay with categories such as politics, science or nature (Fitzgerald 2015b). Chapter 6 then argues that configurations of 'religion' and 'non-religion' are heavily influenced by 'local particularity' (T. Jenkins 1999). Factors that are specific to the Southside are shown to be written into the structure of the religion-related field, leading to the conclusion that locality actively participates in the construction of religion and non-religion in this context.

In Chapter 7 I reflect on what my empirical work says to the critically problematic notion of 'indifference' to religion. My analysis suggests that, in some instances, the *performance* of indifference is a tactic for coping with contextually meaningful difference. Indifference can conceal positive and negative attitudes, mask the hegemony of Christianity and contribute to the maintenance of 'liberal secular principles' (Fitzgerald 2015b: 306). The book then concludes with an epilogue, which draws these conclusions and more together and calls for studies of religion and non-religion to incorporate a range of positions which can act as productive means to further demystify the ideological functions of these categories in the academy and wider society. I end by reflecting on where the field can go from here and appealing for scholars to be relentlessly self-conscious in their approach to religion and the 'other than religious'.

The contemporary non-religious landscape in the UK and beyond

This chapter presents a survey of research on the 'non-religious', 'the nones', 'the secular' and related concepts from a wide range of qualitative and quantitative disciplinary perspectives. The focus is particularly on the UK, but also encompassing key insights from research across the globe. It sets aside important critical issues for the time being (see Chapter 2 onwards) and rather attempts to set the scene in textbook fashion, providing a case for the study of the non-religious, a discussion of key vocabulary and a broad brush-stroke painting of the contemporary non-religious landscape and highlighting some key issues in its contemporary study.

The case for studying non-religion

Lois Lee's early definition of non-religion as 'anything which is *primarily* defined by a relationship of difference to religion' (2012b: 131; emphasis in original) is useful in creating a space for a substantive understanding of non-religion – viewing it as something substantial, rather than an empty remainder – such as she advances in her doctoral thesis (Lee 2012a) and subsequent monograph (2015). She helpfully provides an outline of what might count as legitimate phenomena to be addressed by an emerging field of 'non-religion studies', which

> takes some account of phenomena like atheism, agnosticism, anti-supernaturalism, anti-clericism, blasphemy, hatred of religion, and so-called 'indifference' to religion. It also takes some account of alternative belief systems, ethics, rites of passage, and other matters which point to the way they depart from religion to understand and articulate themselves. Finally, it takes account of the intersections between these areas and gender, sexuality, class, race, ethnicity, nationalism, religious heritage, employment, relationships, health, and happiness. (Lee 2012b: 131)

Such studies are commonly motivated by large-scale social surveys which are taken to demonstrate that 'nonbelievers in God' are the world's fourth largest religious group (Zuckerman 2010: 96). If smaller groups are deemed worthy of scholarly attention, so the argument goes, then the same attention should be directed towards this constituency. Thus, we find a growing body of scholarly work focusing on the 'nones'[1] – a residual category constructed by censuses and surveys – and a further body of material which aims to substantiate what it 'means' to be other than religious.[2]

This work is, in many ways, a logical progression of a broader move away from secularization theory in the academic study of religion,[3] or even its reversal,[4] and the attendant radical particularism in the form of 'lived religion' and related concepts[5] that seems to have overtaken the field in recent years. In other words, given that the currently prevalent view that religion has 'returned', or that it 'never left', seems to be largely based upon a combination of in-depth studies of what people are 'really' doing 'on the ground' and redefining 'religion' to fit this data – speaking of the 'changing nature of religion' and so on (Davie 2015: xii) – it makes sense that some scholars would turn their attention to similarly in-depth studies of social actors who appear not to have this 'religion'. In short, given that vast swathes of the global population seem to be positioning themselves outside established categories relating to religion, it stands to reason that those involved in the study of religion might be curious as to what exactly is going on. However, there are other clear reasons why scholars might be interested in studying 'non-religion' (however defined).

First, studying 'non-religion' allows us to test the perceived or claimed universality of 'religion'. Russell McCutcheon has consistently and convincingly demonstrated that many scholars 'presume that [the term "religion"] points to pre-social and thus universal sentiments' (2007: 182) – the Eliadean idea that we are all *homo religiosus*. Even within the cutting-edge cognitive science of religion, one of the most frequent and heated debates concerns whether human beings are innately religious (Guthrie 1995; Paul 2010: 155; Greene 2011). However, to quote Clifford Geertz,:

> [Whilst it] is probably true … that there is no human society which totally lacks cultural patterns that we can call religious … It is surely untrue that all men in all societies are, in any meaningful sense of the term, religious. (Geertz 1968: 664; cited in Campbell 1971: 129)

By studying non-religion, atheism, agnosticism, religious indifference and so on, we can open up and problematize this perceived universality of religion, if only in a suggestive manner.

Second, studying such topics – which are, in many contexts, necessarily 'religion-related' (more on this later) – allows us to explore relational interactions, contestations and identity politics at different sites: from 'culture wars' between, and identity politics of, 'New Atheists' and the 'Religious Right', especially in the United States, to local grassroots studies of how lay people construct social identities.

Third, studying atheism and non-religion can also contribute to theorizing the concept of 'religion' in relation to the 'secular' and other related categories. The late Jonathan Z. Smith argued that there is 'a marked preference for sharply dualistic or oppositional classes' amongst scholars of religion (2000: 38–9) which sets up the 'religious' and the 'secular' as mutually dependent categories – useless on their own 'but, when used as a binary pair, they set malleable limits that make almost anything possible to say' (McCutcheon 2007: 191). However, what are we to do with phenomena such as Roman emperors, popes of the Roman Catholic Church or the Constitution of the United States of America, which can be argued to be both 'religious' and 'secular'?[6] And what of the prevailing tendency (particularly in the sociology of religion) to (sub)consciously equate 'religious' with generally 'positive' experiences, actions, institutions and so on, which seems to 'entail normative judgements that [are] hardly appropriate for an objective field of study' (B. C. Wilson 1998: 155)? Studying the under-researched side of the problematic religion/non-religion binary can provide a solid basis for its continued and strengthened questioning. Theorizing this relationship not only is of academic importance but lies at the heart of many contemporary problems, particularly concerning legal issues such as individual (non)religious freedoms, charitable statuses, or separation of church and state.

With this case in mind, what can we say about the state of that field of study? Although this chapter serves as my own overview, it is worth reflecting on how we got here. In doing so, I do not aim to be comprehensive and initially draw on Stephen Bullivant and Lois Lee's *Interdisciplinary Studies of Non-religion and Secularity: The State of the Union* (2012). For more recent articulations, readers are directed to articles from a historical (Nash 2019) and sociological (J. M. Smith and Cragun 2019) perspective or my podcast conversation with Lois Lee, *From Non-Religion to Unbelief? A Developing Field* (Lee and Cotter 2018).

The state of the field

Several studies of 'irreligion', 'a-religion' and the 'nones' in the 1960s and early 1970s highlighted the importance of those who were not religious and attempted

> to set a durable research agenda both within and apart from the scientific study of religion … Unfortunately, this was followed by decades of minimal research activity on these topics … Now, nearing the end of the second decade of the 21st century, a growing community of social scientists and other scholars have turned their attention to what is now typically (and variably) referred to by the inclusive categories of 'nonreligion', 'secularity', or 'religion's other'. (J. M. Smith and Cragun 2019: 1)

This opening gambit from Smith and Cragun neatly summarizes the dominant narrative within the study of the other-than-religious which locates its origins in the 1960s and 1970s and acknowledges a recent explosion of scholarly interest. Bullivant and Lee suggest that the 'non-religiosity' of many of the earliest social scientists – Durkheim, Freud, Marx and so on – led them to be fascinated by religiosity and the 'absurd' beliefs of others, yet not to see their own 'lack of belief' as something 'amenable to similar research' (2012: 20–1). Their position seemed natural and not requiring of explanation. That being said, those identifying or being identified as 'non-religious' have, until quite recently, 'made up only relatively small, and diffuse proportions of a given population' outside of particular (post-) Communist societies (2012: 21).

Beyond those who might have considered 'non-religion' to be normative, the situation was somewhat different. As early as 1932 we find a study in the *Journal of Abnormal and Social Psychology*, titled 'Personality and Group Factors in the Making of Atheists' (Vetter and Green 1932). And there was extensive interest in the anomaly of unbelief from Catholic social scientists throughout the 1950s and 1960s. In March 1969, the Vatican convened an international social-scientific conference on 'the culture of unbelief' (see Caporale and Grumelli 1971) – significantly attended by a number of important social scientists including Charles Glock, Robert Bellah, David Martin, Bryan Wilson, Harvey Cox and Peter Berger. A similar event, in collaboration with the Understanding Unbelief research programme and the Nonreligion and Secularity Research Network, took place to mark the fiftieth anniversary in May 2019.[7]

At the time of the original conference there was a coincidental rise of the aforementioned social scientific studies, including Colin Campbell's *Toward a Sociology of Irreligion* (1971). At this time, Campbell argued:

> No tradition for the sociological study of irreligion as yet exists and this book has been written in the hope that it will help to stimulate the development of just such a tradition. (1971: vii)

Describing our present context, Bullivant and Lee note that 'It has become something of a cliché to begin social-scientific studies of non-religion, secularity, atheism, and related topics by bewailing the dearth of previous research' (2012: 19). This is a complaint that no longer holds water: for example, the journal *Secularism and Nonreligion* was launched in August 2011 and has recently been joined by *Secular Studies*; and the bibliography of the *Nonreligion and Secularity Research Network* (founded in 2009), which hasn't been updated since January 2015 (mea culpa), contains over 1,000 scholarly books and articles on atheism, secularity, nonreligion and related topics at time of publication (over 800 of which have been published since 2007).[8]

Several explanations can be proposed for this upsurge of interest. Some of these are societal and relate to the apparent rise in publicly visible forms of 'religion' and 'non-religion' in the West. Setting the scene, McAnulla, Kettell and Schulzke note that although political oppression was connected to a growth of atheism in the UK,

> the more accommodating stance taken by the Christian establishment helped to defuse the potential for a more radical atheist edge. Social and political conditions in the United States inhibited the growth of politicised atheism. High levels of Christian pluralism diluted any common notion of orthodoxy, and the existence of a formally secular constitution prevented the formation of direct links between religion and a political regime. The radical political drive of atheism in Europe was also undermined by a period of economic growth and a gradual rise in living standards towards the end of the twentieth century, as well as by the rise of socialism. (2018: 41–2)

However, the financial crisis of the early twenty-first century combined with the 1979 Iranian Revolution, the terrorist attacks of 9/11 and other high-profile acts of religion-related violence and the mobilization of the 'Christian Right' in the United States have led to increased attention being directed towards 'religion' from scholars, activists, politicians, journalists, anti-religionists and more (McAnulla, Kettell and Schulzke 2018: 43–4). The same period has seen great technological advances, particularly the embrace of innovative online technologies across the West, which have not only provided a means for 'non-religious' consciousness-raising and community-building but also facilitated unprecedented access for scholarly study of so far diffuse and somewhat invisible populations. Furthermore, there 'has also been a shift from modernism to postmodernism', which has 'helped to foster the emergence of new forms of identity politics based around issues such as gender, race, sexuality and the environment', which has both challenged atheistic critiques and provided opportunities for (visible) (re-)assertions of 'non-religious' positions (McAnulla, Kettell and Schulzke 2018: 44).

On the other hand, perhaps this upsurge in interest is emblematic of a movement within the academic study of religion, and within the social sciences generally, towards an appreciation of the multiplicity and situatedness of contemporary religion-related identifications (see, particularly, Chapters 2 and 5) and the apparent disconnect between levels of popular affiliation and levels of practice, belief and holding of traditionally religious attitudes. Before turning to some of the statistics and demographics that have emerged from this scholarly interest, and some key contemporary 'non-religious' formations, a brief overview of some of the vocabulary in this field is in order.

Vocabulary

Given the critical thrust of this volume, this is neither the time nor the place for the provision of proscriptive definitions of key terms for the field that might be called 'non-religion studies'. This would be a laborious task and bring diminishing returns, as others – particularly Conrad (2018), Lee (2015), Lee and Bullivant (2016) and Quillen (2015a) – have done excellent work here. However, a brief dive into the terminological waters will give a sense of the state of the field, as well as some of the critical debates that inform the chapters that follow. Lee helpfully describes three groups of terms that are relevant: first, those related to practice, performance or identification, which take religion as their point of reference and distinguish 'between different ways of relating to that object' (2015: 28); second, those specifically related to belief – or, more narrowly, to theism; and third, those relating to the secular.

Religion-related terms

This group of terms includes the self-explanatory 'anti-religion' and the slightly more obscure 'areligious', that is being 'without' religion (whatever that might mean). Both of these notions were somewhat clumsily fitted into Colin Campbell's conceptualization of 'irreligion': 'those beliefs and actions which are expressive of attitudes of hostility or indifference toward the prevailing religion, together with indications of the rejection of its demands' (1971: 21). Campbell was of the view that an areligious stance is 'merely [an] implicit rejection' (1971: 24–5). This entanglement means that 'irreligion' is seen as implying 'an antagonism or negation with religion that seems to erase the middle, the indifferent, or the spiritually ambiguous' (Conrad 2018: 6), which makes it a problematic notion for those seeking an umbrella term for 'religion's other' (J. M. Smith and Cragun 2019). However, Lee sees the concept retaining some use if it is 'at once generalized and narrowed to indicate the *rejection* of religion – in whatever form this rejection might take and however acute it may be' (Lee 2015: 31). Lee's preferred umbrella term is 'non-religion' – the term that I have chosen as the dominant (though by no means unproblematic) orienting category throughout this book (because of its clear 'parasitic' dependence on the category 'religion', and unambiguous scholarly construction).

I will discuss 'non-religion' in more detail in the following chapter, but, in short, Lee defines this as 'any phenomenon – position, perspective, or practice – that is primarily understood in relation to religion but which is not itself considered to be religious' (2015: 32). For Lee, the 'non-' 'describes a *meaningful* differentiation, as in the sense of "non-violence," used in relation to phenomena that are frequently or typically violent rather than ones that are not' (2015: 32); that is, non-religion is *not everything that is not religious*. So examples of non-religion would include the belief-related terms outlined below, as well as components of humanism and political secularism, which 'both have religious versions' but have 'strong non-religious components' in the UK (2015: 34–5).

Finally, it is worth noting the prominence of the notion of 'deconversion' in many sociological studies (J. M. Smith and Cragun 2019: 3). Whilst much of this terminology is arguably biased and derogatory (R. T. Cragun and Hammer 2011) – consider 'defectors', 'deserters' or 'dropouts' (Pasquale 2012) – others, such as 'apostate', have been appropriated by many who have 'left' religion. Indeed, the prevalence of research in these areas is rooted in the recognition that 'many nonreligious identities are actively built out of critical biographical turning points that involve experience with, and usually steady dissociation from, religion' (J. M. Smith and Cragun 2019: 8).

Belief-related terms

By far the most prominent 'belief-related' concept of relevance to this discussion is the deceptively simple 'atheism'. The term's Greek roots, *atheos* – 'a-', meaning 'without', and 'theos', meaning 'god' – suggest that 'atheism' straightforwardly means being without gods, yet this throws up several critical questions.

First, what are these gods that atheists are apparently without? Is this 'the deity worshipped by ... Judaism, Christianity, and Islam' (Walters 2010: 17), some other god, several gods or the very concept itself? Historically, the term has been associated with the former lineage, yet even here 'atheism' is much less salient 'in many Muslim contexts, such that Arabic, Urdu, and some Persian languages derive a range of terms from the Qur'an to describe different kinds of religious otherness rather than focusing on atheism exclusively' (Lee 2015: 38; cf. Schielke 2013). Importantly, atheism is *not the opposite of* 'religion' (Lee 2012a), whatever that might be. Despite the desires of many scholars, the relationship between atheism and spirituality, deism, polytheism and so on is unclear. 'From the mere fact that a person is [identified as] an atheist, one cannot infer that this person subscribes to any particular positive beliefs' (G. Smith 1989: 21–2), nor is it clear exactly which beliefs they are rejecting. Does the category exclude belief in ghosts, the afterlife or karma? Does it necessitate the rejection of ritual, 'religious' or otherwise? (Eller 2010: 10). Can an 'atheist' maintain a 'religious' identity? These are all open and controversial questions.

Second, what does being 'without' a god or gods involve? Some elaborations on the definition suggest that this is an 'absence of belief' (Bullivant 2013: 13), whilst others imply something more active, such as the 'belief that there is no God or gods' (Baggini 2003: 3) or 'a principled and informed decision to *reject* belief in God' (McGrath 2005: 175). Others prefer to argue that atheism is 'a position (not a "belief")' (Eller 2010: 1), with 'negative atheism' exemplifying the etymologically rooted 'someone without a belief in God' and 'positive atheism' being an explicitly articulated position in which existence claims surrounding god(s) are rejected (M. Martin 2007: 1; cf. Cotter 2011a: 79). We might ask at this point about the implications of the language at play here: what is being implied and constructed through terms such as 'lack', 'absence', 'without', 'positive', 'negative', 'rejection' and 'assertion'? It is clear, however, that atheism

> sets up a false dichotomy that excludes the middle: one is a believer or not a believer … if one looked only for those who called themselves 'atheists,' the study would indubitably leave out a vast number of people who closely fit the description of atheist but never took the name. (Conrad 2018: 1)

This suggests that, as in Ancient Greece and Rome (Bremmer 2007; Edwards 2013; Sedley 2013), atheism is in the eye of the beholder: it matters who is labelled as atheist and by whom. Indeed, such contestations bleed over into another belief-related term: 'agnosticism'.

The term 'agnosticism' was coined by biologist Thomas Henry Huxley in 1869 and elaborated in his later philosophical explorations on that nature of what is and isn't knowable. Once again, this derives from classical Greek 'a-', 'without' and 'gnosis', as in 'knowledge' or 'insight' concerning the transcendent. Huxley 'was unhappy with "atheism" because it was too dogmatic [and] was also being increasingly linked with far-left revolutionary politics, which further tainted the term in polite society' (Hyman 2007: 30). For Huxley, 'agnosticism' was

> not a creed, but a method, the essence of which lies in the rigorous application of a single principle... Positively the principle may be expressed: In matters of the intellect, follow your reason as far as it will take you, without regard to any other consideration. And negatively: In matters of the intellect do not pretend that conclusions are certain which are not demonstrated or demonstrable. (Huxley 1893: 170)

However, Huxley was also keen to stress 'I do not very much care to speak of anything as "unknowable"' (Huxley 1899: n.p.), nor was agnosticism about withholding judgement.

Clearly Huxley's method can apply to any topic, yet it continues to have an association with the 'spiritual', 'metaphysical' and 'religious'. In popular discourse, an agnostic is variously constructed as someone who 'doesn't know', 'doesn't think we can know', 'doesn't care' or 'withholds judgement' on matters relating to the supra-empirical. Agnosticism has been written off as 'negative atheism' by some (M. Martin 2007: 3), with Eller even insinuating some form of deception, referring to the 'cloak of agnosticism' (2010: 8). Yet it can also indicate a distinct philosophical outlook, offering a clear alternative to theistic or atheistic orientations, that can be taken up by rational materialists and postmodern relativists alike but, perhaps, for profoundly different reasons and to different ends.

A final cluster of relevant terms are those explicitly negating belief. Conrad notes:

> 'Disbelief' and 'nonbelief' are functional equivalents to 'unbelief'. ... '[D]isbelief' has the added sense of being unable to believe... [and] 'nonbelief' has the connotation of not believing because of a lack of familiarity. (Conrad 2018: 6)

He deems 'unbelief' a much more open and flexible umbrella term than 'atheism' for describing the phenomena at focus throughout this present volume (2018: 1), siding with Stein's 'open' and 'inclusive' definition of the term as 'not holding orthodox beliefs or traditional opinions – on religious matters' (Stein 1985: xv). The term definitely has a lot going for it: it is salient and intelligent to broader populations, yet also so clearly a folk category that it forces specificity in its scholarly usage (Lee and Cotter 2018: 5–6); it hasn't been claimed by a particular movement and holds space for heterodoxy that doesn't preclude, for example, spirituality (Conrad 2018: 5); and it is tied to 'historical references relevant to the particular culture in discussion' (2018: 3). That being said, this placing of 'belief' front and centre potentially universalizes the notion of belief and, as we will see in the following chapter, 'belief [only] appears as a universal category because of the universalist claims of the tradition in which it has become most central, Christianity' (Lopez Jr 1998: 33). Or, more precisely, of Protestant Christianity.

Secular and related terms

The final grouping of relevant terms is those surrounding the 'secular', namely 'secular', 'secularity', 'secularism' and 'secularization'. In brief, secular is generally understood to identify 'phenomena – objects, spaces, people, and practices – for which religion is no more than a secondary concern, reference point, or authority' (Lee 2015: 39). In this understanding, given 'that religion is centrally relevant to non-religion, irreligion, and anti-religion, they are not secular' (2015, 39).[9] If this is what is meant by 'secular', then 'secularity' is simply 'the condition or state of being secular (as in "locality" and "local")' (Knott 2014: 37), and 'secularization' is the process whereby this state of secularity is reached, 'whereby a) religious institutions decline b) religion declines in importance for society c) religion declines in importance for individuals' (Davie and Woodhead 2009: 524; cf. B. S. Wilson 1966: 14). However, we can clearly see that each of these concepts requires certain agenda-laden definitions of 'religion' in order to make sense. Furthermore, it has been demonstrated that 'secular' is a polysemous concept in public discourse, which can be employed in the same dialogue by the same interlocutors in multiple ways to serve various ideological ends (Blankholm 2014). These are not simple and neutral terms, but intensely political, as is clearly exemplified in the notion of 'secularism'.

Secularism is often defined as an antagonistic 'force which sets itself in opposition to religion, and which shows signs of becoming increasingly militant' (Davie and Woodhead 2009: 524; cf. Warner 2010: 3). However, at its most basic level, secularism is merely 'an account or ideology that demarcates something as secular, notably but not only one advocated by the state' (Lee 2015: 42). Yet in practice, the political secularism that is intrinsic to many modern democracies – and often seen as a proxy for 'liberalism' (Lee 2013: 588) – typically involves a normative commitment to state neutrality in matters of religion (Dalferth 2010). And even the briefest of explorations of the disparate 'secular' structures in the United States, UK, France, Norway or India will demonstrate that secularism is profoundly contextual. The normative entanglements of these terms have led some to describe secularization theory, and even the academic study of religion more broadly, as 'secularist' (Fitzgerald 2000b; Josephson-Storm 2017; Ambasciano 2018).

With this sweeping overview of some of the key terminology populating the field, we now turn to a similarly sweeping and subjective tour through some of the statistics and demographics associated with it.

Statistics and demographics

My focus in this section shall mainly centre on 'Great Britain' and sometimes, more specifically, Scotland. However, I shall allude to other nations and the broader global context throughout. I shall endeavour to provide as much detail on each statistic as possible and state my sources: as I often tell students, statistics themselves do not lie, but confusions, conflations, agendas and manipulations creep in the moment that they are communicated. It is not my intention to offer much in the way of critical commentary here: for that, see the rest of the book!

The terminology 'Great Britain' is used because Northern Ireland is routinely and unjustifiably excluded from the presentation of survey results relating to the 'United Kingdom of Great Britain and Northern Ireland' due to population size (2.9 per cent of the UK population in 2019),[10] and its distinctive religion-related history chequered with sectarianism, violence, problematic entanglements between various forms of Christianity and the state and a peripheral position in relation to the locus of UK power. As shall be seen below, Northern Ireland tends to be an inconvenient exception to the rule in matters relating to 'religion' and 'non-religion', with only 1 per cent of those in Northern Ireland ticking 'no religion' on the 2001 census, although this rose to 'over 5 per cent' in 2011 (C. G. Brown 2017: 7).

Identification

Taking a global view, a Pew Research Center report (2015) concluded that the proportion of religiously 'unaffiliated' individuals in the global population stood at 16.4 per cent, the third largest 'Major Religious Group' behind Christians (31.4 per cent) and Muslims (23.2 per cent) and just above Hindus (15 per cent). Due particularly to disparities in fertility rates, the report predicts that this 'unaffiliated' segment of the global population is likely to proportionately *decrease* from 16.4 per cent (1.1 billion) to 13.2 per cent (1.2 billion) by 2050, falling to fourth place behind Christians (31.4 per cent), Muslims (29.7 per cent) and Hindus (14.9 per cent). On a global level, then, it seems unlikely that the 'unaffiliated' will become a dominant religion-related group any time soon, if at all.[11]

Yet, this global story seems to be playing out quite differently in the West. For example, according to 2018 General Social Survey data, those claiming 'no religion' in the United States now represent 23.1 per cent of the United States population, up from 21.6 per cent in 2016, and now of similar size to the 'Evangelical' population (22.8 per cent) (J. Jenkins 2019). This stands at 33 per cent for those under thirty (Zuckerman, Galen and Pasquale 2016: 4). Approximately 30 per cent of Canadians are 'secular', and in Australia this figure is around 20 per cent (Zuckerman, Galen and Pasquale 2016: 4). Here, there was a 29.41 per cent increase in the population claiming 'no religion' between 2006 and 2011, which is inflated to close to 41 per cent when focusing specifically on Aboriginal Australians or Torres Strait Islanders (J. L. Cox and Possamai 2016: 5). In (Western) Europe, we find significant percentages of populations who claim to believe neither in a god nor any sort of 'spirit' nor 'life force' – 40 per cent in France, 37 per cent in the Czech Republic, 29 per cent in Estonia, 27 per cent in Belgium and Germany and 19 per cent in Spain (Zuckerman, Galen and Pasquale 2016: 5) – and rates of 'atheism' in Denmark, the Netherlands, Norway and Sweden somewhere between 27 per cent and 35 per cent (Lee 2013: 590). Indeed, Lee argues that for

> less religious countries, including both overt and negative forms means that atheism accounts for large majorities in most cases: for example, 78 per cent in Sweden, 76 per cent in the Netherlands, [and] 67 per cent in Belgium. (2013: 590–1)

Turning specifically to Great Britain, 2018 figures from the Annual Population Survey[12] show a 46 per cent increase in those identifying with 'no religion' since 2011: currently 39 per cent of the population (Humanists UK 2019). Drawing on data from the British Social Attitudes and European Social Surveys, Stephen Bullivant has shown that the proportion of self-describing Anglicans in Great Britain declined to 17 per cent in 2015 from 40 per cent in 1983, whilst those self-describing as having 'no religion' nearly doubled from 31 per cent to 49 per cent (Bullivant 2017: 8). He shows that, according to this data, 'no religion' has been the largest religious grouping in Great Britain for two decades, 'with a mean increase of 0.5 percentage points per year from 1983 to 2015' (2017: 8). In 2009, 'no religion' outnumbered all Christians combined, and 'with the single exception of 2011, this pattern has held ever after' (2017: 8).

However, if we take a closer look at these figures, we can see that they are highly location-specific. 'Nones' made up an overall majority in seven of the regions in the report, including Scotland (55 per cent) and Wales (56 per cent) (2017: 7). Recent figures from a 2018 Survation Panel Survey commissioned by Humanist Society Scotland put the Scottish figure at 59 per cent (Sutherland 2018: 6). It is notable that

> the proportion of Nones in the South East (58%), the highest, is almost double of that in Inner London (31%), the lowest. Interestingly, this order is reversed when one looks at members of Non-Christian religions … The Inner London 'microclimate' is all the more remarkable given the close geographical proximity of the two regions. (Bullivant 2017: 7)

What all of this (lack of) affiliation might mean is another question that will be explored throughout this volume. And the reader would do well to note the significant variation in percentages from survey to survey.

As far as self-description is concerned, a recent report from the large-scale, six-nation *Understanding Unbelief: Across Disciplines and Across Cultures* project found that self-describing atheists and agnostics 'are limited to only a very small, and likely atypical, subset of *de facto* atheists and agnostics' and 'there is no single term – or discrete set of terms – for referring to these people which a majority of them would actively choose for themselves' (Bullivant et al. 2019: 11).

Age, gender and ethnicity

Breaking down the recent Scottish figures by age, it is interesting to note that the only age bracket in which 'Christians' outnumber those identifying with 'no religion' is the over 65s, at 59 per cent to 40 per cent (Sutherland 2018: 7). In every other bracket, 'no religion' dominates with 69 per cent of 18–24-, 25–34- and 35–44-year-olds selecting this option as compared to 22 per cent, 25 per cent and 26 per cent 'Christian', respectively (Sutherland 2018: 7). Despite 'common sense' notions that people become more religious as they get older, there is robust empirical evidence which demonstrates that in the UK, at least according to these sorts of survey measures, 'disaffiliation' is generational; that is, each new generation is less likely to identify with a religion (Voas and Crockett 2005; Bruce 2011).

Returning to Bullivant's figures for Great Britain, paying attention to the age profile of the 'nones' helps to destabilize another (justifiably) prevalent theory:

that women are more 'religious' than men (Trzebiatowska and Bruce 2014). Although I will comment more on gender and other intersectional characteristics later in this chapter, the 2015 British Social Attitudes Survey shows that, yes, 'those identifying with "no religion" are more likely to be men than women: 55% vs 45%' (Bullivant 2017: 10). However, not only is this still a huge number of women (10.9 million), in the younger age cohorts there is almost an exact gender balance:

> [O]f the 14% of all Nones who are aged 18–24, half are women and half are men; of the 21% who are aged 25–34, the skew in favour of men is only very slight … In fact, with the exception of the 55–64s, the gender differences in each age category are quite small: within one or two percentage points. (2017: 10)

This suggests that the 'gender gap' in identifying with 'no religion' may become less significant in the future.

I will also discuss the intersections of 'no religion' and race/ethnicity later in the chapter, but at this stage it is worth noting that this is a factor. According to 2015 BSA figures, 95 per cent of those identifying with 'no religion' also identify as 'White' (as compared to the 87 per cent British average) (Bullivant 2017: 11). Among the 'non-religious', '1% identify as Black, 2% as Asian, and 2% as Mixed or Other', which 'puts them significantly behind our other groups, excepting only Anglicans, in terms of racial diversity' (Bullivant 2017: 11). However, these figures do not break down 'White' into further subcategories, which likely masks further diversity. Already, the reader should be internalizing the message that to speak of those with 'no religion' as a coherent group is a fool's errand.

Conversion, transmission and children

Sticking with the British context – although those interested in the United States could do no better than Christel Manning's *Losing Our Religion: How Unaffiliated Parents Are Raising Their Children* (2015) – it has been noted that the 'massive cultural shift from Christian to non-religious Britain has come about largely because of children ceasing to follow the religious commitments of their parents' (Woodhead 2016: 249). Indeed, according to the 2015 BSA figures, whilst 92 per cent of those born with 'no religion' retain this identification, other groups have significant percentages of 'conversions' to this 'no religion' position: for example, 42 per cent from Presbyterian, 41 per cent Anglican, 37 per cent Catholic, 14 per cent Jewish and 10 per cent Muslim (Bullivant 2017: 13). Putting these figures in perspective, Bullivant states that for every 'convert from "no religion" to any religious identity there are nineteen … from a religious identity to having "no religion"', with this figure rising to twenty-six if we substitute 'any Christian identity' for 'religion' (2017: 13).

Politics

A dominant narrative in the study of religion and throughout public discourse is that the 'non-religious' will tend to skew to the left politically and be more liberal and 'progressive' in their outlooks. This is certainly the case in the United States, where 'nonreligious individuals' are 'more left leaning than are those with a religious affiliation', and even more so for the smaller proportion of United States 'atheists' (J. M. Smith and Cragun 2019: 5; cf. Baker and Smith 2015). However, this does not seem to be the case in the UK, where, as we have seen, the 'non-religious' seem to make up a much larger proportion, if not the majority, of the population. Linda Woodhead's surveys with samples of around 2,000 British 'nones' conducted between 2013 and 2015 show that 'nones' are 'spread out across the political spectrum from moderate left-wing to moderate right-wing in much the same way as the British population as a whole' (Woodhead 2016: 251). However, they do seem to have a 'greater sense of global citizenship', particularly when compared to English Anglicans (2016: 251).

Religiosity

Common measures of religiosity among sociologists in the (post-)Christian West involve looking at statistics for church attendance; participation in rites of passage such as weddings and funerals; or engagement in other practices such as prayer, fasting and so on. In the UK Steve Bruce calls attention to the 1851 church census, which showed that between 40 per cent and 60 per cent of the British population attended a Sunday service on 30 March. By 2001 the analogous figure had declined to around 9 per cent (Bruce 2011: 9; cf. Brierley 2006). He also draws on the Mannheim Eurobarometer to demonstrate similar declines throughout Europe from 1970 to 1999 (Bruce 2011: 10): for example, Belgium (52 per cent to 10 per cent), France (23 per cent to 5 per cent), Italy (56 per cent to 39 per cent) and Ireland (91 per cent to 65 per cent).

A similar narrative emerges when looking at wedding ceremonies. In the Republic of Ireland in 2018, Roman Catholic marriages fell below 50 per cent for the first time on record, clocking in at 47.6 per cent as compared to 96.2 per cent in 1980 (Walsh 2019). In Spain, another former Catholic stronghold, 80.2 per cent of marriages in 2018 were civil, standing 'in stark contrast with the reality in 1992, when 79.4 per cent of the marriages were religious – mainly Catholic' (Evangelical Focus 2019). In Scotland, Isabella Kasselstrand has examined the increasing uptake of humanist wedding ceremonies. Legal since 2005, by 2016 humanist ceremonies accounted for 13.6 per cent of Scottish weddings, surpassing the national Church of Scotland (12.6 per cent) to become the second largest provider after civil ceremonies (51.5 per cent) (Kasselstrand 2018: 278). This growth has been almost entirely to the detriment of Church of Scotland ceremonies. Civil ceremonies have remained proportionately stable since 2011, suggesting that a constituency that was turning to the national church now feels satisfied with something apparently 'less than religious' but 'more than civil'.

Looking specifically at the UK 'nones' of the 2014 European Social Survey, Bullivant's key message is that three-quarters 'say that, outside of special occasions such as weddings and funerals, they "never" now attend religious services' with most of the remainder attending on 'special holy days' or less often (Bullivant 2017: 15). When rating their own religiosity, 43 per cent claim to be 'not at all religious', whilst 85 per cent 'rank themselves below the notional mid-point mark' (2017: 14). It is worth noting that these figures imply that almost 60 per cent of 'nones' consider themselves to be in some way 'religious' (whatever that might mean). Finally, through combining self-assessments of religiosity and engagement in prayer, Bullivant constructs a group dubbed 'Nonreligious Nones' who pray on a less-than-monthly basis and who rate their own religiosity at 5 out of 10 or lower. On this basis,

> 'Nonreligious Nones' make up the largest proportion: 85.4% of all Nones, and therefore equating to around 20.7 million British adults. (Furthermore, a very large proportion of this group say that they both never pray, and are not at all religious: these 'Ultranonreligious Nones' alone account for 40.3% of all Nones, and thus around 8.3 million British adults). (2017: 16)

Beliefs

Reporting on Fraser Sutherland's 2018 research in Scotland, a headline in the *Scottish Herald* reads 'We no longer go to church but many Scots still have a belief in angels and devils' (M. Williams 2018). This situation is often seen as contradictory in popular discourse, but those more familiar with the academic literature are unlikely to be surprised. Among Sutherland's sample of the Scottish population, 32 per cent claimed no belief in God or a higher power, 26 per cent said that they didn't know and didn't think that one could find out, whilst 18 per cent were certain that God exists (Sutherland 2018: 8). Wider 'spiritual or supernatural beliefs' received some support among the general population to varying degrees: for example, life after death (34 per cent 'totally believe'), heaven (33 per cent), demons/evil spirits (25 per cent) and reincarnation (21 per cent) (2018: 9). Zooming in on British 'nones', around two-thirds of this population were represented in the 2008 British Social Attitudes Survey by classic 'atheist' and 'agnostic' positions, whilst a further 16 per cent denied 'a personal God' but affirmed 'a Higher Power of some kind'. As Bullivant notes, 'this category, while something of a religion survey classic, is very difficult to interpret – or to guess how others might have interpreted it' (2017: 14).

The recent report from the Understanding Unbelief programme attempts to chart what substantive beliefs 'atheist' and 'agnostics' might hold beyond distancing themselves from traditional theistic beliefs. Drawing on new survey data from Brazil, China, Denmark, Japan, the UK and the United States, four of the project's key findings are:

- 'Unbelief in God doesn't necessarily entail unbelief in other supernatural phenomena. Atheists and (less so) agnostics exhibit lower levels of supernatural belief than do the wider populations.' However, only a minority are 'thoroughgoing naturalists'.
- 'While atheists and agnostics are disproportionately likely to affirm that the universe is "ultimately meaningless" …, it still remains a minority view.'
- 'With only a few exceptions, atheists and agnostics endorse the realities of objective moral values, human dignity and attendant rights, and the "deep value" of nature, at similar rates to the general populations in their countries.'
- 'There is remarkably high agreement between unbelievers and general populations concerning the values most important for "finding meaning in the world and your own life". "Family" and "Freedom" ranked highly for all.' (Bullivant et al. 2019: 3)

These findings have been widely reported as indicating that 'Most atheists believe in the supernatural, despite trusting science' (*New Scientist* 2019) or that 'anti-atheist stereotypes aren't true' (Lesley 2019). Whilst not completely incorrect and coming in the most part from a 'good place', these headlines – and the findings on which they are based – are critically problematic. Emphasizing that atheists believe in the 'supernatural' mistakenly presumes that this is contradictory. We know from existing research (YouGov 2016) that while atheists don't believe in some sort of theistic God, their position doesn't inherently say anything about fate or ghosts or karma or anything else. Responses holding that significant events are 'meant to be', or that 'there are underlying forces of good and evil in this world', were used to bolster claims about supernatural beliefs in this case, but these need not refer to the supernatural. They could be used to explain rational causation of events or societal forces. Furthermore, celebrating the significant emphasis on family and freedom by 'believers' and 'unbelievers' obscures the fact that these are slippery symbols which gather together hosts of incompatible beliefs – for example, freedom for religion and freedom from religion. Yes, they are powerful symbols, but they can mask very real differences. In short, it's too early – and, perhaps, ultimately misguided – to attempt to find unifying beliefs for this 'group' beyond the rejection of certain theistic beliefs.

Summary

My take-home message throughout this section has been that 'it is a mistake to view the nonreligious as a homogeneous group sharing a coherent worldview' (J. M. Smith and Cragun 2019: 4). Across the globe there is enormous variation in the numbers of individuals choosing not to identify with a religion, the contexts which these acts of 'non-identification' happen and the alternative identifications that may or may not be taken up by these individuals. There is no coherent set of beliefs held or rejected by the 'non-religious', and a surprising proportion seem to engage in behaviours that might be traditionally labelled 'religious'. Yet what can be said, in a UK context at least, is that

> a typical none is younger, white, British-born, liberal about personal life and morals, varied in political commitment but cosmopolitan in outlook, suspicious of organised religion but not necessarily atheist, and unwilling to be labelled as religious or to identify with a religious group … They are not a distinct minority, but a confident and rather unselfconscious majority. The choice of 'no religion' seems to be a negative more than a positive choice: a refusal of existing categories and a dis-affiliation from the organised religious groups. (Woodhead 2016: 252; cf. J. M. Smith and Cragun 2019: 4)

Key manifestations and issues

In this final section of this introductory chapter, I will continue this message of diversity by focusing on two related, but contrasting, manifestations of non-religion in the contemporary world – New Atheism and Humanism – before concluding with some final thoughts on key issues that are emerging from the field to date.

New Atheism

> There is simply no programme or manifesto of 'New Atheism' and there is no all-embracing organization, in which all, or even most, of the so-labelled persons are united. (Zenk 2013: 255)

The past fifteen years or so have seen the emergence of a journalistic and scholarly discourse surrounding a 'New Atheism' largely in the anglophone West. As this opening gambit from Thomas Zenk suggests, there is little by way of unifying foundation to this phenomenon. Most commonly the term is understood to point to the 'popular works of a small number of (white male) authors' (Cotter, Quadrio, and Tuckett 2017: 1) – Richard Dawkins, Daniel Dennett, Sam Harris and Christopher Hitchens – and the polemic and counter-polemic continues to this day from atheists, theists, journalists, scientists, theologians and others. However, McAnulla, Kettell and Schulzke have recently argued that New Atheism can also be productively viewed as a 'political movement, expressed through forms of secularist activism' offering 'provocative contributions on issues such as security, multi-culturalism, gender, education and the relationship between the state and civil society' (2018: 1). Furthermore, Ryan Cragun has taken a particularly novel approach using data from social surveys to address the question 'Who are the New Atheists?', suggesting that 'somewhere on the order of 13 to 16 million Americans' exhibit 'New Atheist' characteristics (2015: 210).

In summary,

> the term 'New Atheism' has several conceptual weaknesses, in that it lies in the realm of discursive politics rather than having a clear definition, it 'differs from the self-identification of those labelled as such', and it carries negative connotations in public discourse 'that cannot be subtracted from the label'. (Zenk 2013: 257–8)

Discussion will now turn to some central elements of the New Atheists' critique of religion before considering some other aspects that might make this form of atheism 'new' and concluding with some reflections on why this form of atheism might have emerged when it did.

The new atheistic critique

In a previous article (Cotter 2011a), I argued that the New Atheists' critique of religion occurs within a Christianized, anglophone context, and although devoting space to other religious systems, these authors significantly acknowledge that their 'focus is on Christianity first' (Dennett 2007: xi): their 'atheism is a Protestant atheism' (Hitchens 2008: 11). I demonstrated that their critique of religion is three-fold and focuses upon violence, morality and knowledge/progress. More recently, McAnulla, Kettell and Schulzke have noted six arguments that run throughout the New Atheistic 'critique of religious moral codes':

1. religion interferes with the happiness and well-being that should be the goal of moral life
2. its useful precepts are self-evident
3. it discourages autonomous decision making
4. it fails to constrain immoral conduct
5. it magnifies group differences that encourage discrimination against outsiders
6. its guidelines are excessively vague. (2018: 108)

They also demonstrate that criticizing New Atheism for simply being an intolerant, aggressive repackaging of previous atheist arguments is problematic because this uncritically constructs a homogenous old atheism, against which New Atheism can be counterposed, and ignores some of the arguably unique aspects of this contemporary form (2018: 54–5).

What's new?

A key feature of New Atheism is its naturalistic worldview, with a strong emphasis on reason and science as the best means of understanding reality, in contrast to religious claims regarding revealed truths. In this perspective, 'religion' is reduced 'to a series of assertions (known as "God of the Gaps" arguments) in which a supernatural power is postulated as the causal force for those phenomena that science is as yet unable to explain' (McAnulla, Kettell and Schulzke 2018:

45–6). Furthermore, some of the explanations for 'religion' proposed by the New Atheists make use of cognitive science, evolutionary biology and so on, making it a very twenty-first-century form of atheism.

Another key aspect of New Atheism is the tone of the critique. Drawing on Aaron James's *Assholes: A Theory* (2013), Ethan Quillen discusses how the 'New Atheists' language tends to be overly critical and yet simultaneously exude an aura of being immune to counter criticism because their position is incapable of being incorrect' (Quillen 2015b: np). At the same time, they often fall foul of drawing up straw man positions to attack – even if these straw men do, seemingly, map onto many of their mainly American opponents (A. Johnson 2013). Quillen then goes on to demonstrate how the New Atheists' public image as militant may have outgrown the protagonists themselves: it could be quite difficult, perhaps even impossible, for this image to be shaken even if they wanted to (Quillen 2015b: np).

In another publication, Quillen focuses upon the satirical side of New Atheism and what he calls the 'argument from fictionalization', whereby fictional narratives are used to construct particular versions of religious positions and, in turn, underscore particular Atheistic positions (Quillen 2017: 196). Such fictional narratives range from Bertrand Russell's celestial teapot (1997: 4), Carl Sagan's invisible dragon (1995: 160) and Richard Dawkins' Ultimate Boeing 747 (2007: 113–14), to parody religions such as the Church of the Flying Spaghetti Monster, the Temple of the Invisible Pink Unicorn and the United Church of Bacon (Quillen 2017: 204–4). In the latter's '8 Commandments' we begin to see glimpses of what this sort of atheism might be *for* as well as against: be sceptical, respect boundaries, normalize atheists and religion, have fun, be good, be generous, praise bacon and advocate for fair church taxation.[13]

A third (and for now final) potentially 'new' aspect of New Atheism is its political focus. Stephen LeDrew has argued that 'the new atheism is a secular fundamentalism' which aims at 'the universalisation of the ideology of scientism and the establishment of its cultural authority' and by extension the 'defense of the position of the white middle class male, and of modernity itself' (2016: 2). In contrast, McAnulla, Kettell and Schulzke 'find relatively little that is utopian within new atheism, instead conceiving it more as a movement seeking to assert rights and challenge religious privilege' (2018: 4–5). They go on to argue that whilst this movement seeks to advance a modernist agenda involving the reassertion of Enlightenment principles, 'it does so by utilising distinctly postmodern concerns and strategies', recognizing the fact that beliefs are scarcely more private than actions (2018: 51). New Atheism has also placed a strong emphasis on consciousness raising and atheist identity, in a process 'deliberately drawing on the lessons of previous movements (such as the civil rights and the feminist movements), forming a discourse based on minority rights and explicitly atheist symbols' (2018: 52). Common features that have been identified in New Atheist politics include: 'challenging the public role of religion through promoting secularist arguments', 'challenging the social customs perceived to protect religious beliefs from scrutiny and questioning both in public and private life' and the aforementioned promotion of an atheist identity-politics (Taira 2012; McAnulla, Kettell and Schulzke 2018: 154).

Why now?

The development of atheism from the sixteenth century onwards has been largely shaped by resistance to perceived or actual suppression. Religion was frequently seen as posing a barrier to social, political and economic progress, and thus atheists frequently aligned with more radical causes such as the abolition of slavery, issues of family planning, freedom of expression and so on. As I have already noted above regarding the upsurge in interest in the 'non-religious' (broadly conceived), the contemporary rise of New Atheism is connected to the political climate in the early twenty-first-century West. The technological advances of the same period, and the shift from modernism to postmodernism, have facilitated and to some extent prompted hitherto unprecedented levels of consciousness-raising and the promotion of an atheist identity politics (McAnulla, Kettell, and Schulzke 2018: 43–4).

By way of summary, in their conclusion McAnulla, Kettell and Schulzke note that the popular texts of the 'Four Horsemen' 'all spoke in part to the political context of the time' in which they emerged.

> Each was motivated by concern at the way religion was impacting upon public life, after periods in which many had assumed that its influence would inevitably fade … [New Atheism is] a reaction, in part, to the apparent failure of societies to continue secularising in the way that many social scientists and others had assumed they would. (2018: 160)

Thus, a seemingly diffuse 'intellectual' movement becomes deeply contextual, relevant and comprehensible when placed in its socio-historical context.

Humanism

If New Atheism is regularly constructed in popular and academic discourse as a form of 'bad non-religion' (see Chapter 2), then contenders for its 'good' counterpart might be the Sunday Assembly or Humanism. The Sunday Assembly, founded in 2013, is a movement spanning eight countries and seventy chapters 'where people sing songs, hear inspiring talks, and create community together'.[14] It is often described as an 'Atheist Church' in the media, and the movement is built upon the 'seemingly contradictory mix of rejection and acceptance of both religion and atheism, alongside the notion of "building inclusive community"' (Mortimer and Prideaux 2018: 65). A full doctoral dissertation has been written on the movement (Bullock 2017), as well as articles exploring the movement's 'positive non-religiosity' (Frost 2017) and its valorization of the secular as an object of belief and belonging (J. M. Smith 2017). Clearly the Sunday Assembly has much to say to the contemporary 'non-religious' landscape, yet my presentation now turns to a more established movement – Humanism, particularly in the UK.

Michel Foucault once commented that humanism is a concept with such a 'complex and chequered history that it would be almost impossible to pin it down as a framework of ideals and value commitments' (P. Johnson 2015: 307; cf. Foucault 1984: 44). Current chief executive of Humanists UK, Andrew Copson, argues that the first use of the term 'humanist' in English occurred in 1589, where it referred 'narrowly to a student of ancient languages or more widely to sophisticated academics of any subjects other than theology' (2015: 1). By the nineteenth century this label had been retrospectively applied to the revival of classical learning that occurred during the European Renaissance, and those in the tradition of thought ignited by this revival. At the same time, so the story goes, the term also began to be applied to a range of attitudes to living that were 'nonreligious, non-theistic, or non-Christian' (2015: 2). By the early-to-mid-twentieth century we then – through books, journals, speeches and institutions – started to see this 'humanism' being systematized and given form. It is this 'non-religious, non-theistic and naturalistic approach to life' (2015: 4) that is my focus here.

I shall first address, briefly, what this humanism might be, before turning to its expression in the UK context, with a focus on rituals (funerals and weddings), before concluding with the question of its relationship to religion.

What is humanism?

It should already be evident in asking this question that it will not have a clear answer. Furthermore, when asking it, one will frequently be answered by erudite and scholarly 'insiders'. This need not necessarily be a problem: indeed, 'insiders' write about 'religious' traditions all the time. However, it is always worth keeping potential agendas in the back of your mind.

Most definitions of 'humanism' centre on it being 'a commitment to the value and power of human beings' (Davie, Woodhead and Catto 2016: 568) in 'response to the widespread demand for an alternative to dogmatic religion'[15] or beliefs stressing the importance of 'God, inanimate nature, or totalitarian societies' (Crystal 1990). Copson (2015: 6) highlights the following minimum definition, from the International Humanist and Ethical Union, which has been adopted by humanist organizations in over forty countries:

> Humanism is a democratic and ethical life stance, which affirms that human beings have the right and responsibility to give meaning and shape to their own lives. It stands for the building of a more humane society through an ethic based on human and other natural values in the spirit of reason and free inquiry through human capabilities. It is not theistic, and it does not accept supernatural views of reality.[16]

He then delves into more detail, showing that beyond potentially being described as 'not religious', humanism broadly encompasses a number of threads on the understanding of reality and the self, morality and practical action (Copson 2015: 6–28; cf. Law 2013: 263–5; Engelke 2014: 5299). Stephen Law also helpfully argues that humanism does not include speciesism, utilitarianism, utopianism, scientism, naturalism, materialism or physicalism: 'while some Humanists may sign up to some, even all, of these various positions, they are free to abandon all of them without abandoning their Humanism' (2013: 267).

Much of what has been described above could be dubbed 'humanism with a small h', as opposed to institutional forms of Humanism, such as Humanists UK. This humanism is frequently encountered in the rhetorical construction of a shared 'humanist attitude' – a sort of 'implicit humanism'. Copson writes that 'what we now call a "humanist" attitude has found expression around the world for at least 2,500 years' (2015: 1) and points to an Ipsos Mori[17] poll from 2006, which found that about '36 per cent of UK residents had humanist beliefs in relation to science and morality' (2015: 29 n. 24). Edmund Leach argued that although humanism is 'openly avowed by only a small minority of individuals', it is 'tacitly accepted by a wide spectrum of educated people in all parts of the Western world' (2004), and more recently Callum Brown has decided that the 'most appropriate name' for the relentlessly positive 'new moral cosmos' he sees emerging in the West 'is probably humanism' (2017: 161). We also find this rhetoric in arguments for the inclusion of humanist voices on Thought for the

Day on BBC Radio 4 (Sawer 2018) or in Time for Reflection at the Scottish Parliament (Bonney 2013a, b).

However, this is not *merely* rhetoric – it also plays out on the ground. The whole notion of 'I didn't realize until now that I have been a humanist all along' bears striking resemblance to some 'religious' conversion stories (Bullivant 2008). Humanists UK even offer a 'How Humanist are you?' quiz on their website, stating, 'Many people are humanists without even knowing it.'[18] As with New Atheism, this is all part of the identity politics of institutional forms of Humanism, to which we shall now turn. It is striking, however, to note the relative lack of cogency of the identification 'humanist' even among the 'non-religious' population. In five of the nations studied by the *Understanding Unbelief: Across Disciplines and across Cultures* project, only 2–7 per cent of 'agnostics' and 'atheists' picked 'humanist' as the label closest to how they identify themselves (Bullivant et al. 2019: 10).[19]

Humanist institutions

Before discussing the UK context, it is worth noting a key difference between this and the United States, where one frequently encounters the compound term 'secular humanism'.[20] Some argue that this is a pejorative qualifier (Copson 2015), whilst others contend that Humanism in the United States has its roots in liberal forms of religion, particularly Unitarianism and Universalism. Cimino and Smith state:

> The question of whether to use a religious or secular framework was the main factor in a schism within the primary humanist group, the American Humanist Association (AHA), in the late 1970s. ... Thus, while religious humanists claim that humanism is a non-theistic religion, secular humanists define their movement as a strictly secular philosophy and value system and eschew any religious language. (2007: 409)

In the UK, the additional 'secular' has little purchase.

The British Humanist Association (BHA) was formed in 1896 and has over 28,000 members and supporters, including many distinguished public figures (Engelke 2015a: 217). Eighty-nine per cent of its members are 'White British', 69 per cent are male, 72 per cent have a university degree and 24 per cent are members of a political party (1.5 per cent is the UK average for party membership) (Engelke 2015a: 217). As a charity with an annual income of £1.1 million in 2011, the BHA aims to promote secularism, oppose faith-based education, oppose the teaching of creationism and so on. And although still technically the BHA, in May 2017 the organization changed its operating name to 'Humanists UK'.[21]

The Humanist Society Scotland (HSS) was formed in 1989 in response to a rising demand for nationwide Scottish organizations in an increasingly pro-devolution climate. It remains distinct from Humanists UK, but with close links. A personal communication from the current Chief Executive Fraser Sutherland maintains that in June 2018 the organization had over 14,500 paying members, 120 registered celebrants, 12 recently trained pastoral support workers, 50 trained school visitor volunteers and a successful StreetCare project running in Glasgow with plans to replicate this in Edinburgh. The organization had also performed around 28,000 wedding ceremonies since these became legal in 2005 (see above).

It is these ceremonies that provide Humanism with its most visible presence in the UK. In some nations, such as Norway, humanist ceremonies have strong institutional foundations and have been well-established for many years:

> There has been an alternative in Norway to the church-run confirmation of 14-year-olds since 1951, a 'civil confirmation' that is co-ordinated by the Norwegian Humanist Association and today accounts for 17 percent of all such ceremonies. (Engelke 2015a: 216)

And in 2012 the Belgian government provided €24 million to humanist and secularist organizations – a smaller amount than the €257 million received by the Catholic Church 'but larger than that given to Protestant, Muslim, Jewish, and other communities combined' (Engelke 2015a: 216).

In Matthew Engelke's studies of Humanist funerals in England, we learn that one of the nation's largest funeral providers, Co-operative Funeralcare, classed just over 10 per cent of their funerals as humanist in 2011 (2015a: 220). Engelke argues that the BHA engages in such activities to provide meaningful alternatives to religious ceremonies but also to 'serve constituencies they might otherwise not' (2015b: 35). As far as the motivations of those securing the BHA's services are concerned, Engelke discovered that it was statements with which individuals disagreed strongly – 'rather than those with which they might agree, or even entertain – that mattered most' (2015a: 225). Clients also placed a prime emphasis on 'authenticity', although this is a factor affecting many funerals – religious or not – in the contemporary UK context (2015a: 221). As far as the content of these funerals is concerned, at base there will be a clear message that there is no afterlife but a clear opposition to having a humanist 'master narrative' (versus 'traditional Christian' liturgies) (2015a: 229). Ceremonies will generally incorporate a 'moment of reflection', which, although arguably democratic, contains 'the kernel of an important assertion' that religion 'is just another view' (2015a: 227).

Turning to Humanist weddings, we should first note that these have been legal in Scotland since 2005 and became legal in June 2018 in Northern Ireland. The Westminster Parliament gave the government the power to legally recognize Humanist marriages in 2013 in England and Wales, but no government since then has acted on that power. Indeed, Humanists UK have recently marshalled data showing that, in Scotland, 'humanist marriages are almost four times less likely to end in divorce than others' to argue, once again, that these should be available throughout the UK (Copson 2019). As noted above, Isabella Kasselstrand's research in Scotland has seen Humanist ceremonies increase in popularity to become second only to civil ceremonies in 2016 (2018: 274). Many of Kasselstrand's informants acknowledge the importance of their 'non-belief' in choosing a Humanist ceremony – because they do not want a ceremony that does not speak to their own values and/or because they do not want to be 'discourteous' to religious organizations (2018: 281). However, the choice for a Humanist rather than a civil ceremony was often guided by assumptions surrounding the lack of flexibility or personalization in a civil ceremony. From personal experience, I would contest her informants' bleak assessment of civil ceremonies, yet it is important to note that the striking and relatively sudden growth in popularity of Humanist wedding ceremonies is not at the expense of civil ones but of those provided by the Church of Scotland. Kasselstrand concludes that this 'suggests that Scottish secularisation has indeed created a high demand for secular ceremonies that was not fully met when nonreligious Scots were limited to a civil ceremony', meaning that in other contexts 'it is likely that the popularity of religious ceremonies is, to some extent, inflated as a result of the limited availability of options for nonreligious individuals' (2018: 190).

Humanism and religion

Finally, it is worth considering the relationship between Humanism and the category religion. It must be stated that trying to assess whether Humanism *is* a religion or not is fundamentally an uncritical, normative project which assumes that religion is easy to define. However, strategic claims that Humanism is or is not a religion are frequently made in popular discourse – there is much to be gained or lost when being considered a religion – and thus these are discourses worthy of critical engagement.

First, it is important that we ask who is making a claim about Humanism's relationship to religion. 'Insider' definitions of Humanism will almost invariably emphasize its non-religious credentials. 'Outsider' discourse might be keen to distance Humanism from the category of religion to deny it certain privileges. On the other hand, evangelicals in the United States have been keen to emphasize Humanism's religion-like qualities in order to keep it out of schools (Engelke 2014), that is, in order that it be denied the same privileges apparently denied to evangelicalism.

Second, we might consider whether Humanism is substantively or functionally religious. Engelke acknowledges that, due to substantive similarities, any 'student of religion in Britain might well assume' that he is writing about 'the stereotypical Church of England congregation' when he writes about UK humanist groups (2014: 5299). To this, we might respond by asking, for example, whether 'religious questions' – seemingly important to Christianity and Humanism – are, in fact, simply 'human questions'. Indeed, James Thrower declares that, substantively, 'it would be hard, if not impossible, to maintain that there is a [specifically] religious dimension to humanism' (1990: 45). Functionally, we might look to Humanism's community or ritual dimensions. Engelke argues, 'Organized humanism … is a reminder of the importance of community, of collective action, and of social solidarity to "free thinkers"' (2015a: 230), and he points to the seeming irony of those who are 'often emphatic about their independence, individuality, and autonomy' also seeming to value communities of 'like-minded people' (2014: 5298). Yet, to this we might respond by asking: Are communities of like-minded people religious or human? On the ritual side, my descriptions above should have emphasized that decisions to embrace humanist ceremonies are 'oftentimes, at least in part, … [grounded in] respect for, rather than a rejection of, the religious foundation of churches' (Kasselstrand 2018: 290). Yet, does this make certain (or all) rituals 'religious'? Or is ritual simply a fundamental human activity?

Thrower concludes:

> A blanket definition of religion in which none, or at least few, can be said to be non-religious may give comfort to those religious people who wish to feel that all are for them and none are against them, but one cannot surely sweep away the very real differences that exist between humanists and the religious of the world simply by means of a redefinition of religion. (1990: 48)

Yet he also notes that inasmuch as Humanism is grounded in a rejection of religion (historically and in popular discourse), 'it is open to the charge that it has not passed beyond the sphere of the religious' (1990: 48). This, then, raises a further question: Is Humanism 'non-religious'? In other words, should it be primarily defined by a relationship of difference to religion? Andrew Copson responds that it should not, because most humanists relate to religion with a minor anthropological interest or a mild nostalgia (2015: 27). It might be tempting to dismiss this as disingenuous wishful thinking. Yet it also speaks to what Peter Derkx points to as a divide within the humanist movement, between those 'fighting for the legitimate but limited interest of humanists themselves' and those fighting for their 'view and take on the public interest, the good of all humanity and the world' (2015: 434). He concludes that where the former is prioritized, 'humanism will more often be defined in negative terms as necessarily non-theistic or even non-religious' (2015: 435). Thus, once again, we see that the critical question is not whether humanism is religious/non-religious but who wins and loses by such a classification?

Key issues

In drawing this survey of the non-religious landscape to a close, I wish to focus on a couple of key issues emerging in the contemporary field: intersectionality and 'non-religion' beyond the West. However, there are many other fascinating avenues being explored in contemporary research – from meaning-making (Taves 2018; Taves, Asprem and Ihm 2018; Bullivant et al. 2019) to health and well-being (Cornwell and Waite 2009; Hwang 2013; Speed and Coleman 2019) to pro-sociality (Gore et al. 2019; Nash 2019: 5; J. M. Smith and Cragun 2019: 7) – which readers are encouraged to explore.

Intersectionality

Intersectionality places the multiplicity of social actors' different identifications and (perceived) group memberships at focus. An intersectional approach holds that 'no social aspect, experience, or characteristic may be fully understood without attending to the ways it is shaped and influenced by multiple, interlocking systems of oppression and privilege' (R. T. Cragun and Sumerau 2017: 2), including between the researcher and the researched. For instance, as Cragun and Sumerau argue, a 'non-religious' person

> does not merely experience the world as nonreligious, but rather as a nonreligious person situated within specific historical and contemporary race, class, gender, sex, and sexual hierarchies that shape their experience of nonreligion. (2017: 2)

We will now briefly explore some key findings relating to the intersection of 'non-religiosity' with gender, race and ethnicity and sexuality. Much of what is said below is unfortunately quite binary – particularly when discussing gender – due in part to space but mainly to a dearth of nuanced studies of religion (never mind non-religion) that provide space for more fluid identifications. Furthermore, 'Even within the West, very little is known about atheism and nonreligion among gender, sexual, racial, and ethnic minorities' (J. M. Smith and Cragun 2019: 11).

Despite signs that indicate that the disparity may be levelling off in younger age cohorts (Bullivant 2017; Trzebiatowska 2019), a wide variety of global statistics suggest that, on every measure of religion, women are more religious than men (Trzebiatowska and Bruce 2014; Mahlamäki 2012: 60). A number of explanations for this disparity have been proposed over the years, including focusing upon historical gender roles and an apparent evolved tendency for men to be less risk averse (Brewster 2013: 512–15; cf. Edgell, Frost and Stewart 2017). Given the fact that 'religions' have historically and stereotypically foregrounded male actors and leaders, been transmitted by men to men, founded by men and perhaps with central texts written by men (Mahlamäki 2012: 62; Schwartz 2013; Finger 2017), one might expect women to be attracted to more atheistic positions and for atheism and feminism to go hand-in-hand. However, even among the minority of women who reject religion, 'female atheists constitute a minority within a minority and fewer even actively participate in the organized atheist movement' (Trzebiatowska 2019: 476; cf. Mahlamäki 2012: 64). Recent scholarship has built a convincing case that conventional models of secularization are heavily inflected by the male gaze and based on a myth of liberalism (Scott 2018) and 'a norm of masculine rationality which excludes women and their experiences' (Schwartz 2013: 222; cf. Cady and Fessenden 2013: 6; Guenther 2019). Furthermore, despite avowed support for gender equality in theory, organized forms of atheism are frequently perceived as boys' clubs (Brewster 2013: 517) rife with implicit and explicit misogyny (Mahlamäki 2012: 62; Guenther 2019; Trzebiatowska 2019: 477). This is particularly the case for New Atheism, despite its credentials as a young, post-feminist movement that directly challenges sexist practices, claims to support women's rights and is predominantly present in the United States, where there is an established history of women's leadership in the secular movement (Guenther 2019: 49).

Turning to race and ethnicity, I have already noted above that according to the 2015 British Social Attitudes Survey, 95 per cent of those identifying with 'no religion' also identify as 'White' as compared to the 87 per cent British average

(Bullivant 2017: 11). Callum Brown attests to 'easily 98 per cent of all attenders' at the humanist and atheist groups he has studied in the UK and North America being 'white' (2017: 137). Detailed scholarly work on the intersection between non-religion and race/ethnicity is relatively thin on the ground, although the situation is getting better, with a couple of historical texts from Alexander (2019) and Cameron (2019) appearing recently. A useful 'insider' source focusing on the African American experience is Sikivu Hutchinson's *Moral Combat: Black Atheists, Gender Politics, and the Values Wars* (2011). Here, Hutchinson draws attention to a study (Pew Research Center 2009) which demonstrated that 87 per cent of African Americans described themselves as 'religious', with 79 per cent claiming religion is very important in their lives (compared with 56 per cent among the entire US population). She goes on to argue that organized religion (specifically Christianity) enabled African Americans to 'stake a claim to being human and to being American' in a context of slavery and 'sovereign white manhood', whilst simultaneously prescribing 'a rigid hierarchy of masculinity and femininity based on heterosexist norms' (2011: loc. 1467). It facilitated self-determination and established '"insider" status and racial authenticity' (2011: loc. 2912). In this context, many non-white atheists and humanists are critical of 'white atheists' often 'paternalistic and ahistorical criticism of the role of religion in African American, Latino, and Native American cultures' (2011: loc. 2912). Hutchinson castigates New Atheism in particular for preserving and reproducing 'the status quo of white supremacy' by pointing the finger squarely at 'religion' instead of 'fighting against white racism, sexism, and classism' (2011: loc. 3105). This experience of non-religion as a white preserve is further heightened (in the United States at least) for black LGBTQ people, who frequently find that becoming non-religious means 'breaking ties that alleviate racism' and moving to 'largely white' spaces where they 'encounter racism and discrimination' (Kolysh 2017: 3).

This brings us finally to the intersection between non-religion and LGBTQ identifications. It will hardly be surprising that LGBTQ individuals are much more likely to identify as non-religious than the general population. For example, 46 per cent of LGBTQ people in the United States claim 'no religious affiliation' in 2016, compared with 24 per cent of the general population (Beredjick 2017: loc. 913; D. Cox and Jones 2017). Escaping religious intolerance is a central theme in the stories of many LGBTQ people (Brewster 2013: 518); yet although the language of 'coming out of the closet' has been taken up by many non-religious activists (2013: 520–1), statistics suggest that 'whilst prejudice toward atheists certainly exists, the intensity of such experience appears to be muted' in comparison with the experience of LGBTQ people (2013: 522; Beredjick 2017: loc. 761; cf. Edgell, Gerteis and Hartmann 2006). Simone Kolysh argues that 'some LGBT spaces are religiophobic and some religious LGBT spaces are suspect of non-religious LGBT people' (2017: 3), meaning that many experience a 'double stigma' (Brewster 2013: 518). Furthermore, Cragun and Sumerau's recent research suggests that 'it is more acceptable for nonreligious people, who are still considered "deviant" minorities in American culture, to have additional deviant identities, like being homosexual, bisexual, or transgender' (2017: 8). They use quantitative data to demonstrate that deviation from a religious norm is more socially acceptable than deviating in terms of sexuality or gender (2017: 12). Indeed, 'being nonreligious actually may reduce the ramifications of sexual and gender nonconformity because such an endeavour erases conflicts between religious assumptions and marginalized selfhood' (2017: 13).

The observations above demonstrate the enormous potential of research which takes an intersectional approach to non-religious identification, the rejection of religion and so on and clearly works against naïve ideal-typical approaches to non-religion as a unified phenomenon.

Beyond the West

It has become a familiar refrain among non-religion researchers that 'very little is known about nonreligious individuals and nonbelievers outside of the developed, Western world' (J. M. Smith and Cragun 2019: 11; cf. Lee and Cotter 2018: 8). That being said, several studies have emerged which shed light on the situation in the Islamic/Arab world (Eller 2010; Schielke 2013), India (Quack 2012, 2013), Japan (Roemer 2010; Whylly 2013), Ghana (Yirenkyi and Takyi 2010), China (Liang 2010), South America (Costa 2017) and the former USSR (Thrower 1983; Hormel 2010; Borowik, Ančić and Tyraľa 2013). In addition, Zuckerman, Galen and Pasquale (2016) engage in short discussions of 'secularity' in 'the Sinic and Buddhist Regions' (37–9), Latin America (44–6), 'the Islamic World and Africa' (46–9) and on 'Jewish secularity' (49–51). A few brief comments on the situation in the former USSR, India and Japan will draw this chapter to its conclusion and reinforce my repeated emphasis on the contextuality of non-religion (see Chapter 6 in particular).

During a period from the Russian Revolution of 1917 through to breakup of the Soviet Union in 1991, a swath of nations were subjected to an 'antireligious campaign seeking to disestablish influential religions like Eastern Orthodoxy, to rationalize all church property, and to transfer responsibility in providing public services ... from church to state organizations' (Hormel 2010: 46). This meant that the percentage of child baptisms decreased, rates of atheism increased and success in any sort of career became dependent upon being seen to be 'engaged in the promotion of atheistic views' (Borowik, Ančić and Tyraľa 2013: 624). However, these experiences were not uniform, and in most countries in the region, the Soviet 'period was almost three decades shorter – in most cases, from 1945–1989/1991', meaning 'that in some countries the continuity of religious transfer was completely interrupted, while in others it was not' (2013: 623). This has resulted in rates of atheism from 9.6 per cent in Ukraine to 23.1 per cent in the Russian Federation to 52.1 per cent in Estonia (2013: 630), with evidence supporting the possibility that atheism was internalized by those who spent their entire lives under the Soviet system (Hormel 2010: 58). On the other hand, 'Individuals in post-Soviet societies may seek to reject communism (through baptism), yet still question if they believe in God' (2010: 59).

Writing on the Indian context, Johannes Quack asks two key questions: 'whether it is "anachronistic" to speak of pre-modern atheism and whether it is a form of "mental colonialism" to refer to non-Western people as atheists' (2013: 651). Quack points out that the god that Indian 'atheists' reject could refer to an abstract metaphysical absolute, the inner self, half-gods, ghosts, demons, natural forces, moral principles and more (2013: 652). Furthermore, although there are specific modes of atheistic thought present within Hinduism – critiques of the ascetic lifestyle, moral duty, personalism, afterlife/the soul (Frazier 2013: 376–8) – Quack dubs it questionable to equate these historical currents with 'contemporary atheist positions that draw on modern science, Marxism, utilitarianism, a universal concept of religion and the division between "natural" and "super-natural"' and other discursive developments (2013: 655). In *Disenchanting India* (2012), Quack demonstrates that for the 0.1 per cent of Indians who did not state a religious identification on the 2001 census (2013: 659), the identification 'rationalist' carries much more weight, with an emphasis upon anti-superstition and political activism, and a desire to trace this rationalism to the Vedic age (to combat the charge that rationalists are 'agents of the West') (2013: 49).

Finally, it has become a common argument in recent years – most succinctly expressed in Josephson's *The Invention of Religion in Japan* (2012)[22] – that the concept of 'religion' is intimately connected to the Meiji period (1868–1912), during which Japan experienced increasing 'interaction with Europe and the United States, [which] led to confrontation with many concepts of Western interest, including atheism' (Whylly 2013: 665). The increasing presence of Christianity during this period led to an atmosphere where 'religion' and 'Christianity' were equated and perceived as a threat to Japanese culture and science (2013: 671). This background in part explains why, in contemporary Japan, 'most identify themselves as nonreligious but make a point of carrying out a variety of private and public rituals that connect them with kami, buddhas, or ancestors' (Roemer 2010: 23). Being 'non-religious' in Japan does not equate with being 'atheist', and not only is it unlikely that a Japanese person will disavow 'the existence of all supernatural beings', this issue is 'simply not very important to most Japanese' (2010: 24–5). Whilst there are 'possibly more atheists in Japan than those who claim personal religious affiliation', a combination of these groups makes up less than 40 per cent of the population (2010: 40), and participation in various 'customary' or 'traditional' rituals remains remarkably high.

In each of these contexts, identifying or being identified as 'atheist' or 'non-religious' means vastly different things, demonstrating once again the importance of placing our generalized discussions of religion and non-religion into their socio-historical context and being 'vigilantly specific about the aspect of "nonreligion" that [we] are interested in' (Jong 2015: 20).

Conclusion

The purpose of this chapter was to present a broad survey of the field of non-religion studies with particular reference to the UK context. I began by building the case that non-religion is worthy of study not simply because it seemingly serves as the boundary of the study of religion but also because it allows us to assess claims to the universality of religion, to explore real-world contestations involving some key non-religious identifiers and to continue and develop the highly pertinent questioning of the problematic religion/non-religion and religion/secular binaries. I then presented an overview of non-religion studies to date, proceeding through a discussion of the key vocabulary populating the field, some important statistics and demographics, some key non-religious manifestations and some central issues animating existing scholarship.

My aim throughout was to generally set critical issues to one side and provide a snapshot of research to date that should not only be of use as a survey chapter but also sets the scene for the critical analysis and empirical material that constitutes the remainder of this volume. We have learned that surveys are problematic, that context is key and that ideologies, agendas and political climates animate the production and presentation of notionally objective scholarship. We have seen that terminology matters and will never satisfy everyone, that intersectional approaches have much to offer, that speaking of the non-religious as a coherent group – or even as a group at all – is problematic at best and that asking who wins and loses by the demarcation and labelling of certain phenomena as religious or not can be much more interesting than assessing the validity of such acts of classification.

In the next chapter, I present an account of the critical study of religion, before turning this approach on much of the material presented above. In the process, I outline a discursive solution to many of the critical issues I identify, before focusing in the remainder of the book on my own empirical contribution to the critical study of 'non-religion', rooted in a vibrant district in my adopted home of Edinburgh, Scotland.

Critical religion, critical non-religion

The industry known as religious studies is a kind of generating plant for a value laden view the world that claims to identify religions and faiths as an aspect of all societies and that, by so doing, makes possible another separate 'non-religious' conceptual space, a fundamental area of presumed factual objectivity. (Fitzgerald 2000b: 8)

This book has been written with the aim to critically engage with, reframe and, to some degree, rehabilitate the burgeoning body of contemporary research on non-religion, discussed in the previous chapter, within the framework of the critical academic study of religion, and to explore the benefits of such a reframing for empirical research. Before going any further, it is therefore necessary to provide an account of what I mean by 'the critical study of religion'. I will then continue by reflecting on the research on non-religion and identifying several critical problems which directly relate to one of the central themes in the academic study of religion – namely, the ever-raging debates surrounding the definition of 'religion'. I then turn to one justifiably fashionable approach to these debates – Discourse Analysis – and proceed to outline existing discursive approaches to religion and some of the key terminology employed therein. Finally, I provide a discursive re-reading of studies of 'non-religion' and outline the research agenda for the empirical material in the chapters that follow. This chapter does much of the theoretical heavy lifting for the rest of the book and, as such, is quite densely populated with citations and other scholarly scaffolding. Readers are encouraged to engage with my argument but may wish to jump to the methodological scene-setting in the following chapter or straight into the empirical material that follows. However, I promise to make it worth your while.

Critical religion

It would be impossible and somewhat counter-productive for me to attempt to do justice to the critical study of religion in a few pages, as others have trod this ground many times before. For a thorough, book-length introduction to the field, readers are encouraged to explore Craig Martin's *A Critical Introduction to the Study of Religion* (2017). For a recent example of such critical study in action, there are few better chapters than Naomi Goldenberg's 'Forget about Defining "It" … ' (2018). And readers should also engage with the work of Talal Asad (1993, 2003), Timothy Fitzgerald (2000b, 2007a, 2011, 2015a, b), Aaron Hughes (2015), Tomoko Masuzawa (2005), Russell T. McCutcheon (1997, 2003, 2007, 2014), Jonathan Z. Smith (1978, 1982, 1998) and Bruce Lincoln (1992, 2003) – particularly his 'Theses on Method' (1996). And, indeed, this very book is an example of the critical study of religion in action. However, a few paragraphs of introduction are necessary here.

Throughout this book, I shall use 'critical study of religion' and the more expedient 'critical religion' interchangeably to refer, with Fitzgerald, to the 'critical historical deconstruction of "religion" *and related categories*' (2015b: 303–4). By 'critical', we 'need assume neither cynicism nor dissimulation … and ought to probe scholarly discourse and practice as much as any other' (Lincoln 1996: 226). It is, as I and my colleagues have recently argued, simply part of healthy intellectual life:

> We dismantle ideas, dissect arguments and concepts, consider their limitations, their intellectual and social significance, and place them in their historical, social, political and cultural contexts. (Cotter, Quadrio and Tuckett 2017: 2)

The focus upon religion should not be taken to imply that religion is an 'it' that requires special treatment (Ramey 2015) – nor, indeed, special departments for its study (to follow Fitzgerald's argument in this chapter's epigraph). Indeed, the word has been and can be marshalled to apply to pretty much 'anything and everything that exists in the world and/or that pertains to human beings' (Goldenberg 2018: 83). However, religion is a distinctly problematic and contested category which is implicated in a particular history and bound up in the discourses and power dynamics of modernity. It is a contested domain particularly prone to assertions of self-evidence and the taken-for-granted and is thus especially deserving of critical historical deconstruction (J. Z. Smith 2015: 30).

In Goldenberg's excellent summation of the body of critical religion scholarship, she argues that religion 'is a modern concept that operates as a distorting anachronism when applied to the study of earlier epochs' (2018: 80; cf. Nongbri 2013). It 'has roots in European colonial ambitions and intellectual history' (Goldenberg 2018: 80; cf. J. Z. Smith 1998: 275; Cotter and Robertson 2016b), and many accounts of religion have (implicitly or explicitly) justified the cultural superiority of Christian Europe (C. Martin 2017: 13). Indeed, the very concept of religion is 'a citation of Christianity as idealized prototype' (Goldenberg 2018: 80), generally prioritizing 'belief' and 'doctrine' as preserved in texts as the *sine qua non* (Lopez Jr. 1998: 21). Therefore, any claim that religion is a timeless, universal, ahistorical phenomenon promotes Christian hegemony (Goldenberg 2018: 80). This seemingly innocuous notion can prove particularly problematic in legal cases. Furthermore, whatever is demarcated as 'not religious' in a given context is a function of power (2018: 80): any presentation of 'non-religious' groups 'as more reasonable than "religious" groups' seems just as self-serving as narratives that privilege one 'religion' over another (C. Martin 2017: 11). Similarly, defining 'religion' as somehow more irrational than other 'secular' phenomena 'is a convenient way to justify killing enemies we can successfully label as irrationally "religious"' (C. Martin 2017: 12; cf. Cavanaugh 2009).

In sum, it *matters* that 'there is no such thing that answers to the name "religion"' but only phenomena that 'we habitually label religious' for historically contingent reasons (Jong 2015: 20). Continuing to treat it as an unproblematic, self-evident category 'at best impedes clarity of study and at worst obscures operations of political ideology' (Goldenberg 2018: 80).

The academic study of non-religion

We have been introduced to the fruits of this study in the preceding chapter, yet it is rhetorically useful for me to introduce the academic study of 'non-religion'[1] by returning to the narrative of my research journey outlined in this book's introduction. From an initial undergraduate foray into examining the 'critique, agenda and inherent precariousness' of New Atheism (exemplified in the work of four white male authors) (Cotter 2011a), my postgraduate work began with the construction of an analytic typology (Cotter 2011b) of the narratives of seemingly 'non-religious' students at the University of Edinburgh. Here I adapted an earlier iteration of Lois Lee's definition of non-religion – 'anything which is *primarily* defined by a relationship of difference to religion' (2012b: 131 emphasis in original) – yet, as my own approach began to develop in a more critical direction, I began to take my lead from Johannes Quack's 'relational approach'

(2014). I quickly latched on to 'non-religion' as my preferred umbrella term in my studies – as opposed to Zuckerman, Galen and Pasquale's (2016) preference for 'secular' – precisely because the term is clearly an academic construction, with little colloquial purchase (and thus less potential for confusion), and also because of my positioning within critical *religious* studies.

Quack advocates a ground-up methodological approach which avoids understanding the non-religious through a lens of normative religiosity and, as such, utilizes the notion of non-religion as 'a descriptive term for a certain group of understudied phenomena and not as an analytical term aiming to draw clear boundaries between religion and non-religion' (2014: 441). Non-religion, in this understanding, is not everything which is not religious. Neither does utilizing the term mean that one is defending 'any universal distinction between religion and non-religion' (2014: 441). These are understood as mutually exclusive categories merely for analytical purposes, and they do not cover the full range of extant phenomena. In Quack's model, 'irreligious' covers the full range of phenomena which are not religious, whereas

> 'Non-religious' and 'a-religious' are … mutually exclusive sub-fields of all that is irreligious … any analysis of non-religious phenomena necessarily relates to a specific discourse on 'religion', while a-religious phenomena are generally described and analysed without any reference to religious phenomena. (2014: 446)

Thus,

> 'Non-religion' is not to be understood as a something with thing-like existence, not as something that has clear definitions with primary and secondary features but as denoting various ways of relating to religion (whatever is understood to be religious in any specific case). (2014: 448)

As we shall see below, and in the following chapter, I argue that a discursive adaptation of this relational approach provides an effective means of embracing the study of non-religion within the critical study of religion and avoiding the pitfalls of other approaches. Discussion now turns to a critical assessment of four dominant approaches to the non-religious – which I dub 'subtractionist', 'context-specific', 'substantial' and 'discursive' – and concludes that the latter provides our way forward.

Subtractionist approaches

As noted in the previous chapter when describing the context in which I initially began my research journey, Bullivant and Lee trace a historical neglect of non-religion to the apparent non-religiosity of many of the social sciences' early pioneers who, in trying to understand why so many people could believe in something 'so absurd', 'arguably failed to recognize that their own lack of belief might itself be amenable to similar research' (2012: 20).[2] At the same time, they also point to extensive interest in the anomaly of 'unbelief' from Catholic social scientists throughout the 1950s and 1960s (see Caporale and Grumelli 1971). In his own summary of the state of the field, Frank Pasquale highlights that much of the early research that mentions the non-religious has included them 'as a comparison group, a statistical outlier, or an afterthought' or, indeed, as a *problem* to be dealt with (2012; also Lee 2015: 52). Indeed this seems to hold for a body of work, largely within the sociology of religion, which acknowledges the non-religious but tends to pay them little attention, or treat them as a monolithic minority religious position alongside other minority groups – as a residual category, or abnormality (as in, for example, Sherkat and Ellison 1999: 367; C. Smith et al. 2002: 600; Bryant 2006). For our purposes, these can be understood as exemplifying the first type of academic approach to the non-religious, variously understood: in this case, as *an uninteresting residuum*.[3] Indeed, Lois Lee justifiably devotes a significant amount of space in *Recognizing the Non-Religious* (2015) to charting this subtractionist approach to religion's 'insubstantial' other, which, she argues, 'pervades social scientific research' and 'is visible in religion-centric methodologies, in which the secular is viewed as a context in which religion exists and is enacted' (2015: 50). In other words, these acknowledgements of the 'other than religious' occur in a framework that is dominated by secularization theory and focused upon religion as something substantial and interesting, as opposed to the insubstantial, empty, baseline norm that remains when religion is removed from the equation. As Aaron Hughes argues, this amounts to a reification of 'the "religious" as if it somehow existed independently from more social or political (i.e. mundane) concerns' (2015: 1) and also unjustifiably constructs scholars as rational outsiders studying a bounded phenomenon known as 'religion'.

Context-specific approaches

A second body of approaches to the non-religious are those which are context-specific,[4] though being restricted to very specific contexts – historical, textual, ethnographic and so on. For example, the 'Atheisms' presented in studies of Atheism in Antiquity, such as Bremmer (2007), Drachmann (1922), Sedley (2013) or Thrower (1980), are 'couched in history' and 'affixed to the contexts within which they exist' (Quillen 2015b: 118). Thus, although they are very interesting in and of themselves, they 'should not be seen as merely describing the word "Atheism," but instead understood as descriptions of the historical time and place within which the usage of that word itself is being used' (2015b: 118). This makes it very difficult for scholars to engage in comparisons with Atheism in different historical contexts or for these studies to contribute *directly* to contemporary debates on category formation within the critical study of religion. Similar issues of translation are encountered with studies dealing with restricted bodies of texts – such as my undergraduate dissertation – or social-scientific studies which focus closely on particular non-religious groups and contexts – such as Aston (2015), Cimino and Smith (2007, 2010, 2015), Cotter (2011a), Engelke (2011, 2014), Lee (2015), Mumford (2015), Quack (2012) or Tomlins (2015). As with the historical studies, I am not claiming that these studies do not contain conceptual theorization, which goes beyond the context at focus, nor that there is no merit to such contextually bounded studies. Indeed, Naomi Goldenberg has not infrequently chastised me for my continued use of the abstract, mystifying categories of 'religion' and 'non-religion' – why not use more specific terminology? Yes, doing so 'does not aim to completely dispel the nebulae which surround all meanings', but, she argues,

> By naming groups more specifically as Jews, Catholics, and Hindus, rather than as 'religions,' I momentarily stop propagating the idea that 'religion' exists as an abstraction of which there are only examples. The more specific the name of the group the greater will be the gesture towards particular histories, behaviours and polities. (2018: 92)

However, given that my interest throughout this book concerns discourse on the category of religion – rather than some 'it' pointed to by the discourse – and given that, as we shall see in the following chapter, my chosen field site intentionally mitigated against the consistent application of more specific terminology, this was not an approach I wished to take.[5] By way of contrast, I argue that context-specific studies have much more to say to the central concerns of this volume when they are read critically via the 'discursive' approach outlined later. In this way, they can better help us critically engage with, reframe and rehabilitate contemporary research on non-religion within a critical religion framework.

Substantial approaches

A third approach takes up the baton where subtractionist approaches left off
tempts to give substance to this residual category. Common motivating

factors for such approaches, as noted in Chapter 1, are large-scale social surveys, such as those presented by Zuckerman (2007), which are taken to demonstrate that 'nonbelievers in God' as a group come in fourth place behind 'Christianity', 'Islam' and 'Hinduism', with between 500 and 750 million 'adherents' (Zuckerman 2010: 96). If smaller groups are deemed worthy of scholarly attention, so the argument goes, then the same attention should be directed towards this constituency: the world's 'fourth largest religion' (Lee 2015: 61; cf. Baker and Smith 2015: 1; Zuckerman, Galen and Pasquale 2016: 4–6). Adopting this defensible logic, we thus find a growing body of scholarly work focusing on the 'nones'[6] – a residual category constructed by censuses and surveys which, once in place, has seen many within and outside the academy rushing to 'imbue this group with a material face, social interests and political persuasions, as if this group, always there but now with a name, is available for their commentary and speculation' (Ramey and Miller 2013: n.p.). As Lee notes, the phrase 'the nones' has 'no meaning except in relation to multiple-choice grammars', and thus, 'in accommodating and attending to non-affiliation, academics are implicated in the creation not only of a population but of a social group' (Lee 2015: 132). Thus, in addition to work focusing specifically on the nones of religion-centric surveys, we find a further body of material, including my own Master's dissertation, which aims to substantiate, in some way or other, *what it 'means'* to be other than religious.[7]

Much of the work exemplifying this third approach to the non-religious has a great deal to offer to the academic study of religion and related categories in terms of in-depth qualitative and quantitative studies of identity formation, ritual, parenting, politics, gender, material culture and more. It is also important to note that specific works can and do take multiple approaches. However, from a critical perspective in particular, there are a number of cogent criticisms that can be raised. Discussion now turns to three of these critiques, utilizing Cotter (2011b) and Lee (2015) as particular case studies, before turning to a fourth approach to non-religion that sits much more comfortably within a critical framework. By this point, the reader should be internalizing an accurate impression that my main interlocutor in the substantive study of non-religion is Lois Lee. Lois is a good friend and a long-time colleague and whilst I clearly take issue with a number of aspects of her work from a critical religion perspective (see below), it also contains much of value in empirical and methodological material, and detailed attempts to theorize and provide a vocabulary for an emerging field of study.

The substantial 'non-religious' and the world religions paradigm

I have emphasized *ad nauseum* that I position this book within the critical study of religion, a sub-field of Religious Studies that is particularly focused on the deconstruction of categories and exposing the power dynamics inherent in the utilization of these categories by a variety of interlocutors, including academics. A major target for this critical study has been the 'World Religions Paradigm' (WRP) – a taxonomy of religions that

> typically includes 'the Big Five' … of Christianity, Islam, Judaism, Hinduism and Buddhism – and moreover, almost always presented in that Abrahamocentric order – increasingly with additional 'catch-all' categories such as 'indigenous religions' or 'new religions' included. (Cotter and Robertson 2016b: 2)

The WRP has been thoroughly critiqued for, among other things, repeating and reinforcing a model based on the presumptions of Protestant missionaries, centred on the primacy of belief and evinced by texts and institutions, privileging the accounts of elites, de-emphasizing variation and syncretism and marginalizing constructions which do not fit into the major categories (see Owen 2011; King 1999). The point here is not to rehearse these critiques[8] but to argue that substantive approaches to 'non-religion' are implicated in them.

I have drawn attention above to arguments that the non-religious are worthy of scholarly attention due to significant numbers of '(non-)adherents', and already in this basic argument, we can see a logic of WRP-expansion in play. However, if we turn to Lee's *Recognizing the Non-Religious* as a recent paradigmatic example, we can see this logic being invoked much more subtly. My focus on Lee should not be taken to imply that hers is the only work in which we can see this logic exemplified. Indeed, I could have equally focused upon my own work here.

In Lee's text, we see the non-religious being referred to as a 'group' (2015: 12), the study of which is justified alongside the study of 'traditional and … alternative religions' and spirituality (2015: 3). Lee embarked upon her study of this group alongside other

> empirical phenomena that are typically, if somewhat indeterminately, called 'secular', … [with the] sense that being 'secular' might not only be a matter of being *without* religion but also a matter of being *with* something else. (2015: 5)

Ultimately, she views her work as 'taking seriously the possibility of a substantial aspect to "secularity"' (2015: 69) in contrast to those theorists who 'see the endpoint of secularization processes in the achievement of hollow or insubstantial secularity, and see non-religious cultures as a temporary and incidental feature of that process' (2015: 14).

There is much to commend here. Indeed, if we grant the various 'religions' – 'alternative' and 'traditional' – and 'spiritualities' substance, and view social actors' identifications with various religions as saying something meaningful about their subjectivities, shouldn't the same respect be given to the non-religious or secular? Such an understanding recognizes as legitimate the position of those in society who wish, for whatever reason, to distance themselves from 'religion' and destabilizes presumptions of normative religiosity that accompany viewing society through a religion-coated lens. However, when considered in conjunction with the critique of the WRP, there is a danger that substantiating the secular and non-religious in this manner simply 'rearranges the deckchairs on the Titanic' (Sutcliffe 2016: 27) while 'the band plays on despite the ship taking on water' (McCutcheon 2005: 35). As I have argued with David G. Robertson, although such a move to 'expand the tent' of the WRP 'might seem at first a positive step', it actually further entrenches the typology (2016b: 12). The incorporation of the additional categories such as non-religious or secular enables them to 'act as "pressure valves", allowing for voices which otherwise do not fit' the WRP, and essentially forcing them 'to behave like World Religions', homogenizing differences and prioritizing certain religion-like features (2016b: 12). In this manner, 'differences and contradictions which might potentially challenge the presuppositions of the WRP are co-opted in its service, sometimes against the best intentions of' the author (2016b: 12).

This final point is worth emphasizing, as Lee also goes on to critique the very notion of dividing populations up according to religion, pointing out that 'There is no "opt-out" sub-category in the studies of gender, race, politics, nationality, age, education, ethnicity, or any other major sociological category' (Lee 2015: 196). Clearly something is wrong with this classificatory schema – or, indeed, with the acceptance of religion as a 'major sociological category'. Strategically or subversively employing the WRP can be a useful tool of critique, and Lee clearly sees her work as contributing to this, arguing that the study of non-religion might precipitate a much wider reformation in academic discourse (Lee 2012a: 4–5) and acknowledging that 'non-religion studies' will have failed if the term is still being employed in ten years (Lee 2012c). However, despite this admirable critical intent, the concurrent construction of a substantive non-religion and the life that this category takes on beyond the confines of nuanced scholarly work mean that its problematic implication in the WRP works against substantive non-religion's critical clout.

Ideal types and semantic anarchy

Referring to the 'insubstantial' secular, Lee pithily observes that 'it is not possible to organize absence into types' (2015: 51). However, this is not the case with substantive understandings, and thus my own Master's dissertation set out to produce a typology of non-religion (Cotter 2011b). This project was carried out amongst the undergraduate student body of the University of Edinburgh taking a grounded theoretical approach (Engler 2011a), which elicited narratives via electronic questionnaires and qualitative interviews. Although there is much more that could be said about this previous research, two of the key insights suggested are as follows:

- The ways in which students negotiated (non-)religious terminology throughout their narratives allowed the development of five ideal types which were seemingly independent of established religious categories: *naturalistic, humanistic, philosophical, familial* and *spiritual*.
- Regardless of the salience of the students' (non-)religious identifications, they appeared to be keenly aware of where they stood when religion or non-religion was perceived to interact with what mattered to them. (2011b: 103)

Understandably, any extrapolations that could be made from these insights were highly influenced by the limitations of the methods employed. The narratives analysed emerged from a comparatively narrow demographic, and the practicalities of the investigation foreclosed the possibility of comparing a wide variety of (non-)religious narratives. However, one of the most significant reasons I have felt unease with these insights as they stand is my somewhat lofty and obfuscating attempt to provide an exhaustive ideal-typical account of non-religion.

The concept of ideal types emerged from the work of Max Weber (1949), and they are commonly understood as 'analytical tools to be used to facilitate comparison' (Barker 2010: 188 fn. 2), as 'pragmatic constructs' which can in no way 'be regarded as essential categories or ontological realities' (J. L. Cox 2006: 83). Classic examples of ideal-typical models would be Ernst Troeltsch's three major types of early Christianity (1991 [1911]) or William James's account of the varieties of religious experience (1985 [1902]). More recent examples would be Robert Towler's presentation of five varieties of conventional religion (1984), Alex Norman's 'five modes of spiritual tourism' evident in the 'spiritual marketplace' of Rishikesh (2011: 33–41), Lois Lee's five types of 'existential culture' (2015: 161–72) and my own five types of non-religion. (Indeed, this very typology of approaches to non-religion is itself ideal typical.) Even when writing my dissertation, I was clearly uneasy concerning the correlation between these ideal types and my data:

> These narrative-based types cannot be assumed to be constant, and must be understood as firmly rooted in the context in which they were revealed. However, they reflect what individuals actually say, and give priority to individual self-representations, providing a much 'truer' representation of what (non) religion means to these individuals than wide-ranging, quantitative, typologies which suffer from the same contextual constraints. (Cotter 2011b: 76)

Although I and most other scholars who employ ideal types have never claimed that classifying individuals is a simple matter and have emphasized that there is a large amount of overlap between types, it is almost invariably the case that their artificial and constructed nature becomes lost in translation, giving the false impression that individuals can be easily boxed off into one of a discrete number of types. Whilst such work is very valuable for macro-level analysis, it fundamentally breaks down at the level of the individual where heterogeneity and contextuality abound: there is 'no such thing as a perfect or ideal-typical form' of difference to religion (Lee 2015: 44). As I, and many others, have argued before, 'Religious, spiritual, secular, and non-religious identities are not stable, unitary formations' (Hoesly 2015: 9) but rather 'operational acts of identification' (Bayart 2005: 92). However, in relation to the study of Atheism, Quillen argues that prevalent ideal-typical generalizations are perhaps 'nothing more than a product of the current scholarly study of Atheism's predominant focus on the social-scientific attempt at making sense of "Atheism-in-general", rather than "Atheism-in-specific"' (2015a: 30), the 'attempt at finding an identity in the numerous applications of an ambiguous word' (Baird 1991: 11).

Going further, these problems with ideal types are clearly connected to issues surrounding terminology. The contemporary situation has been described as verging on 'a situation of semantic anarchy, in which individual scholars work with idiosyncratic definitions' (Jong 2015: 19), 'infecting our subjects with language created for our own benefit' (Quillen 2015a: 33). Although I tend not to subscribe to Quillen's hyperbolism when he labels such category construction as 'tortuous' (2015b: 132), he is right to argue that the whole discourse on 'types' of non-religion, or indeed the very terminology of 'ir-religion', 'un-belief', 'non-religion' and so on, is 'not unlike that which complicates the definition of "religion"' (2015b: 132) and falls foul of much of the critique outlined above. In addition, 'The conceptual balkanisation that results from the proliferation of idiosyncratic definitions makes … fruitful collaboration more difficult' between scholars doing empirical work in different contexts (Jong 2015: 19). We need not despair, though: this situation of proliferating ideal types and idiosyncratic terminology can be remedied by the type of context-specificapproach to non-religion discussed above or the discursive approach discussed below, which fit much less problematically within the critical religion approach.

'Non-religion' as parasitic on 'religion'

Concerning the category religion, the basic premise of the critical approach is that

> there is no such thing that answers to the name 'religion'; there are only distinct phenomena that sometimes co-occur and are contingently related to one another, sometimes in things we habitually label religious and sometimes in things that we habitually label secular. (Jong 2015: 20)

As has been implied above through my discussion of Quack's 'relational approach' to non-religion, and as should be quite clear from the very construction of the term itself – for example, Lee's 'anything which is *primarily* defined by a relationship of difference to religion' (2012b: 131) – the concept is explicitly relativized to definitions of religion (Jong 2015: 16). As such, any study taking a substantive approach to non-religion will be plagued by the same issues associated with religion. This allows Jong to quite justifiably conclude that 'The boundary between the religious and the nonreligious – whether conceived of in etic or emic terms – is not so much blurry than simply non-existent, at least in any objective and absolute sense' (2015: 21).

Timothy Fitzgerald succinctly encapsulates the critical issue here when he states that to 'imagine that either side of this binary – "religion" or "non-religion" – can be addressed as a topic of research is an act of reification succumbing to, and reproducing, a central ideological illusion of Liberalism' (2015a: 263–4). In a footnote he continues: 'That those who study non-religion choose to confer at AAR conferences with people who study religion suggests that these are circular, mutually-parasitic sides of the same mystifying, empty binary' (2015a: 264 fn. 22). Now, it goes without saying that these are not the only conferences at which such scholars gather. Furthermore, where are they supposed to gather if not at conferences concerned with the very category their subject of interest is defined in contradistinction to? I would also argue that it is possible for good empirical work to be conducted ostensibly under the rubric of this binary with the potential or explicit aim of contributing to Fitzgerald's critical project (see this book, for example). Indeed, Lee does a good job of mitigating some of Fitzgerald's critique when she argues that 'giving more attention to what it means to be secular' contributes to our understanding of 'religion' (Lee 2015: 3) and, further, that it is Western cultural history itself which reifies the religion from which non-religion, 'spiritual but not religious' and so on are differentiated (Lee 2015: 26). In other words, the study of non-religion is, in many ways, simply a study of a culturally dominant reification. However, the heart of Fitzgerald's critique still stands: through not being able to shed its alter-ego religion, empirical studies of non-religion seem doomed to be tarred with the same brush, to 'focus on the negation and not the object being negated, although we do not accept the object in the first place' (Engelke 2015b: 136).

A particularly stark example of the impact of this entanglement concerns the bleeding over of a problematic rhetoric of 'good' versus 'bad' religion into scholarship on 'non-religion'. We'll hear more on this in later chapters, but Aaron Hughes has highlighted what he calls the 'rhetoric of authenticity' in public discourse about religion, whereby 'good religion', which is 'egalitarian, progressive, pluralistic, democratic, and so on', is constructed as 'the real or authentic version' and set against its dichotomous opposite, 'bad religion' (Hughes 2015: xiv–xv). He demonstrates that this rhetoric manifests in much scholarship on religion – or, in his case, a sub-field he dubs 'Islamic Religious Studies' – and concludes that, for the scholars he critiques,

> Religion, or at least 'good' religion, is something real and is supposed to be based on equality, justice, pluralism, and so on. In holding this position, however, scholars of Islamic religious studies inadvertently maintain a host of Christian assumptions that reflect the all too Christian heritage of the term 'religion'. (2015: 120)

So, too, we find this rhetoric in substantive studies of non-religion. For example, Phil Zuckerman argues in *Society without God* that religion is not 'a necessary ingredient for a healthy, peaceful, prosperous, and … deeply good society' (2010: 183) and sells *Faith No More* as finding that apostates are not 'the cliché of the angry, nihilistic atheist' but are 'life-affirming, courageous, highly intelligent and inquisitive–and deeply moral' (2011: back cover). More recently. Callum G. Brown sees his *Becoming Atheist: Humanism and the Secular West* focusing on 'the millions of people of a new ethical Western world who have discovered themselves to be good without god' (2017: vii). He is proud that his book 'doesn't regard the loss of religion as a catastrophe' and approaches atheism as 'a positivity, as an enhancement of the individuals' sense of their self' (2017: 17). While I agree that – when looking at the majority of non-religious who don't identify with labels – 'being label-less is not being value-less' (2017: 168), here we have the key, problematic, conflation: (good) religion = values, and so too for (good) non-religion. My point is that this persistent academic effort to demonstrate that atheism, agnosticism, non-religion and so on are good, proper and authentic mirrors and tacitly endorses the similarly problematic academic discourse on good, proper and authentic religion. Not only are the concepts in a parasitic relationship but so too the problematic discourses surrounding them.

One possible solution would be for scholars to be 'vigilantly specific about the aspect of "nonreligion" that they are interested in' (Jong 2015: 20) and clear about 'the instance to which it is applied and the meaning to which it is used' (Buckley 1987: 6; cited in Quillen 2015b: 118), resulting, once again, in context-specific approaches (see above). Another, however, is to take up Fitzgerald's challenge: 'Surely the only topic here that makes sense as an object of study is the discourse [on "religion" and "non-religion"] itself?' (2015a: 264 fn. 22). It is to such an approach that we now turn.

Discursive approaches

Above I alluded to some of the key findings of my Master's research and the discomfort I have retrospectively felt about placing individuals into ideal-typical categories. No participant was easy to classify into one of the five types I proposed, and each made statements which could be associated with other types. When I revisited my Master's dissertation after having placed some distance between myself and the project, and with the above discussion in mind, I realized that many of the difficulties associated with such generalizing classifications can be overcome by reframing these types in terms of *what my informants said*; that is, in terms of *discourse*. This shifts the focus to 'the *social effects* of the way people talk, rather than the apparent meaning of their words' (C. Martin 2017: 104). People can employ multiple discourses in particular situations; they can say things in many different ways, depending on the discursive resources available to them in a particular cultural context. A shift in focus from the individual to the discourse they employ – from the person to what they say and how they say it – allows the social reality of the individual to be incorporated analytically into the wider societal conversation of which they are inherently a part. As Bayart argues, drawing on Mikhail Bakhtin, no speech act can be attributed to a single individual, but is a product of the broader complex social situation in which it occurs, as well as its historical context: 'every utterance is related to earlier utterances' (2005: 112).

A nascent version of this move can already be detected in my shift from speaking of types of non-religion in my Master's dissertation to 'types of narrative' in a resulting publication (Cotter 2015). Reframing the key insights from this project in a discursive fashion, coupled with a discussion of other discursive studies of non-religion, provides the basis for the research agenda discussed at the end of this chapter. However, before this discursive re-framing can take place, I should introduce discursive approaches, and the benefits that they bring to the contemporary critical study of religion and related categories. These approaches are directly related to more formal forms of Discourse Analysis, which have emerged, primarily from scholars within linguistics, over the past twenty years or so (Wodak and Meyer 2009: 2–3), although the origins of a discursive line of thought can be traced to the late 1960s/early 1970s (see van Dijk 2007). I will now introduce this Discourse Analysis before turning to the looser discursive approaches I have in mind.

Discourse Analysis

Discourse Analysis has been applied to many varied social situations, from the macro-level analysis of discourses on the Information Society in Romania and the EU (Fairclough 2005), or the revival of Austrian anti-Semitism since 1945 (Wodak 2011), to the more micro-level analysis of racist discourse in a conservative broadsheet newspaper (T. van Leeuwen 2008: 25–32), ethnographic studies of multilingual neighbourhoods to demonstrate relationship between local linguistic and material processes and globalization (Blommaert, Collins and Slembrouck 2005) and a wide variety of educational contexts (Rogers et al. 2005). These distinct applications share common roots in the social constructionist epistemologies of theorists such as Foucault and Bourdieu, the four basic premises of which are:

> that our understandings of the world are necessarily informed by preconceived notions which need to be deconstructed; that knowledge is always culturally and historically specific; that knowledge is produced in human interaction and communication; and that knowledge informs social interaction, and vice versa. (Granholm 2013: 47)[9]

Every study that incorporates Discourse Analysis is unique, requiring its own research design (Hjelm 2011: 142), and this study-specific nature extends even to conceptualization of discourse. Discourse can be understood to mean 'anything from a historical monument, a *lieu de mémoire*, a policy, a political strategy, narratives in a restricted or broad sense of the term, text, talk, a speech, topic-related conversations, to language per se' (Wodak and Meyer 2009: 2–3; cf. Fairclough 2003: 4). Here, I adopt Reisigl and Wodak's 'discourse historical' understanding of discourse as 'a cluster of context-dependent semiotic practices that are situated within specific fields of social action', which are 'socially constituted and socially constitutive', 'related to a macro-topic' and 'linked to the argumentation about validity claims such as truth and normative validity involving several social actors who have different points of view' (Reisigl and Wodak 2009: 89). However, as shall be made clear below, such precision of language is not necessary for the exploratory and polymethodic analysis I propose, and for the most part Teemu Taira's concise definition of discourse as a 'relatively coherent set of statements (action through speech) which produce a particular version of events' (2013: 28) should suffice. Discourse is 'a *social practice*' (Hjelm 2014a: 6, emphasis in original). Consequently, in this context, Discourse Analysis 'addresses the relationship among communicational practices and the (re)production of systems of meaning', the various conditions that underlie these processes, and their reciprocal 'impact on social collectives' (von Stuckrad 2013a: 10). It 'considers the relationship between language and the contexts in which it is used' (Paltridge 2006: 3).

This focus upon discourse, and the accompanying social constructionist agenda, has encouraged charges of postmodernist 'relativism' – getting so caught up in discourse that we forget that there 'is a real world independent of how we talk about it' (Bruce 2009: 11). Whilst there are some who would dispute this ontological claim, an important counterpoint to this charge is that there is nothing vague about defining a field of discourse (von Stuckrad 2010b: 165). Discursive study allows scholars to remain fully reflexive about the fact that their studies are entirely contextual; discourses are both socially constitutive and socially shaped (Fairclough, Mulderrig and Wodak 2011: 358), and any good qualitative research must always keep this in mind. Discourse is much more than just language, speech or text; it is 'language in action' (Blommaert 2011: 2) and a fundamental medium for the construction of beliefs and practices (Barker 2010: 200). Far from being an intellectualist enterprise, Discourse Analysis is not limited to oral or written discourses but extends to 'other modes of communication', such as 'gesture, music and clothing' (Bayart 2005: 110), and focuses on the constitution of social identities, relationships and objects of knowledge (Fairclough and Wodak 1997: 258).

As hinted at above, Discourse Analysis is not a specific method, but 'follows certain steps and rules that have proven useful' within certain distinct schools of analysis, such as the 'discourse historical approach', the 'sociocognitive approach', or the 'social actors approach' (Wodak and Meyer 2009: 20). For example, Reisigl and Wodak provide an ideal-typical eight-stage recursive programme for the discourse historical approach which includes such stages as 'specification of the research question and formulation of assumptions', 'qualitative pilot analysis' and 'detailed case studies' (2009: 96), which seem strikingly similar to the basic components of any qualitative analysis. Because of its linguistic focus, and a somewhat-crippling reflexivity on the power dynamics inherent in the research process, Discourse Analysis is most suited to dealing thoroughly with small amounts of naturally occurring written text (Taira 2013: 29), and does not easily lend itself to the large amounts of wide-ranging data from interviews, questionnaires, or participant observation that have come to characterize the qualitative study of contemporary religion.[10] It is for this reason, amongst others, that scholars of religion who employ discourse analytical techniques prefer, in the main, to take a 'discursive' approach: an approach which is guided by the principles and methodological positioning of Discourse Analysis, whilst taking a more active role in the generation of qualitative data, without being bound by the more strict, detailed linguistic focus, characteristic of Discourse Analysis 'proper'.

Discursive approaches to religion

In my positioning of this present work within the critical study of religion, and in my discussion of the entanglement of substantive approaches to non-religion with the World Religions Paradigm, I have already introduced a dominant theme in the contemporary study of religion: the acknowledgement that religion is a relatively recent, Western and Christianized construct, which serves a variety of political and ideological purposes. This historicization of the concept encourages us to

> reconsider the now widely shared, seemingly commonsense presumption that there is such a thing in the world called religion, that it takes different forms in different regions and eras, that it is a feature of all human beings, and that it is inherently or properly distinguishable from that nonreligious thing that goes by the name of politics, the secular, the profane, or, simply put, the mundane. (Arnal and McCutcheon 2012: 3)

This line of argument is generally traced back to Jonathan Z. Smith (e.g. 1978, 1982) and to Talal Asad (e.g. 1993, 2003) who argued that 'different kinds of practice and discourse are intrinsic to the field in which religious representations (like any representation) acquire their identity and their truthfulness' and that, therefore, 'their possibility and their authoritative status are to be explained as products of historically distinctive disciplines and forces' (Asad 2002: 129).

The recognition of religion's constructed nature,[11] and also of its implication in power structures such as 'law courts', 'the hegemonic discourse of the national media', 'parliamentary forums' and so on (Asad 2003: 12), has understandably led some scholars to be increasingly wary about defining religion. One recent manner of addressing this issue 'is to move away from attempts at defining the term "religion"' (Quillen 2015a: 30) and instead focus on discourse, on 'the processes that *make* certain things […] recognizably religious' (Bender 2012: 275).[12]

One of the most influential exponents of a discursive study of religion is Kocku von Stuckrad, who has published extensively on the area in general (2003, 2010b, 2013a, b), with a particular focus upon discourses on esotericism and mysticism (2005, 2010a). Much of von Stuckrad's terminology forms the basis of the theoretical vocabulary that will be utilized through the remainder of this book and is worth introducing briefly. In von Stuckrad's model, the religion that is approached via discursive study is conceptualized as 'an empty signifier that can be filled with many different meanings, depending on the use of the word in a given society and context' (2010b: 166). Von Stuckrad combines Pierre Bourdieu's notions of field, capital and habitus with Michel Foucault's argument that epistemological categories are instruments of power, and his 'archaeological' as opposed to 'historical' approach, to suggest 'that religious studies should focus upon the analysis of *fields of discourse*' instead of attempting to 'define categories substantively' (Robertson 2016: 27–33).[13] A *discursive field* is 'a structured system of social positions, occupied either by individuals or institutions, the nature of which defines the situation for their occupants' (von Stuckrad 2010b: 160). These fields are hierarchical, may overlap and contain multiple competing discourses which make use of forms of capital which are specific to that field. They 'contain a number of competing and contradictory discourses with varying degrees of power to give meaning to and organize social institutions and processes' (Pinkus 1996). In addition, and importantly, elements in the field interact both with each other and with the field itself (Quack 2014: 450 fn. 12).

In order to emphasize that *discourse on religion* is the focus of analysis, von Stuckrad makes a distinction in typeface whereby '"religion" refers to contributions to a discourse on religion, while "RELIGION" refers to the discourse itself' or, further, 'the societal organization of knowledge about religion' (2013a: 12). Although I shall not be adopting this distinction, it is worth noting here that 'religion', in this rendering, acts as a *discursive object* (Potter and Hepburn 2008: 275). In my usage of the terms, *discourses* are 'about how a certain *object* is constructed' (Taira 2013: 29 my italics). Thus, concerning discourses about religion, 'religion' is the discursive object; that is, 'descriptions, claims, reports, allegations, and assertions' *about* religion are the topic of the analysis, rather than 'religion' itself (Potter and Hepburn 2008: 275). Thus, we have *discourses* which are manifested in *discursive fields* surrounding particular *discursive objects*.

One example of such a discursive study would be Timothy Fitzgerald's magisterial *Discourse on Civility and Barbarity* (2007a), in which he presents an analysis of the historical vicissitudes of religion and related categories (such as 'politics', 'secular', 'profane' and 'civility') and demonstrates that 'our ancestors had an entirely different view of the meaning of "religion"' and that 'scholarly practices tend to hide this by constructing a past which conforms too uncritically to what we assume to be the "natural" generic categories in which we think today' (2007a: 144). In a similar vein, Russell McCutcheon's *Manufacturing Religion* (1997) focuses upon a prevalent discourse in the academic study of religion, the discourse on religion as *sui generis,* demonstrating how this marginalizes naturalistic explanations of religion and proselytizes 'for a kind of modern theology, an ideology with hidden transcendental ... assumptions and biases' (Fitzgerald 2000a: 99–100). These analyses would fall somewhere in between what Marcus Moberg refers to as 'first-' and 'second-level' discourse analytic approaches in the study of religion – those which focus on meta-theoretical issues and those which 'highlight the character of scholarly theorizing, and its problematic aspects and flaws, within their respective sub-fields of research' (2013: 13–19). Other works, however, fall into the category of 'third-level' discursive analyses – those which employ 'actual discursive analysis' (2013: 19–22). One example is Kennet Granholm's text- and actor-based study of esoteric currents as discursive complexes (2013). Another is Teemu Taira's intricate portrayal of the political discourse surrounding the application of the Finnish Free Wicca Association to attaining the status of a registered religious community in Finland in 2001 (2010). For reasons that will be made clear in the discursive re-reading below, I see my own work sharing most in common with such ground-up micro-level approaches.

With this vocabulary and background in mind, we are now able to turn our attention to discursive approaches to non-religion, beginning with a discursive re-reading of my previous research.

Approaching non-religion discursively

Although discursive questions were not the driver for my Master's project, it can clearly be interpreted as having focused on the way 'religion is organized, discussed, and discursively materialized' (von Stuckrad 2010b: 166) in a particular context, by individuals who self-described aspects of their individual practice, beliefs, attitudes and/or identity as different from their subjective self-definitions of religion. As such, the project can be viewed as discerning a range of *discourses,* which could be classified as spiritual, familial, philosophical, humanistic and naturalistic, surrounding a variety of negotiated phenomena – identities, practices, attitudes, beliefs – which acted as *discursive objects,* in a *field of discourse* with boundaries dictated by the logics of the research project, that is, substantiating the 'non-religiosity' of students, at the University of Edinburgh, in 2010–2011, whose self-descriptions were 'non-religious', and so on.

Returning to the two key insights of the project – discussed above – this discursive re-reading allows them to be reframed as follows:

- In these particular narratives, these students primarily invoked five types of discourse when they engaged with a variety of topics related to religion, non-religion, and related categories. These discourses appeared to operate at a level independent of the specific terminology – the discursive objects – in question. For example, two of my interviewees – Niamh and Séverine – both employed 'familial' discourses, despite Niamh's complex mix of identifications as 'agnostic', 'atheist', 'Catholic', 'freethinker', 'humanist' and 'nonreligious', and Séverine's deceptively straightforward 'atheist'.
- Regardless of the salience of these discourses in individuals' lives, they were invoked when the students were confronted with phenomena that were deemed to be related to – which meaningfully intersected with – the field of discourse on religion, non-religion and related categories.

We are now starting to see the emergence of some of the key questions motivating the empirical component of this book: Would it be possible to flesh out these insights with more rigour, based on the analysis of a broader set of discursive data? Could this approach be expanded to include the voices of those who are ostensibly religious and non-religious, those who are 'indifferent' to religion and those who are in between? What would this say to academic constructions of non-religion? Are religion-related discourses dependent upon specific configurations of discursive objects? What are these points of meaningful intersection and just how contextual are they?

These questions and more animate the chapters that follow and, as I have demonstrated in this chapter, fit comfortably within a critical (non-)religion framework. They take up Fitzgerald's call for scholars to study the discourse that distinguishes between the religious and the non-religious, whilst simultaneously providing space for an empirical component that goes beyond the 'merely' intellectual and discursive. In the next chapter, I turn explicitly to the task of operationalizing the present chapter's theoretical argument in an empirical setting in an attempt to address these questions.

Approaching non-religion: Edinburgh, the Southside and the religion-related field

> One of the tasks of studies of nonreligion could be to specify where there are possible landmarks, boundaries, and borderlands by researching specific kinds and ranges of relationships between a religious field and nonreligious phenomena. (Quack 2014: 450)

In Chapter 1, I presented a broad survey of empirical research to date related to the contested notion of non-religion. Chapter 2 then critically assessed this research, identifying several problems with it but proposing a discursive solution. In this chapter, I turn my attention to putting this solution into practice, to making the abstract concrete and address the task described above by Quack. It's time to get empirical.

Religion-related discourse

Lois Lee's[1] early definition of non-religion as 'anything which is *primarily* defined by a relationship of difference to religion' (2012b: 131; emphasis in original) is useful in creating a space for the substantive understanding of non-religion discussed in the preceding chapters, such as she advances in her doctoral thesis (Lee 2012a) and subsequent monograph (2015). However, this definition seems to exclude phenomena such as humanism, naturalism and rationalism because they are ontologically autonomous from religion (see critique in Quack 2014). Lee has since refined her definition further, in acknowledgement of this critique: 'Non-religion is therefore any phenomenon – position, perspective, or practice – that is primarily understood in relation to religion but which is not itself considered to be religious' (2015: 32). However, Mortimer and Prideaux have challenged the emphasis on primacy, through their work on the Sunday

Assembly (see Chapter 1) – a movement which many would consider to be non-religious. They argue that 'while the Sunday Assembly as an organization and the majority of its individual attendees do show a relationship of difference with religion… this is not always primary' (2018: 79). However, Lee has offered the following clarification of her position:

> I argue that these should not be considered *intrinsically* non-religious (as they often are in more essentialist approaches), but in fact are only relevant to nonreligion when they are understood in contradistinction to religion (whether explicitly or implicitly). (personal communication, April 2018)

The key issue, therefore, is relationality.

In his 2014 article, Johannes Quack has added some nuance, proposing locating non-religion in a 'religion-related' field comprising

> all phenomena that are considered to be not religious (according to the constitution of a concrete object of inquiry, a larger discourse on 'religion,' or according to a certain definition of 'religion'), while at the same time they stand in a determinable and relevant relationship to a religious field. (2014: 12)

This 'determinable and relevant relationship' can take the form of criticism, competition, collaboration, mirroring, functional equivalence, interest and so on (see Quack and Schuh 2017a). Such an understanding sees non-religion as part of a wider field of phenomena associated with religion, which, after all, is how non-religion is defined – by Lee, or more colloquially. Indeed, Quack acknowledges that it is consistent to speak of the religion-related field as part of the religious field since each can be conceptualized as extending their reach to other fields which feel their influence through what Bourdieu would call their 'field effects' (2014: 450–1).

James L. Cox has criticized both Lee and Quack's models of non-religion for 'employing language in an obscure and at times convoluted manner', holding that 'it would be much easier and clearer simply to define what is meant by religion and non-religion quite explicitly' (2016: 30). My immediate response to this critique is that Cox is somewhat missing the point – both Lee and Quack are taking a broad view, allowing scholars such as Cox to come in and use the definitions that suit his empirical study. Furthermore, the model Cox proposes – based on Jean Marie Guyau's *The Non-Religion of the Future: A Sociological Study* (1897) – is that non-religion studies should 'analyse trends in contemporary society that are characterized by an emphasis on individual autonomy, governed by self-interest and whose values are thoroughly relativistic' (2016: 36). Not only does this model simply reinforce common secularizationist tropes, but it is quite theological, equating religion with a variety of positive sociological traits and non-religion with negative ones. Cox falls into the very trap that Lee, Quack, myself and others seek to avoid. Thus, while I am sympathetic to his case regarding the problematic vagueness inherent in Lee and Quack's model, I see this as a strength that can be marshalled to the advantage of the critical study of non-religion.

Via Lee and Quack we thus arrive at a nuanced relational model for the study of non-religion which *need not* result in essentializing the religious or the non-religious – though, as the previous chapter has demonstrated, this frequently occurs. Furthermore, this is a model which can be developed and repurposed for the study of *discourse*, allowing non-religion to be fully integrated into the critical study of religion due to their discursive interrelationship and respective field effects. This is, as I shall argue repeatedly throughout the remainder of this volume, the logical outcome of discursive study in a context where the discourses on religion, non-religion, secularism and related categories 'have perpetuated the importance of religion in Western Europe' and beyond (von Stuckrad 2013b: 4; cf. Asad 1993; 2003; Fitzgerald 2007b).

Take materialism, for example: as Lee points out, it is in principle 'possible to think about materialism independently of religion; in practice, however, materialism is, in Western contexts at least, explicitly and implicitly understood in contradistinction to religion, [and] frequently specified as or conflated with a non-theist orientation' (2015: 33). Here, Lee is arguing that in practice, in Western contexts, materialism be conceptualized as non-religious because of the way in which it is 'made meaningful' through a relationship of difference to religion (2015: 33). However, although many conceptualizations of materialism might have a non-religious character, constructing it as such is arguably going too far. What of, for instance, the 'prosperity gospel' (Bowler 2013) or the 'Protestant Ethic' (Weber 2001)? Although constructing materialism as non-religious might not necessarily be inaccurate, it is much less problematic to note the *relationship* to religion (as Lee does) and conclude that, in practice, materialism is discursively entangled with religion rather than being non-religious per se.

This discursive development of Lee and Quack's relation models allows the analytical incorporation of *any* discourse that is contextually associated with religion in particular historical contexts, whether that be on evolution, secularism (which, though inherently religion-related, is not necessarily non-religious), spirituality or indeed potentially any discourse which occurs outside of (non-)religious contexts amongst individuals who may fall under the radar of (non-)religion studies. This echoes Kennet Granholm's argument concerning 'discourse on the esoteric', where scholars must, 'instead of simply focusing on "esotericists", … examine the whole field which engages with the esoteric in one way or another' (2013: 51). Discursively appropriating Quack's 'religion-related' notion effectively encapsulates the similarly motivated catch-all phrase 'religion and related categories', which has seen increased usage since the publication of Fitzgerald's *Discourse on Civility and Barbarity* (2007a).[2] In this sense, although the study of religion-related discourse can simply be seen as taking the discursive study of religion to its logical conclusion, the term usefully provides a wider encapsulation of discourse on religion which can be operationalized empirically to incorporate non-religion in a non-stipulative manner and which rhetorically reminds both the reader and the researcher that 'religion' need not be a dominant, normative or positive term in the discourses studied.

Operationalizing a discursive approach

With this relational model now established, how might we put it into practice empirically? I began this volume by introducing three individuals (Keith, Mohammed and Niamh), whose everyday narratives – in the sense of being non-expert, outside of organized institutions and rooted in life history and in experiences of both the 'mundane' and the 'extraordinary' (Ammerman 2007) – raised a number of important critical questions relating to the religion/non-religion binary and provided the impetus for this book. An interest in these questions – what makes a particular act '(non-)religious', what contestations are particularly entangled in the religion-related field, who decides, why do these classifications matter and so on – in combination with the relational, discursive model outlined above meant that I wished to empirically analyse religion-related discourses as employed in social interaction by non-elite social actors who strategically place themselves, and/or are placed by others, in a variety of positions within a bounded context. My task was to address Quack's call in the epigraph to this chapter for empirical studies of non-religion to map the religion-related field of discourse in specific contexts, focusing upon landmarks, boundaries, borderlands and 'specific kinds and ranges of relationships' (Quack 2014: 450).

Every research project – particularly when involving the non-religious (see Lee 2012a, 2015; Cheruvallil-Contractor et al. 2013) – must jump its own methodological hurdles, and a critically engaged study even more so.

Determining which discourses might be in a relevant relationship with religion is a complex and contextual task, and any pre-determination runs the risk of biasing the research from the very start. The study of organized groups such as Humanists UK or the Sunday Assembly is all well and good, but such approaches require the pre-determination of groups that will produce relevant data – something which perpetuates prevalent reifications of what 'counts' as data for Religious Studies and which potentially neglects those individuals who do not join religion-related communities, or even regularly gather in communities at all (Cheruvallil-Contractor et al. 2013; cf. Campbell 1971: 42). My desire to incorporate as wide a range of subject positions as possible, and on an 'everyday' level, meant that it was important for my empirical work to be small-scale, focusing upon the individual, rather than filtered through various official channels. This suggested an interview-centred approach. Yet as Martin Stringer acknowledges, individuals employ different discourses in different contexts, and to rely *only* on interview data might 'force them to bring the[se] various discourses into a single space and encourage a level of coherence that may not exist in the real world' (Stringer 2013b: 168). This is not to say that interviews should not be utilized – indeed, a precedent has been set for this by Wijsen (2013b). However, an awareness of the impact of context – particularly the 'genre' of the discourse (interview, presentation, formal worship, pub conversation, etc.) – meant that it was desirable for me to explore discourses in several different, yet connected, contexts.

Ultimately, I adopted three strategies to operationalize my relational, discursive approach empirically: a multi-method approach prioritizing interviews and utilizing historical data sources for triangulation; a maximum variation sampling strategy; and challenging the 'established orthodoxy' of the World Religions paradigm by sticking, in part, to its own premises (in the spirit of Baumann 1996: 32). Discussion of each of these strategies is interwoven throughout the following pages, but it is first necessary to discuss the type of context at focus: *locality*.

Discourse and locality

Given the limited timescale and resources at my disposal (despite receiving a generous AHRC stipend), it was essential that the nature of the discursive field under investigation be such that it would facilitate access to the narratives associated with a broad range of religious and non-religious identifications, within a manageable context that could be defended as coherent. I was also keen to avoid foregrounding the very divisions between religion and non-religion, and between different 'world religions' that this project was undertaken to critique. Building upon my prior research, it was desirable that the field facilitate access to a broader demographic base than students in higher education, and that by conscientiously targeting informants from a range of ages, educational backgrounds and socio-economic statuses, I might better avoid the production and analysis of highly intellectualized discourses. However, given that my prior research had been conducted within a UK context, and given the large and ever-growing body of research that has been conducted in said context (as discussed in the preceding chapters), it was desirable that the discursive field be UK-based. Thus, I was looking for a UK-based field that was not inextricably linked to societal discourses on religion but which would facilitate access to a broad range of everyday discourses relating to religion being deployed by a diverse group of social actors.

In seeking an appropriate field, I was acutely aware of the perils of entering uncritically into 'the completely unregulated market of the "religion and … " genre' (McCutcheon 2014: 146). For example, as Tuckett and Robertson have noted concerning the study of 'religion and video games', this field is marred by a lack of conceptual clarity (2014: 103): Are these studies intended to focus upon 'religious responses to video games', critiques of 'meat-world' religions in video games or the religions that one encounters in video games themselves? However, it is possible to avoid such critiques by being specific about what we intend to study – for example, religion-related discourse in UK-centred debates surrounding certain video games. A quick spontaneous list illustrates the sheer number of potential fields that could have been explored: the media, politics, law, the internet, fiction, conspiracist narratives, nationalism, education and so on. There is much valuable work being conducted in each of these fields, and all could potentially have been utilized as sites for investigating religion-related discourse. Some – such as law or the media – do not easily lend themselves to the kind of micro-level analysis I propose, and many approaches to these fields (but not all) seem to uncritically construct religion as having agency *in itself*, rather than taking a critical discursive position whereby religion 'does not have agency to teach or do anything' but is constructed by social actors who interpret discursive objects 'in ways that relate to their particular context and the range of interests that enliven that context' (Ramey 2014: 109).

Another type of field that presented itself as a potential 'orienting metaphor' (Tweed 2008)[3] for my empirical work was *locality*, which I characterized in the introduction as spaces, whether material or discursive, that are 'practical working environment[s]' which are meaningful for those social actors within them, 'important for individual and group identity' and amenable to academic study due to their size and relative internal coherence (Knott 1998: 283–4). As Michel de Certeau argued, discursive studies have an unfortunate tendency to extract texts 'from their historical context and eliminate … the operations of speakers in particular situations of time, place, and competition' (1984: 20). An approach which foregrounds locality can avoid this pitfall, by being rooted in the 'particularity [and] … complexity of its social relations and the sum of the stories told about it' (Knott 2005: 33). As noted in the introduction, space and locality have been theorized in a manner which makes them eminently compatible with a critical discursive approach, by being dynamically social constituted in language. Viewing localities as discursive fields facilitates setting aside the particularities of individual and community 'identities', viewing them rather as 'operational acts of identification' (Bayart 2005: 92), as acts of positioning 'in relation to other locations, with a sense of perspective on other places' (N. Smith and Katz 1993; cf. Marten 2014).

Perhaps most importantly for my purposes, examination of specific places challenges our conceptions of religion, religions, non-religion and so on 'as unities focused on discrete, systematic sets of traditions, and normative beliefs and practices' (Knott 2009: 159). A locality-based discursive study would therefore allow me to more easily (though, undoubtedly, not entirely) avoid reifying the very categories under examination, whilst simultaneously providing a relatively bounded and coherent context within which to conduct my analysis. Additionally, as Joseph Webster found in his research on folk-theologies of salvation and eschatology among Scottish fishermen in Gamrie (2013a), or as Martin Stringer has noted through sitting on buses in the city of Birmingham and listening to 'discourses on religious diversity' (2013a), religion-related discourses can occur in the most unpredictable of places, and a focus upon and immersion within a locality increases the likelihood that they will be encountered by the researcher. Such a focus raises the status of the locality to much 'more than a mere context or backdrop' for the study of religion-related discourse (Knott 2009: 159). Indeed, such is the nature of all discursive fields, which invariably define the situation for their occupants (von Stuckrad 2010a: 5). Specific localities 'cannot be said to exhibit agency by [themselves]' but affect 'agency in those who experience and participate' in them (Knott 2005: 129). Thus, in pursuing locality as a framework to organize my discursive analysis, it was essential that an appropriate location be selected for data gathering, one that is diverse yet characterized by 'coherence and conceptual manageability' (Knott 1998: 283).

Edinburgh's Southside

With the above in mind, it was important that I select a demographically diverse locality to act as a porously bounded discursive container which was not merely a collection of explicitly religious or non-religious institutions, and where I would be able to access the discourses of individuals who exempt themselves (for whatever reason) from such institutions. It was also important that I capture discourses of 'indifference to non-/religion', and discourses in more naturally occurring situations than just researcher-led interviews.

I initially considered searching for an appropriate locality in cities with 'super-diverse' (Vertovec 2007) neighbourhoods such as London, Birmingham, Manchester or, to a degree, Glasgow. In my reading of Vertovec, super-diversity occurs when 'diversity' reaches such a critical mass that there is diversity within diversity – where it makes no sense to refer to a small number of majority/minority social groups within a local environment, but where there are multifarious groups, and 'there may be widely differing statuses *within* groups of the same ethnic or national origin' (2007: 1039). I eventually ruled this out primarily due to logistics and familiarity, but also because of the (at the time) quite under-theorized nature of such super-diverse contexts and the potential impact this might have upon my work as a distraction and by muddying some already complex waters. This situation has changed remarkably in recent years, with a veritable explosion in publications, such as Chimienti and Liempt (2015), Eriksen (2015), Meissner and Vertovec (2015), Vertovec (2015) and Wessendorf (2014b). However, this came too late, and thus I turned my attention towards my adopted home of Edinburgh, where I had already conducted empirical research, and decided on the area known as the 'Southside', where I have lived for over fourteen years. I thought that this would provide appropriate diversity in terms of religion-related identification, age, educational background and socio-economic status, as well as a beneficial level of familiarity and a desirable degree of continuity with my previous research.

Edinburgh today

Edinburgh is the capital city of Scotland – populations approximately 477,000 and 5,295,000 respectively, according to the 2011 census (National Records of Scotland 2012) – one of the constituent nations of the UK.[4] While Scotland retains notably higher levels of church attendance than England and Wales (Guest, Olson and Wolffe 2012: 64), statistics tell a familiar story of declining church attendance and loss of normative Christian culture over the last fifty years (C. G. Brown 1992: 75–6, 2000; C. G. Brown and Lynch 2012: 344; Bruce 2013: 371).[5] In 2011, 93 per cent of the Scottish population answered a question on the Scottish decennial census which asked, 'What religion, religious denomination or body do you belong to?' According to the National Records of Scotland,

> 54 per cent of the population stated they belonged to a Christian denomination (a decrease of 11 percentage points from 2001) whilst the proportion who stated that they had 'No religion' was 37 per cent (an increase of 9 percentage points from 2001). All other religions made up the remaining 3 per cent, an increase from 2 per cent from 2001. (2013: 4)

More recently, a poll by Humanist Society Scotland seems to show that 72.4 per cent of people in Scotland say they are 'not religious' (*Herald Scotland* 2017).

Turning to other factors, it is worth noting that, whereas in 1900 Scotland had around 3,600 Presbyterian clergy (the national Church of Scotland is Presbyterian), this had fallen to around 900 in the year 2000 (Bruce 2013: 374; drawing on Brierley 1989: 55). It is also significant that Scotland has been alone in the UK in granting 'humanist' weddings legal status since 2005. By 2016 humanist ceremonies accounted for 13.6 per cent of Scottish weddings, the second largest category after civil ceremonies (51.5 per cent) and surpassing the national Church of Scotland (12.6 per cent) (Kasselstrand 2018: 278).[6] Of course, there are enormous regional variations across Scotland in terms of religious practice and affiliation, with conservative Protestantism remaining strong in rural fishing villages in the north-east (see Webster 2013a, b) and Catholic/Protestant sectarianism – 'particularly in the west (around Glasgow)' and 'strongly linked to the footballing rivalry between the Glasgow teams of Celtic and Rangers' – remaining a major social and political issue (Nye and Weller 2012: 37; cf. Bruce et al. 2004; Robinson 2016). In Edinburgh, 45 per cent of the population selected 'No religion' on the 2011 Census (8 per cent higher than the national average), in comparison with 48 per cent for all other religious identifications combined (National Records of Scotland 2013: 33), and although some Christian congregations (see Roxburgh 2012) and other religious identifications are growing, the situation remains one of clear decline. Although these are by no means the only potential measures of religion or religiousness (and problematic measures at that), this brief discussion indicates that Scotland, and Edinburgh in particular are sites in which a growing and significant section of the population self-describe as being other than religious – a prime site for investigating non-religion.

Defining the Southside

Much like religion and related categories, the 'Southside' of Edinburgh is a contested but meaning-infused concept. As one surveys the built environment to the south of Princes Street, one comes across pubs, letting agents, dentists, community centres and major pizza delivery chains that incorporate 'Southside' into their names. Various groups and organizations identify with the term, from the Southside Heritage Group to the Southside Community Choir, as well as local newsletters, circulars and art projects. The stock phrase 'once a Southsider, always a Southsider' is in the discursive repertoire of many an Edinburgh resident, and the term has found its way into the (auto)biographies of local centenarians (*Edinburgh Evening News* 2008) and rabbis (Daiches 2001), and the pages and titles of local histories (J. G. Gray 1962c; C. J. Smith 2000; Sherman 2000; Pinkerton 2012). As shall become clear, this is not to say that the term holds universal appeal or is even universally acknowledged (due, in no small part, to an ever-growing transient student population). However, the most significant contestation surrounding the Southside concerns not whether there *is* a Southside but where its boundaries might lie.

It is impossible to discuss the boundaries of Edinburgh's Southside without first sketching something of the history of this area within the City of Edinburgh. As far as the city itself is concerned, it is generally agreed that substantial settlement in the area began some time before the seventh century CE, with the large rock upon which Edinburgh Castle now rests being a site of fortification from at least the twelfth-century reign of King David. Until the middle of the eighteenth century, the town of Edinburgh consisted largely of what is known today as the Old Town, the area surrounding the historic Royal Mile, the High Street which runs from Edinburgh Castle in the West down to the Palace of Holyrood House in the East.

In the first centuries of the second millennium, if one walked south from the now High Street, one would soon have encountered an expanse of water later known as the South or Burgh Loch (now Edinburgh's popular 'Meadows' park), the northern side of which formed the southern boundary of the old town. Beyond the Burgh Loch lay the Burgh Muir, a section of the 'dense forest of Drumselch' (C. J. Smith 2000: 1). During the fourteenth and fifteenth centuries, the Burgh Muir remained densely forested, 'providing vagrants and outlaws with a retreat from the city authorities' and also serving as a quarantine area for plague victims (C. J. Smith 2000: 3). Following a 1508 charter of King James IV to open up the Muir for commercial uses, and a further devastating plague in 1585, the Muir was cleared and gradually developed (C. J. Smith 2000: 3–5).

Fast-forwarding a couple of hundred years to the mid-eighteenth century, these clearances contributed to a situation where 'most citizens were residing in the Old Town', and a large 'green swath' stretched to the south 'between Arthur's Seat and Blackford Hill' (Sherman 2000: 3). There,

> [d]otted amongst the orchards and farms were small villages and hamlets such as Causewayside, the Pleasance, Powburn and Nether Liberton. There were also country estates belonging to wealthy city merchants, incorporating their prominent manor houses. (Sherman 2000: 3)

In 1772 the North Bridge was opened, which 'led to the exodus of Old Town citizens of means ... northwards across the drained Nor' Loch to a new style of elegant residence in James Craig's classical New Town' (C. J. Smith 2000: xi). Following soon after, in 1788, was the South Bridge, a 'new southern highway' which 'stimulated a significant movement of people to the districts of Newington, the Grange and Morningside' (C. J. Smith 2000: xi) and facilitated the development of what is commonly referred to today as 'the Southside'.

This brief historical sketch provides a convenient cut-off point for the Southside in terms of its northern boundary: the Southside is to the south of the Royal Mile. However, this tells us nothing of the other three boundaries and ignores contestations surrounding where the Old Town stops and the Southside begins. Charles Smith writes that '[w]hen Edinburgh people talk of the city's "South Side" they usually mean the relatively small area comprising South Clerk Street, St Leonard's, Causewayside, Sciennes, Newington and the Grange' (C. J. Smith 2000: xi). Robin Sherman's account is somewhat narrower, placing the Grange (to the south-east), Marchmont (east) and Gilmerton (south) outwith the Southside (2000: 3). This narrower definition is the one adopted by the Southside Heritage Group and became my own working definition following an examination of the areas covered by the South Central Community Council, the Southside Neighbourhood Partnership, the Southside Advertiser, Newington Churches Together, the catchment of Southside Community Centre, the relevant City Council Wards and Holyrood and Westminster Constituencies and postcodes. Figure 3.1 shows a simplified map of the area that was used as a visual aid in interviews, which corresponds roughly to the area covered by the EH8 9 and EH9 1 postcodes, which can be utilized when browsing the 2011 census results online.[7] Ultimately, I took a pragmatic approach, calling for participants who considered themselves to have (had) a relationship with the Southside, resulting in a wide catchment area. Yet all participants considered the same core to be the Southside – the difference lies in the periphery.

Figure 3.1 Simplified map used as visual aid in interviews. Produced by author.

The contemporary Southside

As the preceding discussion surrounding the contested boundaries of the Southside has indicated, this is an area that is steeped in history. The keen-eyed observer of the built environment will note plaques commemorating Robert Burns's 1787 lodgings in Buccleuch Pend (J. G. Gray 1962a: 73) or his meeting with a young Sir Walter Scott in Sciennes House Place that same year (W. F. Gray 1962c: 13). Those who take an interest in the origins of street names might be aware that the area known as Sciennes, including Sienna Gardens, Sciennes House Place, St Catherine's Place and so on, is so named due to the brief presence (1518–1567) of the Convent of St Catherine of Siena, with the name being 'corrupted colloquially into Sciennes or (in the eighteenth century) Sheens' (W. F. Gray 1962b: 30; cf. C. J. Smith 2000: 6–7). And who could fail to notice the presence of the University of Edinburgh in and around George Square,[8] a number of imposing Victorian neo-Gothic churches and the simple yet striking Archer's Hall on Buccleuch Street, which opened in 1777 as 'the headquarters of the Royal Company of Archers or King's Bodyguard' (W. F. Gray 1962d: 45) and which hosted the Queen, Prince Phillip and Princess Anne as recently as July 2016.[9] Yet despite all of this, it would be misleading to say that 'historic' was a term that many would immediately associate with the Southside, with this term being more readily attached to the adjacent 'Old Town'.

Writing in 1962, John Gray lamented that it 'sometimes seems that Southsiders are unaware of their heritage and that much is being whittled away and lost simply because a generation has arisen that has ceased to care for that which is worthwhile and seeks only after material values' (1962b: 5). Much as we might be tempted to put this down to resentment directed at 'young people these days', Gray was writing at a time of enormous change for the Southside. The contemporary visitor would be largely unaware of the Southside's former status as a thriving industrial centre, yet older residents remember a rather different place. Writing of his childhood in the 1950s, James Beyer describes how

> Biscuits, confectionery, food colouring and flavouring, heavy engineering, upholstery, cardboard box making, printing and bookbinding, mapmaking and even pipe organ construction were just some of the many enterprises thriving in Causewayside, all being found within an area of less than a quarter of a square mile. (2009: 34)

This narrative of a vibrant commercial and industrial neighbourhood is augmented by his description of accompanying smells and a delicious description of the embodied boredom associated with the hegemonic religion of the time:

> Drifting from the factory of confectioner John Millar and Sons Ltd. was the tantalizing bouquet of boiling sugar, chocolate, fruit flavourings and, above all, mint, for this was the home of the celebrated Pan Drop, one of the most popular sweets ever to have been manufactured in sweet-toothed Scotland and a boon to bored church-goers throughout the land as they slowly sucked their way through many a long, tedious sermon, the air over the pews becoming more heavy with mint than piety. (2009: 34)

As is the case in cities across the UK, this thriving industrial scene is now no more, with demolitions or conversions into tenements being the norm (indeed, the flat in which I resided for the duration of my doctoral study is part of a former Southside brewery).

Another change that Gray would have witnessed was the clearing of many of the more dilapidated tenements in the Southside, the moving of many Southside residents to newly constructed council estates on the periphery of the city and the beginnings of the rapid expansion of the University of Edinburgh, with its main Pollock Halls of Residence being a major new addition to the Southside landscape in the 1960s. As we shall see in the chapters that follow, this change was felt as traumatic by many of the Southside's residents, and a resentment against both the University of Edinburgh and the City Council runs deep throughout many of my interviews with older residents.

The Southside can thus be described as post-industrial and historic, although the history is somewhat layered or sedimented, and not immediately visible to the casual user of the space. The presence of the University of Edinburgh in the area means that the Southside serves as an arrival point for many individuals who latterly decide to remain in Edinburgh after their period of study but who tend to move out of the area as they seek to buy property or start families. Two dominant groups in the area are thus a core of longer established residents, and a larger, more transient population who remain for a few years and arguably push up rental prices due to the demand on accommodation near the university.

As far as religion is concerned, the Southside is home to many Christian groups, including Church of Scotland, Roman Catholic, Episcopalian, Orthodox and Pentecostal congregations and features many church buildings that have been repurposed as community centres, libraries, lighting showrooms and so on. The area is also home to the Edinburgh Central Mosque (completed in 1998), the synagogue of the Edinburgh Hebrew Congregation – its foundation stone laid in 1931 (C. J. Smith 2000: 13) and a small Jewish burial ground opened in 1818 (W. F. Gray 1962a: 35) – in addition to a number of shops offering alternative therapies, crystals and the like. Table 3.1 shows the census results for this area, broken down according to 'Ethnicity' and 'Religion' and compared with the results for Edinburgh and Scotland as a whole. From this table, we can see that the Southside has a much higher proportion of 'non-White' residents (15 per cent) when compared to the Edinburgh (8 per cent) and Scotland (4 per cent) averages, which yet remain predominantly 'White'. In terms of 'religion', more than half of the Southside's residents identified with 'no religion' (53 per cent) as compared to 45 per cent of Edinburgh's population, whilst just 11 per cent of Southside residents identified with the Church of Scotland, which is half the percentage for Edinburgh and only one-third of that for the whole of Scotland. A marginally higher number of residents identified as Roman Catholic, but these percentages were also slightly smaller than the Edinburgh and Scotland averages. Finally,

Table 3.1 'Ethnicity' and 'religion' statistics from census 2011: 'Southside',
Edinburgh and Scotland

Ethnicity	Southside Population: 22,494 (%)	Edinburgh Population: 477,000(%)	Scotland Population: 5,295,000(%)
White	85.20	91.80	96.00
Mixed or Multiple Ethnic Groups	1.81	^	0.40
Asian, Asian Scottish or Asian British	10.88	5.50	2.70
African	0.79	^	0.60
Caribbean or Black	0.20	^	0.10
Other	1.12	^	0.30
Religion			
Church of Scotland	10.64	24.30	32.40
Roman Catholic	10.79	12.10	15.90
Other Christian	9.82	6.90	5.50
Buddhist	1.25	*	0.20
Hindu	1.15	*	0.30
Jewish	0.62	*	0.10
Muslim	3.23	2.60	1.40
Sikh	0.20	*	0.20
Other religion	0.54	*	0.30
No religion	53.05	44.80	36.70
Religion not stated	8.69	7.10	7.00

Source: http://www.scotlandscensus.gov.uk/ods-web/standard-outputs.html. 'Southside' results generated using 'Local Characteristic Postcode Sectors' EH8 9 and EH9. Edinburgh and Scotland populations rounded to
the nearest 1,000. All ^ are amalgamated as 'other ethnic groups' in the Edinburgh data, at 2.80 per cent. All
* are amalgamated as 'other religions' in the Edinburgh data, at 2.10 per cent (Accessed 29 September 2016).

notably higher percentages of Southside residents identified with Islam, other
forms of Christianity and 'other religions' than in either Edinburgh or Scotland.

Aside from its more historic buildings, the built environment of the Southside
is largely divided into tenement residences and various elements of the service
industry, including the increasingly rare independent shop, chains of (mini)
supermarkets, extraordinary numbers of takeaways, some restaurants and coffee

shops, dozens of pubs and bars, barber shops and hairdressers, betting shops, pawn shops, a couple of Chinese supermarkets and about a dozen charity shops. Despite being quite a dense urban area, the Southside is bounded to the west by the well-utilized Meadows Park and to the east by Holyrood Park featuring Arthur's Seat and the Crags – imposing geological formations which loom large in the Edinburgh skyline. These parks combine with numerous smaller landscaped squares and tree-lined streets to produce a general feeling of leafy suburbia, despite the grittier urban aspects of the Southside and its presence on a busy commuter artery between the city centre and its southern suburbs.

The Southside also never feels very far from power and privilege, having the University of Edinburgh within its boundaries; the Scottish Parliament Building only just outside of these; and the notably more opulent areas of Marchmont, Morningside and the Grange surrounding its southern borders. This is juxtaposed by the all-too-real deprivation experienced by many in the Southside, with food banks and homeless shelters providing essential services throughout the area, and the Scottish Parliament buildings sitting firmly in the accusatory gaze of its next-door neighbour, Dumbiedykes council estate. This juxtaposition is just one of the many dichotomies – urban/green, transience/permanence, historic/contemporary, privilege/poverty, religious/non-religious – that seem to characterize the contemporary Southside and make it a particularly fascinating context in which to examine non-religion.

Locating religion-related discourse in the Southside

Much of the data that has informed this study has emerged due to my personal familiarity with the Southside, where I have lived for the past fourteen years. In addition to consulting a variety of local histories sourced through the National Library of Scotland, the Edinburgh City Library and the University of Edinburgh's Scottish Studies Library, a major boon to my research was my regular participation in meetings of the Southside Heritage Group, who maintain a large archive of texts, photographs and assorted artefacts relevant to the Southside. I also paid attention to the discourses at play in the built environment, the changing landscape of advertising banners and fly postings and news stories that are of relevance to the local area. However, while this combination of elements has helped to contextualize my research, my discursive analysis has focused upon three discrete sets of interview data: the eleven interview transcripts and sixty-two questionnaire responses generated in 2011 as part of my Master's project, thirty-seven transcripts of individual and group interviews conducted in 1995/6 for the *Peoples of Edinburgh Project* (PEP) and twenty-three new interviews that I conducted between February and November 2014 with new research questions in mind. As hinted at above, some scholars prefer the use of 'naturally occurring data' as opposed to material such as interviews because this means that 'the researcher has not influenced the formation of the discourse' (Taira 2013: 29). However, my triangulation with other data sources, my being embedded in the Southside, my linking to broader national discourses and my use of the PEP material mitigate some of the issues associated with this charge. Furthermore, as I discuss below, the resulting reflections on my own involvement in the co-construction of religion-related discourse in the Southside is a further strength of this approach.

MSc by research

My MSc research – which has been discussed in some detail in Chapter 2 (see also Cotter 2015) – was carried out at the University of Edinburgh, as a broad investigation into non-religion among the student body, with core aims of avoiding imposing preconceived categories onto informants (see Day 2011) and engaging with this constituency beyond institutional forms of 'non-religion'. Electronic questionnaires were disseminated to seventeen student societies (clubs) intended to provide access to a wide range of ideological and 'faith-based' perspectives,[10] motivated by Edward Dutton's argument that student societies act as contexts where students 'assert or find a strong identity' in the face of the 'liminal' character of university life (2008: 83). Ultimately a wide net was cast over the non-religion side of the supposed religion/non-religion dichotomy, and I excluded only those students who did not self-identify in terms deemed non-religious *and* who scored highly on self-declared measures of religious attitudes, beliefs and practices. My subject group at the time comprised forty-eight students, average age twenty-one years, two-thirds female, but given the nature of my investigation in the present volume, the full set of sixty-two completed questionnaires could be included as discursive data. Eleven interviews of sixty to eighty minutes also took place with a cross-section of respondents, resulting in a rich set of discursive data, to which I return in this project, with a different research objective.

As with the individuals involved in the *Peoples of Edinburgh Project (PEP)*, to which discussion I shall now turn, the students involved in my 2011 project did not necessarily (though most likely did) live in the Southside and, as with most student populations, might have been quite transient or remained relatively aloof in terms of their connection with the area. However, given that the University of Edinburgh is considered part of the Southside – even by the narrowest of definitions – and that all interviews took place in the Southside, with individuals who were clearly familiar with the area, this collection forms a coherent and bounded body of discursive data with clear connections to the present volume. It also provides a large cohort of younger participants to augment my contemporary Southside data which, as we shall see below, was predominantly produced with older interlocutors.

The Peoples of Edinburgh Project

The *Peoples of Edinburgh Project* (PEP) was a joint project between the City of Edinburgh Council's Museums and Galleries Division and the Workers' Educational Association. A prime example of a multiculturalist endeavour, it was born out of a desire to more fully 'reflect the life of all the people in the multi-cultural city of Edinburgh' (City of Edinburgh Council 1996: 3). The PEP ran from 1995 to 1996 and aimed 'to promote understanding between the peoples of Edinburgh and celebrate the richness of multi-cultural society' by collecting reminiscences from, and developing an exhibition concerning, 'as wide a range of community groups as possible', most of whom had migrated to Edinburgh at some point in the recent past (1996: 3).

The project began with group reminiscence sessions 'with the Chinese Elderly and Residents of Cathay Court Sheltered Housing, NKS Bangladeshi Women's Group, Milan: Senior Welfare Council, Wester Hailes Asian Women's Group, Leith Sikh Women's Group, the Bengali Association, Queen Margaret College and a group of young Chinese women at the Black Community Development Project, Pilton' (1996: 8) and continued to include thirty-six individual interviews. These interviews were conducted mainly by postgraduate students at the University of Edinburgh's School of Scottish Studies, in English and a few other first languages. The English versions of these transcripts and some of the reminiscence sessions 'provided the text for the book and exhibition' (1996: 9) and the material that I was given access to.

Religion was one of fifteen themes to be explored in the interviews, with the interviewers being given the following mandate:

7. Religion
- What is family religion?
- How, where worship/pray?

- Where is place of worship/how often attend?
- Describe festivals, celebrations, ceremonies, customs?
- Where do you obtain items for prayer/shrine at home?
- Day of rest, which day, what do you do?
- How does your religion affect lifestyle of self/family?

Given the broad focus of these interviews (and the nature of interviews in general), occasionally the topic of religion was not raised at all, and in other cases, these areas were not strictly focused upon. The exhibition itself began with a section focusing on journeying – where the people of Edinburgh had come from – before turning to sections on 'ways in which people keep their culture through dress and jewellery, language, food, music, dance and entertainment, cultural organizations and religion' (City of Edinburgh Council 1996: 16) and, finally, 'adaptation and integration'. Religion also features prominently in the published book, with a section entitled 'keeping the faith' running for fifteen of the sixty-six pages, making up the majority of the central 'keeping the culture' section where 'religion' is declared to be 'part of everyday life. People keep their culture through religious observations and festivals' (Clark, Dick and Fraser 1996: 27).

In general, the PEP was pronounced a resounding success and, in the words of Edinburgh's then Lord Provost, provided an 'opportunity for all of Edinburgh's people to share and learn from each other. This initiative ... enhance[s] our knowledge of one another and it represents an important step towards eliminating ignorance and prejudice' (Clark, Dick and Fraser 1996: 4). It was decided by stakeholders that, although discussion of racism and other 'obstacles and barriers' to integration should not be ignored, 'any treatment [of these] should not detract from the exhibition's main message of celebration' (City of Edinburgh Council 1996: 10).

The motivation for including this data in the present study was firstly to allow a pilot analysis to test the analytical techniques discussed below (see Cotter 2016: Chapter 4) and secondly to provide an historical data source that is connected spatially and chronologically to the Southside, and which enabled a degree of methodological triangulation and accountability for the resulting conclusions. Although many of the Edinburgh residents involved in the PEP did not have a clear connection to the Southside, many did, and it provided a rich historical source of religion-related discourses of a similar scale and from a sufficiently similar context to enable my analytical framework to be rigorously established and tested, and on a body of data that was generated independently of my agency as an interviewer.

The contemporary Southside

Finally, I conducted a further twenty-three interviews with individuals from a variety of religious and non-religious identifications who considered themselves to have a connection to Edinburgh's Southside. I avoided specifying what I understood the Southside to be, or what kind of connection I was looking for, to enable potential interviewees to respond in their own ways, and not to appear too restrictive from the outset. I set up a project website, and potential interviewees were informed that I wished to include a wide variety of people in my study, whatever their background and no matter how important or unimportant religion was in their lives. The main thrust of my communications and publicity material was on the Southside (although religion was, of course, mentioned) in the hope that this would encourage greater participation from those who might position themselves as largely 'indifferent' to religion, or who prefer to avoid discussing it.

My strategy for sourcing interviewees was multi-stranded. I made use of my own social network within the Southside, and an element of snowballing (Atkinson and Flint 2001), to disperse a call for interviewees, making particular use of Facebook and Twitter. I also capitalized upon the relationship I had built up with the Southside Heritage Group and was invited to attend one of their Monday meetings as a warm-up for the guest speaker that week, where I was able to detail my project and successfully solicit interviewees. More passively, I strategically placed posters calling for participants around the Southside in local pubs, shops, the Southside Community Centre[11] and the Nelson Hall,[12] and had an advert placed in the Meadows Directory[13] and several local (online) message boards. E-mails were circulated around the Causey Development Trust,[14] the creative writing group, drama group and community choir who meet at the Southside Community Centre, the Southside Elderly Group, the South Central Neighbourhood Partnership,[15] the Dumbiedykes Writers Group, the Braidwood Centre[16] and the Southbridge Resource Centre.[17] Finally, several religion-related organizations were specifically targeted with information and posters. I adopted a maximum variation sampling strategy, much like Lois Lee did when conducting interviews and engaging in ethnographic work with explicitly non-religious populations in and around London (2012a). This meant that, while I generally remained passive in allowing interviewees to approach me, as the interviewing phase carried on, I more actively pursued interviews which would ensure a broader range of ages, socio-economic statuses, nationalities and religion-related identifications, in addition to achieving as close to gender parity as was practicable.

Unsurprisingly, of course, the process of sourcing interviewees was not a smooth one. I frequently met with the response 'I've got nothing to say about that' or 'You wouldn't want to speak to me', and although some individuals were subsequently persuaded to be interviewed (and did, in fact, have quite a lot to say), I can only assume that many other potential interviewees were dissuaded from participating due to the focus on religion or due to not feeling sufficiently knowledgeable about the Southside. I also attempted to include the perspectives of a group who might have a very different perspective of the Southside – those who are at the lower end of the socio-economic spectrum. I was given valuable access to a local food bank and café which I attended as a participant observer for four sessions, and although I had several incredibly valuable conversations with service users and volunteers, the logistics of the setting, difficulties in finding or arranging time to conduct a formal interview and my uneasiness surrounding my apparent position of power over these vulnerable individuals led to no interviews taking place. However, the interactions that occurred there, as well as my frequent interaction with members of the Heritage Group, provided worthwhile opportunities to listen in on unsolicited conversations surrounding religion (many of which were, of course, initiated in response to my presence).

In the end, I conducted twenty-one individual interviews and two interviews with married couples, all of whom (had) lived and/or (had) worked within the boundaries I set for 'the Southside'. The interviews lasted between 45 and 100 minutes and were conducted either in University of Edinburgh meeting rooms, the interviewees' residences or cafés. These interviewees (had) worked primarily in a range of industries from (higher) education and IT consultancy, to secretarial and catering work, although it would be fair to say that all were reasonably comfortable financially. The majority claimed to have, or have had, some personal connection with various forms of Christianity or to have never identified as 'religious'. Tables 3.2–3.5 provide demographic breakdowns of my interviewees by gender, nationality, age and initial religious identification. See Appendix 1 for a full list of interviewees.

Table 3.2 2014 Interview participants by gender

Gender	M	F
	14	11

Table 3.3 2014 Interview participants by nationality

Nationality	
Scottish	14
English	5
Australian	1
Scottish/Italian	1
Scottish/German	1
Scottish/American	1
Polish	1
Syrian	1

Table 3.4 2014 Interview participants by age

Age	
18–24	2
25–34	3
35–44	2
45–54	2
55–64	5
65–74	8
75+	3

Table 3.5 2014 Interview participants by initial religious identification

Initial Religious Identification	
Church of Scotland	4
Atheist	3
Atheist/Agnostic	3
Agnostic	2
(Former) Catholic	1
None	2
Catholic	1
Episcopalian	3
Pagan	1
Muslim	2
(Secular) Jew	1
Other Christian	1
Buddhist	1

The interviews were semi-structured, and all followed a set pattern that I developed during three initial test interviews (which were incorporated into the final data set). Discussion initially focused explicitly on the Southside and the interviewee's relationship to it. Topics that were covered included the boundaries of the Southside and a free-listing (Stausberg 2011) exercise on characteristics that they would ascribe to the Southside. We also discussed a map of the Southside (that I provided), and the interviewee(s) took me on a virtual tour, pointing out the places that they felt were most significant, and then after prompting, the locations they would associate with religion. Our attention then turned to a photo elicitation exercise (Banks 2001: 87–98), where three key images from the Southside were discussed: (a) the Southside Community Centre (formerly Nicolson Street Church, see Figure 3.2), (b) a halal meat market, (c) an advert on a local bus for the 'trypraying' campaign (see Figure 3.3).[18] Discussion then turned explicitly to religion, with the interviewee being asked for a brief 'religious biography', before being presented with a pre-produced list of religion-related terms and invited to provide definitions, whether or not they would consider the term to apply to themselves, any stories they might have connected with the terms and so on. After asking any contextually relevant follow-up questions, discussion returned to the Southside, with the interviewee being directed to consider the religion-related terms in relation to their experiences there. Finally, most interviewees were asked for their opinions on then UK prime minister David Cameron's comments concerning the UK's status as a 'Christian country' (BBC News Online 2014), and all were asked about their responses to and opinions of the religion question on the UK 2011 Census.

The development of this interview approach was highly influenced by the schedules utilized during my MSc, in addition to the work of many other scholars engaged in similar projects, particularly Rebecca Catto and Janet Eccles (2013), Abby Day (2009), Lois Lee (2012a, 2015) and Simeon Wallis (2014).[19] It has recently been noted that within the field of Religious Studies, 'there are at present no widely recognized normative standards or guidelines, no professional code of ethics to set the standard for both how we should engage in our investigations and how we should communicate what we learn in the process' (Bird and Lamoureux Scholes 2011: 82). In studies of this nature, focusing upon potentially sensitive religion-related discourses, in the narratives of non-elites – co-constructed in this case with the researcher, and with other researchers in the past – it is essential that research ethics are given due consideration. Beyond standard measures to anonymize and protect personal data, seek informed consent and so on, I was also acutely aware – particularly given my analysis of

Figure 3.2 The Southside Community Centre, Nicolson Street. Photograph taken by author.

Figure 3.3 Bus with 'trypraying' advert, South Bridge. Photograph taken by author.

interviews conducted by interviewers other than myself – of the impact that the agenda and perspective of the interviewer can have upon the discourses that are deployed in interview situations. As Valentine and Sadgrove acknowledge, 'how the self is narrated may differ according to the specific performative encounter between a given respondent and interviewer', meaning that the interviewer 'is not merely the passive recipient of the narrative but an active, authorial agent' (2013: 1983).

There is a view among some scholars of religion that the researcher should be explicit about their own position in the religion-related field, both in their academic writing and in face-to-face contact with their informants (Neitz 2011: 61–3; Hopkins 2007; Cheruvallil-Contractor et al. 2013). Although I did adopt this practice in one of my test interviews, I decided that this was unnecessary and unhelpful. Yet I fully subscribe to the view, articulated by Kim Knott, that '[t]here is no neutral ground from which to view the field of struggle between the "religious" and the "secular". No position to take which is not implicated in its force relationships' (2005: 89). As a researcher who has lived and worked in Edinburgh's Southside for over fourteen years and engaged in the study of religion for over twelve of those, I consider myself entirely implicated in the field of discourse on religion in the Southside. Consequently, I have not merely analysed the statements of my interviewees but have self-reflexively included my own statements within the analysis and taken a perspective on the interviews as co-constructions. Given that this project involved, among other things, investigating whether the discursive field surrounding religion is coherent regardless of the identifications of the individuals in question, I deemed it irrelevant and counter-productive to the research process for me to be explicit about my own, equally irrelevant, perspective. Suffice to say, I view questions of whether or not religion is a force for good in the world as effectively meaningless – like asking whether the weather is a force for good in the world – and I prefer to focus upon the effects of social actors' claims surrounding the supernatural, the nation or morality, rather than evaluating the substance of these claims.

As with all research, but particularly research involving interviews, 'participants tend to come to the situation believing that they will learn something' from their participation, and it is therefore worthwhile to give due consideration to 'the quality of the learning experience' provided by the research process (Breen 2006: 468). As with many things in academia, this is an ongoing process, but I plan to continue engaging in knowledge exchange activities whereby the results of my research – particularly concerning the history of the local area – are communicated through publications and presentations (including this volume), and lodging materials with the Southside Heritage Group.

Analysing religion-related discourse

The collections of interviews that provide the empirical backbone to this project and are viewed as *particular* instantiations (texts) of multiple, intertwined discourses which surround a variety of objects (terms, buildings, individuals etc.), flow throughout a particular field (the Southside of Edinburgh) and are invoked by contextually relevant social actors. These discourses are entangled with each other and embedded in the text(s) and require excavation through discursive analysis. The following chapters contain the results of this excavation and relate these discourses to broader societal discourses and theoretical frameworks. However, in concluding this chapter it is necessary for me to outline the analytical approach I take.

My methodological framework was rooted in a desire to allow discourses to emerge from the data through a process of close-reading and open-coding, and Discourse Analysis in the sense outlined below. This framework was tested and refined in late 2013/early 2014 using the thirty-seven transcripts from the PEP, before continuing to apply it to the new interviews conducted specifically for this study. In describing my approach, it makes narrative sense to describe the process mainly from the perspective of my pilot analysis with the PEP.

To begin with, I undertook an initial reading of the thirty-seven transcripts which had been generated during the PEP, many of which were handwritten, and proceeded to make contextual notes on each interview and to pragmatically deduce which sections could be considered religion-related. I cast a wide net in making these decisions, utilizing my existing knowledge of cultural systems commonly understood as religious, in combination with a helpful coding list provided by Knott, Poole and Taira's 'Main Categories and Subcategories Used in Coding References to Religion and the Secular Sacred in 2008–2009' (2013: 191–5). This resulted in 135 pages containing religion-related material which were then digitized, re-read and subjected to discursive analysis. This analysis was primarily informed by two sources, an article by Stephanie Garling (2013) and unpublished guidance notes for the Discourse Analysis undertaken in Knott, Poole and Taira (2013). In her article, Garling suggested that texts can be approached through three levels of analysis – the thematic, the grammatical and the argumentative – to extract the underlying discourses. She states:

> At the thematic level overall topics of the text and its outlines are set and the themes unfold. At the grammatical level, different linguistic means are used to make these themes understandable and plausible to the audience. And finally at the argumentative level convincing and evaluative strategies as well as presumptions are to be found. (2013: 19)

At the first level of analysis, one looks for themes which are appealed to (implicitly and explicitly) throughout a single text or a collection of discursive data and which 'connect the argument(s) with the conclusion' (2013: 19). In other words, this level of analysis corresponds loosely to what we might colloquially label as 'close reading', whereby the substantive content of the text is examined and categorized according to (multiple) emergent themes, such as 'Islam as alien to the UK' or 'religion as a private matter'. The second and third levels involve analysis of linguistic conventions, whereby the term 'excavation' becomes more applicable – i.e. going beyond the surface level of the text. At the second level then, one can look for 'referential strateg[ies] or strateg[ies] of nomination, membership categorization […], metaphors and metonymies and synecdoches' (M. Meyer 2001: 26–7), in addition to 'in/out group representation', 'emotional references' and 'over-lexicalization (exaggeration)' (notes on discourse analysis, Knott, Poole and Taira n.d.). The final level examines what are 'understood as procedures for persuasion and argumentation' (Garling 2013: 21) – essentially the use of disclaimers, comedic paradigm, decontextualization, stereotyping, attribution and so on. Approaching the PEP and subsequent transcripts through these three levels (in a non-sequential but systematic process) allowed me to disentangle several religion-related discourses at play in each transcript and proceed to the next stage of analysis.

Once the relevant pages of each transcript had been analysed in this manner, eighteen transcripts were selected for further analysis, due to markedly higher occurrences of religion-related discourses. These transcripts, along with the full material from my own interviews, then underwent a process of open coding within NVivo,[20] and the resulting coding structure was revised and hierarchized according to emerging themes. The discourses that emerged from this analysis will be discussed in detail in the chapters that follow, where I also make use of extended interview extracts to provide concrete examples of the practical application of this complex analytical process and provide space for Southsiders' own voices to shine through.

Discursive entanglements: The religion-related field in Edinburgh's Southside

> Material spaces matter because they bring people together in a location where abstract discourses and positionings in diffuse social networks become outworked as tangible, sedimented social relations through collective imaginaries and the production of community normativities (unspoken rules/codes of behaviour) and forms of regulation. (Valentine and Sadgrove 2013: 1982)

Edinburgh's Southside is a densely populated district of the city with contested boundaries, just to the south-east of Edinburgh's historic Old Town, sandwiched between the iconic Meadows and Holyrood Park. The area saw enormous growth during the nineteenth century and became a thriving industrial centre, but nowadays most of that industrial history is invisible to the casual user of the Southside. Much of the industrial infrastructure was demolished in the middle of the twentieth century, along with dilapidated tenements, to make way for more modern housing and to provide space for the University of Edinburgh to expand. As such, a simmering resentment against the City Council and the University of Edinburgh is clearly present amongst the older population. This older population forms the core of longer-term residents of the Southside, which is augmented by a large, transient, multicultural population attracted to the area by the university. According to the 2011 census, most Southside residents identify with no religion, and the area is notably characterized by a significantly lower proportion of 'Christian' residents than the rest of Edinburgh, or Scotland as a whole, and with notably higher proportions of all other religion-related identifications. In the preceding chapter, I proposed several dichotomies – urban/green, transience/permanence, historic/contemporary, privilege/poverty, religious/non-religious – as characteristic of the contemporary Southside. In this chapter, I present a broad map of the religion-related discourses I have encountered in my work there.

Throughout this chapter, my main concern is to demonstrate the viability and utility of treating the entire religion-related field as a coherent whole. However, I go further and demonstrate that the religion-related field in the Southside of Edinburgh is entangled in discourses that are effectively 'a-religious' in that they can be 'described and analysed without any reference to religious phenomena' (Quack 2014: 446), yet with '(non-)religion' appearing as a contextually more or less useful trope throughout. I also address a further question identified in Chapter 2 concerning the dependence of these discourses on particular configurations of religion-related identifiers (discursive objects). I conclude that religion-related identifiers are theoretically interchangeable, but the particularities of the Southside mean that some arrangements will be more prevalent than others. I also reflect on some of the discursive shifts during the twenty-year timespan of the data, on the role of the researcher and on some significant implications for modelling non-religion.

My empirical data has been discussed in the previous chapter, and it is derived from participation in local heritage groups and food banks, consultation of local histories and newspapers, observation of the built environment and linguistic landscape, thirty-four interviews and sixty-two questionnaire responses generated by my own research from 2011 to 2014, and thirty-seven transcripts of individual and group interviews conducted in 1995/1996 by the City of Edinburgh Council for the *Peoples of Edinburgh Project*. The sources that will receive most attention in the chapters that follow were the twenty-three interviews I conducted between February and November 2014 with individuals who considered themselves to have a connection to the Southside. Discussion in these interviews began with a focus upon the Southside and the interviewees' relationship to it, the boundaries of the Southside and characteristics they would associate with it. Interviewees then took me on a virtual tour of the Southside, before participating in a photo elicitation exercise. Discussion then turned to the interviewees' 'religious biography', before focusing upon a pre-prepared list of religion-related terms and relating these to the Southside. Let's now turn to a section of roughly five-and-a-half minutes from my conversation with Keith in November 2014, which begins immediately after the photo elicitation exercise.

'As I've got older, I've gone to more and more funerals'

I began the introduction to this book with a brief extract from my interview with Keith, and it is only fitting that he enters the fray as my first major empirical example. You might remember that Keith is a man in his late forties who is Southside born and bred, has lived there for almost his entire life, has managed a pub in the area for many years and claims to have never been 'big on religion'. The following extract sets the scene and acts as an anchor point for the presentation of discourses that follows.

C: ... but we've been talking a little bit around religion there, and you've said, um, that you're not really religious, and you've said that you went to the church there for some school stuff ...

K: Aye.

C: ... so maybe if you could just tell me your, sort of, story relating to religion ... just, you know like <pause> you know, yeah just tell me a bit about you and religion. It doesn't have to be ... there doesn't have to be anything, but em ...

K: Right. I never, em, <pause> I was never, I was never big on religion. Eh, I've probably been in ... I've probably been in Catholic churches more now, coz my wife's Catholic, so I'd probably be more at church now, eh, with her and her family, than I have been <pause> for anything else. I notice as I get, as I get older, I seem to be going to more funerals as well ... eh, which is weird. I'm getting to know hymns a lot better. But, me ... but me growing up, I was ... I was never. I wasn't ... my mother and father weren't religious either, so we weren't ... we were never a religious family and, em <pause> em, not that I had any, I never had a faith, but eh ... when I lost my mum and dad to cancer ... that just sorta put [an end to it], coz they weren't, I mean, they were a good age but then I just sorta ... any interest, any interest I had <pause> I probably lost ... eh, when they died, aye. And, various other members of my family. So ... <pause> But [saying that] I suppose since I met my wife and gone to ... Catholic church, and ... a couple of times, four or five times, em ... I've probably, <laughs> I've realized I'm glad I'm not a Catholic, because they're very long-winded ... services, so <laughs> eh, yeah ... but it, it doesn't inspire me to change my religion and become a Catholic ... after being there. Em, as I was saying, as I've got older, I've gone to more and more funerals ... em, and I've found <pause> that's probably the closest I've got to religion is being ... is going to funerals ... More and more funerals, eh <pause> and I just, I just find ... they always seem to use the same sermon, which doesn't ... which never makes it feel, em, very personal ... Which puts me off as well. Em <pause> yeah, it puts me off.

C: Alright. How do you ... <pause> so, how do you end up going along like with your, with your wife and stuff ... like, does she go like every week? Or ...

K: She doesn't … no she doesn't go as regular, I mean we go to, em, what's it? We go to her nephews' and nieces', eh, communion, em … and, we were at her father's funeral not that long ago. Em, and a couple of other things, and [that's just … <inaudible>] what's that thing the kids get? It's not communion. Is it communion they have?

C: Aye they have the, the first communion …

K: Aye, yeah so and she's got a lot of nephews and nieces, so we've been to five or six of them, funerals … maybe a couple of other things that I didn't know what they were.

C: That's alright.

K: They have to … but when they go, I mean they're from East Kilbride, so when they go it's the family thing, the … the family chapel, church … em, and they've all got, you know, it's like the family seat …

C: Right.

K: … eh, but then my wife, my wife's mother, she's very religious. Eh, she's in, she's in church twice a week, three times a week. Eh, so when we go to see her, we sometimes go, go on a Sunday and then we go, go to church with her … [any time we go on a Sunday <inaudible>] But, eh, she's very religious.

C: Yeah. Um, and how did you find <pause> how did you find it growing up? Like, you know, so the school would have things, and things like that … so was there <pause> yeah, like what was … what was the normal sort of thing for you?

K: I mean it was … when we went with the school it was, it was, eh … we always went at Christmas, we did a … just at the church up the road, we did all the carols and stuff, and then we went at, em, <pause> I can't remember what it's called now, at harvest time … went then. Easter, went then. Em <pause> yeah, I mean I'm, I'm going back to … I'm going back thirty-odd years … it was, eh <pause> I liked going and singing the songs, I don't think I would… it would never, it would never, eh <pause> it wasn't like a crowd-puller for me … you know what I mean? <laughs>

C: Yeah.

K: <inaudible> To make me go back. And then we, I did, I had a, eh, we did RE at secondary school, eh <pause> I didn't pay much attention in RE. It was just a … it was something that I've never ever got, got involved in. … Although, as I say, as I've got older I've probably been involved with more, em <pause> and sometime … eh, especially if it … let's say, if we're at funerals, especially if, you know, if it's close friends or family, and you sitting there … especially if they were young, and <inaudible, pause> I don't understand why, I don't … I still don't understand why people, some people have to die so young … when there's arseholes still alive, like you know what I mean? That's the bit I don't get. … I don't think anybody could ever explain it to me, so …

There is a lot going on in this extract, and in another publication, I take readers systematically through it, line by line, to demonstrate my analytical process and the potential of discursive analysis for the study of 'non-religion'. However, that is not my purpose here. What I shall do now is make a few general comments about some of the complex religion-related discourses evidenced here – including in my own contributions – before launching into a broad overview of the religion-related field of discourse in Edinburgh's Southside.

Throughout this extract, we encounter a variety of discourses on engagement and identification. Religion seems to be something that Keith has been aware of throughout his life, but his initial response positions him as indifferent: he's not *anti-religious*, or even *not religious*, but 'not big on religion'. This deprecating phrase seems to imply that being 'big on religion' means going to church. Yet, later in the extract we learn that he does not consider his own increasingly frequent attendance at church to make him religious – it seems that something deeper needs to occur or some explicit declarations need to be made. Yet, at the same time, he is willing to use the participation of others as a barometer of their subjective religiosity. Further, we can also sense a shift in his engagement with religion from a position of disinterested indifference to one with more hard-and-fast boundaries. This is evident in his aside about not changing his religion, where we also learn that Catholics/Christians are seen to have an agenda directed towards changing or supplying him with a religious 'identity' and that he makes a distinction between Catholicism, Church of Scotland and 'not big on religion' as different religions.

Keith's initial response also invokes the notion that others *are* 'big on religion', setting up a dichotomy between 'normal' and 'excessive' interest. He consistently hints at wider societal discourses on Catholics being more inclined to be active in their religion or, indeed, that Catholicism demands more of its adherents: a view bolstered by the fact that '[a]t 62%, the Catholic Church's retention rate is the strongest of the main British denominations' (Bullivant 2016: 185). Indeed, Catholics are a 'they' who 'have to' do certain things. Further, the normative framework within which Keith positions our interaction is non-Catholic – indeed the Roman Catholic population of the Southside (10.79 per cent) according to the 2011 census is less than half of that in East Kilbride (22.8 per cent). In the Southside, Keith does not question the right of churches to perform funerals, nor does he engage with potential reasons why these commemorations occurred in churches in the first place. Here, 'the Church' writ large is constructed as the hegemonic default option for life cycle rituals. We also see an unproblematic and hegemonic link between the practices and routines of (certain) schools and (certain) churches in the Southside.

This ties in to other discourses on belonging and insider discourse. For Keith, hymns and other learned behaviours are constructed as banal but important indicators of 'proper' insider status. At times he indicates that he is aware of an insider discourse that he is not part of – or at least he wishes to present himself as not being part of – and he constructs himself as an outsider experiencing another's community. This experience has made him 'glad I'm not a Catholic', yet, importantly, doctrinal aspects are not discussed: what Catholicism means to Keith is an embodied experience that is uninspiring and boring. What he remembers of religion in his childhood is a similarly benign experience of some appealing songs and little else – certainly nothing to encourage him to investigate further. Could this be indifference *par excellence*? Similarly, religious education (RE) is remembered merely as something that everyone had to go through; it just happened. His memories of RE aren't invested with any negativity – indeed, it is barely remembered at all, as he 'didn't pay much attention'. This view is echoed in his contemporary construction of religion as both harmless and boring.

Another theme in this extract concerns common-sense notions that people engage in religious activity because of the desires or habits of other members of the family. For Keith, being married to a Catholic means that certain events happen as a matter of tradition; because his wife and her family participate, he does so too. Indeed, this may be to avoid causing offence, with Keith explaining away the religious behaviour of his immediate family as a matter of obligation and keeping the peace with an older family member who (still) places significant weight upon such behaviour. Keith emphasizes how the religiosity of parents influences that of their children, and we also hint at the importance of children to religious institutions, religion and education and religion in the public square.

Finally, we turn to the major themes of death, mortality and morality. Keith notes that the death of his parents caused him to 'probably' lose 'any interest I had' in religion and describes how he perceives his interactions with religion to be increasingly dictated by attendance at funerals as he gets older. Because of these interactions, religion relates to death, mortality and theodicy, and is perceived to be attempting (inadequately) to provide solace, comfort and explanations for why people die and where they go after death. Ultimately, Keith dismisses such attempts: 'I still don't understand why … some people have to die so young when there's arseholes still alive.' He also castigates a faceless 'they' for preaching superficial sermons 'which never [make] it feel … very personal, which puts me off'. Thus, for Keith, religion *should* be personally meaningful and relevant; it *should* provide comfort, solace and answers to the deep questions of life. He clearly has an ideal model of what religion *should* be, yet his subjective experiences stand in stark contrast with this model and thus religion is found wanting.

To summarize, here we have encountered a multitude of religion-related discourses, on engagement and identification, moderation, hegemony, family transmission, offense and obligation, death, mortality and morality, belonging and insider discourse, the meaningfulness of practice, indifference, embodiment, superficiality and sincerity, ritual, tradition, friendships and more – all of this in one short extract from one of over seventy interviews. I'll now present a succinct summary of eight discourse groupings encountered throughout my body of data, before reflecting on their relative entanglement in the religion-related field, on some of the discursive shifts during the twenty-year timespan of the data, on what this says to the role of the researcher and on some significant implications for modelling 'non-religion'.

Religion-related discourses in Edinburgh's Southside

The eight discursive groupings presented below were constructed when I analysed my body of transcribed data using the approach outlined in the previous chapter, that is, a process of close reading, open coding and discourse analysis. The groups are discussed in no particular order and are presented in summary form. More detail shall be provided where appropriate throughout the remainder of the book. Readers may also wish to consult my doctoral dissertation (Cotter 2016) for a fuller explication.

Power

The discourses on *Power* are those which are most explicitly implicated in hierarchies and power relationships and can be usefully presented as falling into one of two strands. The first consists of discourses which construct particular religion-related terms as 'power categories' (Fitzgerald 2015b) that are applied to contexts within which power is exerted and oppression occurs. The second concerns the implication of religion-related terms, through legitimation or opposition, in hierarchies and power relationships which are not inherently religious, but which are contextually entangled in the religion-related field in the Southside.

Concerning power categories, I concur with Foucault that 'power is everywhere', not in the sense 'that it engulfs everything, but that it comes from everywhere' (Foucault 1998: 63). However, my point is the application of religion-related terms to *particular* contexts or spaces. The logics and scale of these spaces can vary contextually, from narrowly conceived institutions constraining and oppressing those who are discursively placed within their walls to more nebulous localities and nations. Religion-related terms act 'in dialectical interplay with other power categories such as "politics," "science," or "nature," [to construct] … a world and our own apprehensions' (Fitzgerald 2015b: 305).

In the Southside, Christianity was backgrounded as a minority concern alongside a narrative of decline from a past state of 'ubiquitous religiosity' (Naomi) and placed outwith the realm of phenomena that must be given serious attention, into a category that can be viewed with benign – if mildly amused – indifference (Cotter 2017a; see also Chapter 7). Declining religiosity was correlated with youth and the shift from rural to urban life, echoing some of the tropes of 'classical secularization theory' (Warner 2010: 7–40); and also high levels of existential security, echoing more contemporary developments (Norris and Inglehart 2004; Silver 2006; Harskamp 2008). These discourses on normative secularity and religious (Christian) decline were entangled with the construction of the Southside as 'post-Christian', reflecting a pervasive internalization of the historical roots of 'the secular' as detailed by Taylor and others (see Taylor 1998: 31 ff; Fitzgerald 2007b; Cavanaugh 2009).

Peter described the Southside as

> a kind of post-Christian, or a kind of Christian society, full of Christian symbolism, it's all over the place – so you see the churches, you see those things, and you see those things all the time – but there's nothing that's actively Christian.

It is 'post-Christian' not in the sense that Christianity 'has become irrelevant per se' but that 'its effects are diffuse and indirect' (Lee 2015: 30). (Protestant) Christianity is granted dominance, being seen as embedded in local and national rituals, in institutions such as scouts and schools, in the very fabric and skyline of the Southside itself (cf. Davie 2014: 615). Indeed, 'the overwhelming presence of Christian buildings in this country' creates expectations and in some senses 'impinges on the secular' (Davie 2015: 78). Much as would be the case in contexts with relatively homogeneous 'Christian' identification across the populace, many of these manifestations of Christianity are viewed as inoffensive, unproblematic, banal or simply not comment-worthy. Indeed, as a cultural marker, Christianity 'continues to frame the borders of inclusion and exclusion' in UK contexts (Wells and Watson 2005: 268). Those who are positioned in the majority might – as many of my interviewees did – view Christianity as a positive social force, a benign curiosity or a laughable non-problem, yet feel threatened by mere perceived manifestations of Islam. This brings in other discourses on power and oppression, with the very category of religion potentially being understood to oppress, with Keith effectively banning conversations on the topic in his pub because 'it leads to arguments'. Many individuals who identified with established religions felt an aversion to being described as 'religious', seeing religion as a 'toxic brand' (Woodhead in Elgot 2014; cf. Lee 2015: 5). Furthermore, notions of religion and conflict were intimately bound together. Whether the individual saw religion as a/the cause for conflict, a (potent) contributing factor or as nothing to do with it at all, these notions were intimately connected in such 'discursive knots', where 'several discourses are entangled' (Jäger and Maier 2009: 47; cf. Garling 2013: 22). These associations between religion and conflict are common parlance in the West, even if their empirical basis is much more complicated and rhetorical (see, for example, Schäfer 2004; Cavanaugh 2009; Gunning and Jackson 2011; Murphy 2011; Francis 2015).

The second strand of discourses on *Power* implicates the religion-related field in hierarchies and power relationships which are not deemed religious in and of themselves. Due in no small part to the focus on locality in my interviews, the field is particularly entangled in power relationships, pitting the harmonious locality against disruptive external forces. Positively or negatively, the state was invested with power over the regulation or monitoring of religion at the level of the individual, primarily through official state apparatus such as the census, and through legislating for the freedom of, or protection from, expressions of religion in public spaces. Here, religion is constructed as a social domain over which a totalizing state exerts, or should exert, control through 'regulation, opposition, exclusion and silencing' (Woodhead 2012a: 25; cf. Stack, Goldenberg and Fitzgerald 2015). It becomes what Naomi Goldenberg (2018) refers to as a 'vestigial state', a resource that can be both co-opted by the state for its own ends and utilized by social actors in their interactions with the state. Indeed, it seems that in these discourses 'only the liberal secular nation state and its agents have the right to decide what is and is not a genuine "religion"' (Fitzgerald 2015b: 306).

A further power dynamic in this body of interviews concerned a perceived conflict between the locality of the Southside and external powers. The Southside itself was routinely constructed positively as a coherent, vibrant, tolerant, safe, friendly and diverse locality. Where this positive image of the Southside was disrupted, the source was frequently traced to something considered external – whether that be the University of Edinburgh destroying the area through rapid expansion of infrastructure, and the attendant government-fuelled influx of students,[1] or multinational 'corporate capital' (Wells and Watson 2005: 275) gradually eating away at the Southside's character one shop at a time. The presumed decline in the number of churchgoers, and subsequent closure of many Southside churches, was not solely blamed on a *sui generis* secularization narrative but also upon the declining sense of community in the Southside brought about by the aforementioned student industry, and upon the 'decanting' of much of the population to council estates on the outskirts of Edinburgh, traced to an alliance between the University of Edinburgh and Edinburgh City Council. In other words, just as the discourse on the state versus the individual was not inherently religion-related but became contextually entangled in the religion-related field, so too the discourse on the local versus the external is entangled with the discourse of secularization in the Southside. Similarly, where religion-related conflict or intolerance was discussed, this tended to be placed outside the Southside or at least traced to external sources. This scans with studies acknowledging a 'positive attribution' of the 'political or cultural nation' to 'members or institutions in a given scheme of the local civic society' (Kurczewska 2008: 147) or a 'proximity bias' in charitable giving (Songhorian 2014: 61; Bowen 2015;). In this way, the Southside is an exemplum of Kaplan's account of the 'rise' of religious tolerance, which 'has a circular, self-confirming power' and 'encourages us to view intolerance as someone else's vice, not our own' (2007: 6).

Civic space

The discourses on *Civic Space* are those which relate to the Southside as a shared, local space, the character and atmosphere of that space as experienced by its users and the social norms and expectations that accompany that experience. Although the term 'public' could arguably be substituted for 'civic', I have opted for 'civic space' as this conveys more of the sense of shared ownership of the Southside felt by my interviewees (Amin 2006). Those discourses which most explicitly intersected with the religion-related field can be separated into two strands: discourses of multiculturalism and discourses of moderation.

The discourses of multiculturalism construct the Southside as multicultural and propose strategies for managing multiculturalism. Some of these discourses also promote it (i.e. are multicultural*ist* discourses) and express opinions on it. Here multiculturalism is understood as 'the political accommodation of minorities formed by immigration to western countries from outside the prosperous West' (Modood 2007: 5). As was the case with some of the discourses on *Power*, these discourses were not exclusively invoked in relation to religion, but the link was frequently made. Indeed, when it comes to the broader discourses on multiculturalism, it is quite difficult to imagine these *not* making reference to religion,[2] at least in the UK and Western Europe (R. H. Williams 2015).

At the most basic level, interviewees were open and unambiguous about the diverse and multicultural nature of the Southside and in many cases were very keen to emphasize how positively they viewed this multicultural mixing in the Southside, instantiated in the mundanities of day-to-day commercial transactions in 'public or associational space' (Wessendorf 2014a: 12). Much as Martin Stringer discovered in the city of Birmingham, this multiculturalism was negotiated by many through a form of convivial 'indifference to difference', whereby the heterogeneity of the locality is celebrated as allowing individuals and groups the space (a beneficial anonymity?) to manifest their identities without fear of censure (Stringer 2013a: 54–5, 65–7). However, entangled with this positive multiculturalist discourse, there lurked a more oppressive discourse of political correctness. This was exemplified through hints of a pressure to be seen to be celebrating diversity, to not be seen to be intolerant or to have negative views of 'others' and to place intolerance outside the Southside, both spatially and temporally. This is not to say that interviewees refrained from offering negative comments on expressions of difference, with, for example, Keith criticizing those who 'don't want to integrate, don't want to speak English', or Brian lamenting the 'Islamification' of Nicolson Square. However, such comments were a relatively minor thread in these interviews and were focused upon isolated *expressions* of difference and not upon particular groups of people and so on.

There is also a clear discomfort over who owns the public space within which multiculturalism is instantiated. Is the space value-free? Is it owned by all? Or are its characteristics dictated by the dominant post-Christian secularity discussed in the discourses on *Power*? On the one hand, these discourses of multiculturalism combine to construct a Southside that is dominated by a political correctness, where immigration and diversity *must* be celebrated and where the 'other' *must* abide by the rules of *our* secular public space: 'they' should speak 'our' language, not promote messages or ideas that 'we' don't agree with and certainly not try to change anyone's mind. However, they were also seen to construct a Southside that is vibrant, welcoming, both celebratory of and indifferent to difference and a place where encounters with the other facilitate positive, life-enhancing changes. Much as Wessendorf found in her ethnographic study of Hackney, in the Southside we see the 'co-existence of positive attitudes towards diversity more generally, and stereotypes against specific groups' (2014a: 18), with residents able to develop a sense of belonging 'because they can find their own "niche" of like-minded people' (2014a: 32).

Turning to moderation, these discourses essentially relate to what are deemed acceptable incursions of religion-related phenomena into public space, although it is clear from the interviews that these standards apply broadly to conduct in public spaces in general. They reflect the internalization of a pervasive form of liberal secularist discourse that extols moderation concerning questions of religion in interpersonal interaction and demonizes militancy or extremism: to quote Samantha, 'I'm definitely not a fundamentalist'. This discourse is detailed by Fitzgerald, who summarizes: 'Good religion is what conforms to, and does not challenge, liberal secular principles. Good religion stays out of "politics." Bad religion takes a critical stand against liberal categories and is, therefore, fanatical' (2015b: 306; also Casanova 2009: 139). Holding – or more importantly expressing – 'strong opinions' was dubbed by many as inherently problematic, although this view was frequently articulated alongside the notion that it is not the substance of the message that matters, so much as the manner in which it is expressed. Immoderate assertions of exclusivity were dubbed 'extremism', and whilst tendencies to extremism were generally viewed as an inherently human problem, some viewed religion or being religious as potent correlates with such extremism.

Liberal and moderate, Christian or secular, messages were thus regularly constructed as acceptable and inoffensive; they are compatible with the secular state and with the norms of civic space and can almost be ignored. However, alien messages, such as those of (non-moderate) Muslims, Atheists, Scientologists or American televangelists, cannot be ignored so easily. They should, according to the dominant discourse of moderation, keep themselves to themselves and steer clear of the liberal, tolerant public space of the Southside. This is a perfect exemplar of Aaron Hughes's 'rhetoric of authenticity' that is dominant in public discourse about religion (see Chapter 2). We also see this rhetoric in, for example, the writings of New Atheists such as Sam Harris (e.g. 2007) and philosophers such as Rawls and Habermas.[3] As I argue in Chapter 7, this dominant discourse of moderation in the Southside is what Michel de Certeau (1984) would dub a 'strategic' discourse, entangled with and negotiated through a variety of related 'tactical' discourses of indifference.

Space and the built environment

Given the local focus of my interviews, and the incorporation of visual representations of Southside religion into the interview schedule, it is unsurprising that a major theme concerned the interplay between religion, space and the built environment. However, Knott has argued that, despite tensions in local specificity and global connections, historic presence and new innovations, 'if you ask people to identify religion in an urban context most will point to a building' (2015: 18). In the Southside, these discourses primarily related to utility and heritage, the identity or character of the Southside and the subjective inner experience of users of the Southside. We will discuss these discourses in much greater depth in Chapter 6.

Concerning utility and heritage, discourses focused almost entirely upon the (former) church buildings in the Southside and their place within an 'urban heritage economy' (Knott, Krech, and Meyer 2016: 127). My Southsiders were unanimous in the view that the historic churches of the Southside are beautiful buildings that are embedded in the (hi)story of the area and thus worthy of preservation. This is quite apart from their perceived status as (former) religious buildings. Significantly, the (former) churches that were granted this 'beautiful' and 'historic' status were those that *looked like churches* – this status was not extended to other churches, or the premises of 'other' religions. Related to this desire for the preservation of heritage were discourses surrounding community use. The Southside Community Centre, that is, the reuse of the former Nicolson Street Church, was universally hailed as 'a great idea because it's sorta still based on what it was built for' (Keith). This reflects broader correlations between long-term establishment of national churches and a 'welfare-view of religion' (2000b; cf. Schenk, Burchardt and Wohlrab-Sahr 2015: 6; Woodhead 2012a).

Turning to the identity or character of the Southside, these discourses relate to the power that buildings deemed religious were perceived to exert over the locality. I have already demonstrated how the Southside is imbued with a lingering Christian character for many of my informants – there are 'traces of the Christian past in [this] urban space' (Knott, Krech and Meyer 2016: 129). Non-Christian buildings – where acknowledged at all – seemed particularly worthy of comment, with an underlying discourse of the threat of Islam 'taking over' reflective of a UK-wide anxiety about Islam (see, for example, Gilliat-Ray in

Bluck et al. 2012: 117–18; Wells and Watson 2005: 268). However, the way these identity dynamics generally played out was intimately tied to the identifications of the interlocutors concerned. In other words, certain buildings or types of buildings in the Southside were bound up in specific discourses on religion, dependent on the lens through which the individuals in question viewed them.

Taking up this subjective element, other discourses concerned the more visceral aspects of my informants' interactions with religion in the Southside, how they *feel* when they interact with elements of the built environment deemed religious. These feelings ranged from feelings of threat and intimidation (whether associated with *all* religious spaces or merely *others'* religious spaces), via feelings of majesty, awe and transcendence, to feelings of togetherness and belonging, or of 'nothing' or exclusion, that were traced to the community associated with a space, synchronically and diachronically, rather than to the space itself. Despite this variety, each informant operated with a working model for identifying religion in the built environment; associated this model with remembered, embodied and emotional experiences; and was able to utilize this model as a lens through which to retrospectively analyse their experiences in the Southside (cf. Mumford 2015).

As Birgit Meyer argues, perceptions are 'always subject to cultural framing', and 'people learn to direct their attention, tuning out certain stimuli while emphasizing and developing a sensibility toward others, generating certain emotions in the process' (in Meyer et al. 2014: 217). The 'cultural framing' in the Southside includes the language of 'religion', which is attached by some to elements of the built environment that 'do more than merely represent' but that 'interplay with bodily sensations' (Beekers and Tamimi Arab 2016: 152; see also Meyer 2015: 20). Put simply, 'religion' and 'religious' were meaningful terms for understanding embodied experience in the Southside.

Living

The discourses on *Living* consist of discourses surrounding the meaningfulness of individual and social practices that are considered religious and discourses surrounding the embodiment of religion. I have utilized the term 'Living' to intentionally bring these discourses into conversation with academic discourse on the 'Lived Religion', that is, on 'religion as expressed and experienced in the lives of individuals' (McGuire 2008: 3). As shall be discussed in Chapter 5, the critically problematic notion of 'lived religion' as 'real religion' that has gained popularity among some scholars in recent decades also permeates discourses in the Southside, suggesting that the turn to the everyday from the elite model exists in popular as well as academic discourse.[4] These discourses were particularly resonant throughout my entire body of data – a point to which I shall return at the conclusion of this chapter.

A cornucopia of competing, complementary and overlapping discourses surround the meaning(s) with which practices deemed religious are invested or not. At times the sincerity of social actors' religious beliefs and/or religious identifications was measured by their (regular) engagement in specific practices. Indeed, for some, practice – the 'living out of belief' – was seen as much more significant than (mere) belief (Day 2010; Vincett et al. 2012). This discourse was invoked by interviewees in relation to their own (lack of) practice as well as that of others. In a similar manner, interviewees inverted (and, thus, reinforced)[5] this discourse when they 'defended' their own participation in certain practices as mere 'tradition', or as 'keeping the peace' with family members, judged certain practices to be meaningless, harmless or benign or castigated others for their unthinking or disrespectful practice. Although such performances of difference are not inherently religion-related, it remains difficult to talk about cultural difference (in the Southside at least) without invoking religion. In this context, religion seems to remain a major fault line along which people articulate social difference, regardless of whether they are talking from experience or they are talking in the abstract.

Turning to embodiment, it must be said that for the most part, religion was perceived as invisible – given that religion was understood in the main to imply Christianity, and most 'Christians' in the Southside are not perceived to stand out from the crowd, due to the post-Christian hegemony discussed above. Where religion was located in the Southside's inhabitants was frequently in unusual dress and in visible practices as just discussed. Thus, the Southside sits comfortably in wider scholarly constructions of cities as 'prime arenas in which the public presence of religion – through, for instance, modes of dress, buildings, sounds, rituals and performances – is displayed and discussed' (Knott, Krech and Meyer 2016: 125). Unsurprisingly, it was Islam that stood out the most in terms of visibly different dress, although allusions were also made to visible activities and dress associated with 'other religions'. Furthermore, as I'll discuss in Chapter 5, the dynamics surrounding 'Islam' in this context can be viewed as a contemporary instantiation of dynamics that historically surrounded 'Catholicism'.

A key point is, again, that it isn't essentially religious difference that is being embodied here, so much as difference in general. Acknowledgements of diversity and difference seem to bring with them the *assumption* of religious diversity (and thus we return to the implication of religion in discourses on multiculturalism discussed above). By way of contrast, whilst other religions in the Southside were discussed primarily in terms of (external) sights, sounds and smells, those that were subjectively more familiar were frequently discussed in terms of (internal) emotions and embodied experience. Personal encounters with religion – positive, negative or banal – were spoken of in terms of emotional content and feelings, not with intellectualized notions and theological discourse. In fact, changes in subjective 'beliefs' were seen as unproblematic in social interaction, but (attendant) changes in behaviour and practice – which can be observed by others – are disruptive to the hegemonic order in particular contexts and were, thus, constructed as problematic.

Social identity

The discourses on *Social Identity* concern the relationships between religion, the individual and society. These discourses include: first, those that focus on the relationship between religion and society, constructing religion as a social force – positive, negative or benign; second, those focusing on the subjective relationship between religion and the (autonomous) individual; and third, those that focus on the individual's place in relation to ideal-typical constructions of religion-related identities as mediated by society.

The first group of discourses construct 'religion' and 'society' as substantive entities that interact and exert power over each other. Given the context of these interviews – in a study focusing on religion in the Southside – it goes without saying that I am implicated in potentially overplaying the social significance of religion. More on that later. Yet, discourses I encountered ranged from 'common sense' statements of religion's centrality to society and its importance for governments and academics to monitor and study, through various forms of indifference, to feelings that religion is only relevant to insiders and plays little to no part in day-to-day interactions in the Southside. These discourses can be placed along a continuum addressing 'the question of whether the discourse is essentially positive or essentially negative' (Stringer 2013a: 33). Yet, to complicate matters, religion was frequently constructed as a private matter for the individual and an inappropriate conversation topic in polite interaction – thus paradoxically constructing a private matter as something surrounded by a significant social taboo.

This brings us to the second group of discourses, on the relationship between religion and the individual, particularly concerning questions of individual choice and autonomy, and the subjective nature of belief and practice. In my conversations I regularly encountered discourses echoing Rational Choice Theory (Stark and Bainbridge 1985, 1987; Stark and Finke 2000), whereby the idealized individual was constructed as an autonomous social actor in the religious field, picking and choosing how they position themselves within that field based upon seemingly idiosyncratic criteria. At the same time, groups were perceived as complementary to the individual's religion-related journey, providing resources, comfort, meaning and a context within which to interpret material and make decisions. These discourses were further supported when interviewees highlighted a felt conflict between their own personal choice/ satisfaction and a sense of duty or reflected on whether religion was a choice or a 'state of being', a way in which one was brought up, 'hard-wired into my DNA' (Naomi). Perhaps unsurprisingly, a related discourse was that religion is primarily about belief, and hence, again, a notionally private matter for the individual. Yet, informants were also highly aware of the performative aspects of belief.

Finally, we have those discourses that focus on individuals' relationships with ideal-typical constructions of religion-related identifications that are dominant in society. Some instances consisted of a general positing of an idealized (non-) religious individual by an interviewee as a kind of foil. More often, however, these discourses concerned the paradoxically normative deviation of individuals from presumed norms of consistency in identification and ideal-typical behaviour. Many interviewees acknowledged fluidity in their identification with certain religion-related terms, painting their identifications as tactical and contextual discursive acts rather than permanent states of being, with some expressing profound discomfort with labels, in general, and with situations in which one feels forced into making declarative statements. This general willingness to impart fluidity and individuality to oneself and to others sharing one's identifications (one's 'in-group') was somewhat less evidenced in interviewees' discussions of others.

Containment

The discourses on *Containment* concern the interaction between various constructions of religion, particular social actors and the metaphor of containment. These discourses construct religion as a container, as a context within which action happens, within which social actors move, where their movements are constrained, which strongly influences social interaction and which cannot be abandoned lightly. Furthermore, religion is constructed as one container among many, acting in combination and competition with other contextually relevant containers such as culture, education, gender and sexuality, which similarly influence and constrain social action.

The metaphor of containment was extensively invoked throughout these interviews, through a variety of mutually reinforcing discourses. Religion was frequently described as analogous to a context in which social actors interacted with and made sense of the world. Religion is something within which one can be brought up – or not, in Keith's case, above – a tradition stretching back through time and made manifest through the broader context in which one finds oneself – indeed, it forms and informs that context. Many individuals related positively to these notions, finding (or hypothesizing that others might find) grounding, meaning, continuity and a positive lineage in religion, or describing religion in terms of comfort, safety, contentment and freedom. Many others related more negatively to religion, focusing on the (potentially) restrictive nature of the container, conceptualizing 'traditional' as 'backward' and feeling constrained or misrepresented by religion-related terms – indeed, even the designation 'religious' itself.

As was indicated above, however, the positioning of social actors in religion-related containers also raises the possibility of these containers interacting with others, whether these are explicitly understood in religious terms or as religion-related by virtue of the interactions. An especially good example of the interaction between containers explicitly related to religion is the notion of (de-) conversion, which tended to be conceived as moving out of/into a container and potentially into/from another. If these containers were perceived to overlap, sharing a significant portion of dimensions in common, this change would conceivably be less problematic. Other 'conversions' – such as Aisha's (from 'secular Scot' to 'Muslim'), David's (from 'active' to 'lapsed Catholic') or Naomi's (from the centre to the periphery of 'Judaism', and back again) – were loaded with much more meaning and trauma.

In many cases, this significance was rooted in the entanglement of explicitly religion-related containers with other forms of containment, including ethnicity, culture, education, gender, sexuality and nationality. Immigration acted as a locus for these discussions in relation to the Southside, being visibly linked to the changing religious character of the area. At a more individual level, religion was viewed as a particularly gendered and heteronormative container, with resulting misalignments meaning that some felt the need to reassess their relationship to religion in the light of these competing 'sacreds' (Knott 2013). In summary, the discourses on *Containment* construct religion-related identifications as socially significant containers acting in combination and competition with other contextually relevant containers which similarly influence and constrain social action.

Relationships

In the discourses on *Relationships*, the religion-related field is entangled with several binaries – unity and division, homogeneity and heterogeneity, belonging and exclusion – across three main strands: one's family, one's friendship circle and the broader community.

As far as 'family' is concerned, it is no real surprise that the connection between 'family' and 'religion' was frequently made, given the autobiographical nature of some lines of questioning. Yet, despite the normative convention of beginning one's autobiography with one's family, this type of response is suggestive of three themes. First, as we saw exemplified unequivocally in Keith's narrative, family members' relationships to religion are constructed as relevant to one's own. Second, we see the dominance of the transmission model, whereby religion (and non-religion) is presumed to be passed on from parent(s) to children down a family line (see Regnerus, Smith and Fritsch 2003; Arweck and Nesbitt 2010; Voas 2010; Woodhead 2010), regardless of how 'sticky' this transmission might ultimately be (see Bullivant 2016; Woodhead in Academy of Social Sciences 2016). And third, we have the notion that issues arise when there is a mismatch between family members concerning matters relating to religion.

Some participants described issues that have arisen due to changes in identification. Others spoke of arguments concerning religion or of mitigating their opinions out of concern for family members. Although notions of what counts as 'family' are subjective and extend beyond simple biological relationships, it is worth highlighting that these discursive themes were prevalent in the *Peoples of Edinburgh Project* and in my previous research (Cotter 2015) and that it appears that it is not the specifics of the religion-related identifications that matter here, but changes and differences within family groups.

Turning from the more narrowly conceived family to the broader friendship circle, the discursive dynamics are somewhat similar, yet with much of the negativity absent. A significant theme for a minority of my interviewees was that religion is, among other things, about shared experiences and relationships, with Eileen telling me that 'a lot of my close friends are Episcopalian, so when we're together although we're not actually talking about church things … we just feel we're, we're in it together … you know? And it's quite nice'. As we have seen above, the discourse was also negatively invoked by Keith when he criticized impersonal church funerals. It is not insignificant that this point was made by someone claiming not to be religious but who participates occasionally in church services; like those who positively invoked this discourse, Keith is speaking from experience, and not in the abstract. Similarly, when these same individuals spoke with a more-than-passing familiarity about religions with which they had no *direct* personal experience, their accounts were framed around friends' engagement with them; religion was still being constructed *relationally*.

Finally, the interaction between the religion-related field and 'community' can be discussed first in terms of religion(s) *as* community and second in terms of the interaction between religion(s) *and* (the) community. It was not uncommon to encounter the view that religions act as communities for those who are involved. For some, these communities were conceptualized as extending beyond the Southside, providing 'somewhere to belong' (David), and contrasted with a perceived lack of secular community. This notion of a secular void is furthered by the entanglement of the presumed decline of religion as encountered in the secularization discourse discussed above with a discourse on the decline of community in the Southside. This connection was made whether religious decline was considered the causal factor – one of the 'reasons for having church is it keeps people together in communities and groups' (Samantha) – or vice versa – 'when people moved out … a lot of these churches all closed down' (Alastair).

This connection to the Southside brings us to those discourses surrounding the interaction between religion(s) and the local community, or community in general. On the one hand, there was a clear emphasis that 'good' or 'proper' religion should be oriented towards the local community. On the other hand, there were many more references to religion being connected with division and militancy, whether historically, contemporaneously or in more general terms. Regardless of the specifics, a common theme is that religion has the potential to serve as a boundary marker, whether between religion and the secular world, or between different groups.

Each of the discourses on *Relationships* shares a common focus upon boundaries of belonging and exclusion, and the contestations that occur when subject positions are marked, or become marked, as different from contextual norms.

Science and meaning

The discourses on *Science and Meaning* encapsulate two main themes: the first is that of religion versus science or rationality, and the second is that of religion and what I term 'The 4Ms' – mystery, meaning, morality and mortality.[6] None of these themes was explicitly raised in questioning,[7] but discussions frequently turned to issues of epistemology, ontology and ethics.

Science and religion were particularly entangled in this body of data, with a prevalent theme concerning the conflict, or lack of it, between the two, or their (in)compatibility. In some instances, (bad) religion, or being highly spiritual or religious, was associated with credulity, naivety and irrationality; with intentionally restricting science and knowledge (particularly in educational contexts); or with being 'based on faith' rather than an 'historical or analytical' approach (Brenda). At other times religious belief was viewed as the only rational choice, with science being castigated for its fallibility and its inattentiveness to experience, feelings and mystery. Further, some individuals attested to feeling little conflict as they navigated between these two domains or to this so-called divide having little to no meaning in their subjective lives:

> I mean, yes I believe in God, Jesus … but then I know, I mean … you don't turn a blind eye to Darwin and the theory of evolution and things like that <laughs>.
> (Lily)

However, the unifying feature of these varied and oppositional discourses is the conceptualization of science and religion as separable realms or 'magisteria' (Gould 1998: 269–83) and the reification of the distinction(s) between them. Whether these are constructed as (partially) overlapping or as 'non-overlapping magisteria' (Gould 1998: 269–83), these discourses concern the seeming (lack of) competition and boundaries between science and religion as epistemological frameworks.[8]

These discourses concerned the construction of religion in relation to epistemology, as a particular *episteme*: 'a specific, contingent "configuration" within the epistemological field' (Robertson 2016: 45; on Foucault 1973: 168). Religion was discursively connected with questions concerning the meaning and purpose of life, and frequently with death, the afterlife[9] and existential (in) security, suggesting an entanglement between the perceived domain of religion and those 'gaps' that are (currently) perceived to be beyond the grasp of empirical reason.

Religion was also caught up in moral issues and theodicy, with the general thrust being that religion *should be* about morality, even if many/most religious social actors (occasionally) act immorally. This instantiates a dominant discourse in the contemporary UK described by Bruce, whereby 'religious people are not condemned for having the wrong religion: they are condemned for misunderstanding the proper nature of religion, which is simply to be nice' (2014b: 18). Religion was also connected with the very notion of the unexplained/unexplainable – the ubiquitous *gap in our empirical knowledge*. For each of these questions, the religion-related field could be positively or negatively implicated in the issue at hand. This includes non-religion, with Knott, Poole and Taira citing news stories which castigate Dawkinsian 'bad secularism and atheism' for not allowing 'space for imagination and fantasy, for the sense of mystery, myth and morality' (2013: 115). For example, for those who turned to, or claimed that others would turn to, religion at times of crisis and when dealing with death, there were (a smaller number of) others who cited crises and dealing with death as the reasons they, or others, would not be interested in, or ceased having any interest in, religion (see Keith's narrative above).

To summarize, it appears that religion in the Southside is deeply embedded in social thought concerning mystery, meaning, morality and mortality. It is constructed as an episteme whose (in)compatibility with the dominant cultural ethos of science and empiricism must be accounted for in the narratives of social actors in the Southside and beyond.

The Southside in context

In the section that follows, I place the Southside into its broader socio-historical context before reflecting on some of the discursive changes that have taken place, the role of the researcher in the production and interpretation of discursive data, and what these findings say about our modelling of non-religion.

A persistent theme in the sociology of religion in recent years is that the 'nature of religion' has been changing in the contemporary UK, 'a country with a deeply embedded Christian culture, which at one and the same time is becoming increasingly secular and increasingly diverse with regard to its religious profile' (Davie 2015: xii). There has been a shift in the 'discursive objects' in UK religion-related discourse, due to significant events such as the Dunblane massacre, the death of Princess Diana and the sacking of Glen Hoddle, 'all of which provoked – or were provoked by – an unexpected "religious" response and associated debate' (Davie 2000a: 117), and, of course, 9/11, 7/7 and other acts of violence associated with Islam. In the twenty-first-century UK, religion is increasingly associated with a broad range of social issues, such as leadership, political party choice, abortion, homosexuality, foreign policy issues, free speech, terror, moral panics, gender equality, environmentalism, euthanasia, stem cell research, dress, views of the body, discrimination, immigration and community relations (see Clements 2015: 7; Nye and Weller 2012; Guest, Olson and Wolffe 2012: 161; Ganiel and Jones 2012: 308; C. G. Brown and Lynch 2012: 342; Knott, Poole and Taira 2013: 82).

Linda Woodhead describes a variety of changes in UK society in the post-war period, including the rise of the welfare state and the eventual loss of faith in socialist institutions (2012a: 10), combined with the diminishing prestige of science in the face of epidemics, rising natural disasters, competing holistic therapies, entanglement with big business and so on (2012a: 9–10). In the post-9/11 and post-7/7 world, the UK has seen 'an attempt to extend greater state control over religion' (2012a: 22), which was somewhat paradoxically prompted by a prolonged phase of deregulation and disinterest (2012a: 24) which led many to the view that religion had somehow 'reappeared'. This bureaucratic situation is compounded by new legal measures and equalities legislation introduced via the EU, changes in charities law and the

> state's growing concern from the late 1990s onwards to enter into more regularized forms of consultation with a range of 'faith communities', rather than simply relying on historical forms of relationship with the major churches and with the long-established Jewish community in Britain. (2012a: 23)

Early twenty-first-century discourse has seen a rise in New Atheism (potentially in response to the aforementioned diminishing prestige of science) (2012a: 8) and a neoliberalism that is increasingly willing to make alliances with religion (2012a: 11) – think of former prime minister David Cameron's short-lived 'Big Society' agenda, for example. As we have seen above, these alliances map onto a dominant dichotomy in UK discourse between 'good' and 'bad' religion, whereby 'good' correlates with socially beneficial, private, moderate and tolerant, and 'bad' correlates with public, extreme, intolerant, demanding, interfering and fundamentalist (Hjelm 2014b; Hughes 2015; Fitzgerald 2015a). This period has also seen the continued shift from the communal to the individual, with institutions being invested with less authority (Clements 2015: 25), religion being viewed as a field in which individuals engage in choice (Bruce 2014a: 131) and the more 'open' and 'individualized' language of spirituality being preferred over the rigidity and traditionalism of religion (Vincett and Woodhead 2009: 320; Davie 2015: 37). It has also seen the rise of 'the failure of multiculturalism' discourse in popular politics (Modood 2014).

Woodhead summarizes the contemporary religion-related setup in the UK in four key points. First, the visibly or actively religious have become 'a numerical minority, and the open expression of religion in many public arenas … became highly contentious' (2012a: 25). Second, 'the fastest-growing forms of religion' are no longer 'those which are most closely allied with political power and social prestige' (2012a: 25). Third, religion has become 'the place where some of the tasks which are not being carried out by other social actors are attended' (2012a: 25). And fourth, religion is increasingly constructed as a 'minority interest' (2012a: 25) with weakened linkages to the state and increasing ties to 'consumer capitalism and a wide range of media' (2012a: 27). Yet despite the fact that Christianity and 'the Church' are becoming a distant memory for many, or a vague cultural memory for others, this has left an indelible imprint on UK discourse, with 'legacies of the past remain[ing] deeply embedded in both the physical and cultural environment' (Davie 2015: 4), and in the rhythms of everyday life and the national ritual cycle (Bruce 1995: 46, 70; Knott, Poole and Taira 2013: 57–78; Davie 2014: 615). Furthermore, all of this is occurring in the face of growing indifference among the population as a whole (see Chapter 7), described by Bruce as 'the biggest change' in Scotland's religious culture in recent decades (2014a: 3).

Discursive change in the Southside

The *Peoples of Edinburgh Project* (PEP), introduced in the previous chapter, was produced as part of a much broader multiculturalist project in the mid-1990s. Religion was a relatively minor feature of the conversations in this body of data and was present alongside other more prominent topics such as family, education, food, leisure time and 'integration into Edinburgh society'. As such, the discourses that were excavated from that body of data were somewhat more circumscribed than those in the contemporary Southside (CS). There were many continuities, however, and every discourse evinced in the PEP was present in some form in the CS. This is not entirely unsurprising, given that the genre of discourse (a semi-formal, semi-structured interview) was the same and given the commonalities among the interlocutors. Further, each project took place in a context of diminishing but hegemonic Christianity, the effects of which were felt quite strongly in the CS and were amplified for those of minority traditions in the PEP. This helps to explain, for example, the continuities in discourses of secularization and those that constructed religion-related terms as 'power categories'. Third, the PEP was conceived at a time when 'diversity' and 'communities' started to be conceptualized along religious lines, rather than by country of origin or ethnicity. The CS, particularly through the impact of contemporary discourses on Islam-related violence and the 'resurgence' of religion, is very much still working within this framework, and thus 'almost inevitably prioritizing religious over other features (such as occupation or locality, for example) and promoting religious Muslims as the representatives of Muslims as a whole' (Modood 2007: 133). With this consistent thread in the conceptualization of diversity comes consistency in metaphors of containment being associated with religion, and in discourses on religions as/and community. These commonalities aside, there were five major areas of change evident between the PEP and CS.

The first concerns the discourses on *Containment*. In the PEP these discourses were dominated by constructions of religion as *the* preeminent container in social interaction. An overriding assumption here was that religious identities were discreet and decontextualized silos into which social actors could be placed. By way of contrast, these discourses in the CS tended to relativize religion as one container among many, acting in combination and competition with others that were contextually relevant, such as culture, education, gender and sexuality. The CS thus speaks to a much more fluid, multiple and contextual understanding of religious 'identification' (as opposed to 'identity'). This is largely to be explained by my own critical position and its influence upon conversation, and by the extended focus upon religion in my interviews as compared to the more peripheral engagement in the PEP. However, it also fits with the continued shift in UK discourse on religion towards more open and individualized models, the exercise of choice and the rise of neoliberalism discussed above.

Second, and in a similar manner, the discourses on *Community* in the PEP frequently ascribed global homogeneity – generally in terms of (idealized) practice – to those individuals and communities who share a particular identification. This stands in marked contrast to the CS, where many interviewees acknowledged fluidity in their strategic and contextual identifications with certain religion-related terms (although this was somewhat less evidenced in interviewees' discussions of out-groups in the Southside and beyond). This unevenness can be somewhat explained methodologically, due to a differing emphasis in interview contexts. The participants in the PEP were of interest to the project because they identified as members of minority communities with explicit links to communities overseas. Whilst these individuals might well have been speaking for themselves, the line of questioning pursued by the PEP interviewers, and the way interviewees' narratives were presented, resulted in a greater prevalence of discourses of homogeneity.

Third, discourses on the meaningfulness of practice in the PEP were augmented by a discourse on the near-exclusively benign to positive or even 'safe' quality of said practices. In contrast, the CS material had more of an ambiguous flavour. Furthermore, although both bodies of data contained discourses on religion's continued relevance to the Southside and beyond, discourses in the CS tended to construct this relevance largely in terms of novelty and difference from a hegemonic and (admittedly, post-Christian) secular norm. The first of these points can be explained by the fact that participants in the PEP were commenting on *their own* practices, and as representatives of *their own* 'community', whereas the contemporary Southsiders were focusing upon religion in general, and on manifestations of this 'othered' religion in the Southside. Due to attribution biases, a focus on the conduct of one's own religion-related group is much less likely to prompt negative discourses than those focusing on the religion-related groups of others. Furthermore, the twenty years between these two projects has seen the rise of public discourse on 'good' versus 'bad' religion, which will undoubtedly have been a factor. The second point, on the shift from religious relevance to religious novelty and difference, makes sense in the context of the rise of the 'failure of multiculturalism' discourse (Brighton 2007; Modood 2014; Wise and Velayutham 2014), as well as increasing indifference to religion-related matters.

Fourth, due to the guiding principles behind selection of PEP interviewees, the majority of the discourses surrounding religion and oppression were invoked by individuals who identified as religious, and, as such, religion in general did not tend to be constructed as the oppressor, and the power relationships with which religion was connected were of a particularly personal nature. While these discourses were certainly not absent in the CS, here we encountered hierarchies and power relationships on a much bigger scale, most significantly concerning the machinations of the nation state, the relationship between the individual and said state and the perceived effect of external forces on the locality. Further, whilst the CS and the PEP both evinced a coherent discourse associating religion with individualized experiences of patriarchy and heteronormativity, this tended to remain unchallenged in the PEP material (i.e. it was described rather than criticized). The most obvious explanation for these shifting dynamics is the prevalence of non-religious subject positions in my data from the CS, but we must also think to the changing local, global and national context. The CS exists in a context of increased state control and regulation of religion, controversies and legal cases surrounding more established forms of religion; the rise of popular and vocal critics of religion; and a general cynicism surrounding the entanglements of religion with power, capitalism and so on. It is little wonder, in this context, that the very notion of religion itself is diminishing in popularity, as individuals and groups find alternative, less tarnished, terms to describe their beliefs, practices, traditions and ideologies.

Fifth, the discourses of the PEP were often inflected with an emphasis on the boundaries between a geographically (and chronologically) distant context labelled 'home' and the 'alien' context of Edinburgh (or the UK generally). Many interviewees also invoked a discourse whereby living in Edinburgh made it difficult to maintain their religion in their preferred manner. This discourse was clearly invoked in the CS in the more negative aspects of the discourses on *Civic Space*; however, these discourses also contained much more in the way of positivity whereby diversity brought benefits for the individual and the Southside, where the Southside was welcoming and celebratory of difference, and where the performance of indifference acted as a viable tactic for negotiating a dominant, *strategic* discourse that extols moderation concerning religion-related questions in interpersonal interaction and demonizes militancy or extremism. Given that the interviewees in the CS were explicitly solicited on the basis of considering themselves as having a connection to the Southside, no matter how tenuous, and given that locality was my chosen means to approach religion-related discourse, it is unsurprising that the main spatial dichotomy in the CS was between local and external forces, rather than between an 'alien' Southside and some longed-for 'home'.

Finally, it is worth noting that several discursive groupings were evident in the CS that were largely or totally absent from the PEP data, including those focusing on the utility and heritage of buildings, intersections between the built environment and Southside identity, friends, science and meaning-making. Concerning the built environment, my main explanation for the effective absence of these discourses in the PEP is to point to Knott's argument that 'if you ask people to identify religion in an urban context most will point to a building' (2015: 18). The participants in the PEP were not asked about religion in general or in Edinburgh, nor were they asked about the spaces in which they practised their religion. This is not to say that religious buildings weren't mentioned at all in the PEP, but simply that they were more peripheral to discussion. This could possibly be because interviewers might have assumed that minority communities are less likely to have made permanent or significant additions to the urban landscape. Also, as we saw above, the religion-related built environment in the

Southside is entangled in discourses surrounding Southside identity – it is a site of contestation. A project which sought to celebrate Edinburgh's diversity, at a time when such a celebration was presumably felt to be needed, would be understandably unlikely to focus on an area where 'locals' might feel particularly threatened by said diversity.

The absence of discourses connecting religion with friendships can once again be explained by looking to the rubric of the PEP. The interviewers' schedules contained prompts on the 'family religion' and how religion affects 'lifestyle of self/family', but nothing about friendships. It was also noted in the CS that interviewees tended to speak about *other* religions relationally, through the experiences of their friends and acquaintances. Once again, the PEP participants were not asked to speak about other religions – a topic much more likely to encourage negative commentary than one's own religion. Finally, when we consider the discourses on science and meaning, my first point is methodological and again concerns the motivations behind the PEP. Death, mystery, morality, meaning and the relationship between religion and science are controversial and emotional topics, at least in the UK context. They are not typically the topic of polite conversation and typically relegated to the private realm of 'belief'. It is little wonder that the mandate of the PEP – 'to promote understanding between the peoples of Edinburgh and celebrate the richness of multi-cultural society' (City of Edinburgh Council 1996: 3) – did not encourage conversations on such topics. Indeed, interviewers actively steered conversations away from them. However, as I shall now discuss, had the organizing rubric been different – focused on meaning or belief, for example – these discourses might have made an appearance in the PEP. Furthermore, the shifting UK discourse on science and religion, with the attendant rise of 'New Atheism', might have contributed to a heightened sense of urgency surrounding these issues.

The mystification of meaning

Ann Taves has rightly identified that 'we cannot compare religion and nonreligion without specifying an overarching rubric that encompasses them both' (2018: 1). In seeking such an overarching rubric, Taves nods approvingly at Lee's concept of 'existential cultures' (Lee 2015: 161–72) or Coleman, Silver and Holcombe's (2013) 'profoundly meaningful experiences' but latches on to 'worldviews' as a way forward (Taves 2018; Taves, Asprem and Ihm 2018). Taves argues that this concept 'provides a neutral starting point … that is not biased toward religious categories' (2018: 2) and points out that in many educational contexts, religion is now becoming broadened and subsumed under the notion of 'religions and non-religious worldviews' (Jackson 2016) or 'religion and worldviews' (Commission on Religious Education 2018).

With Egil Asprem and Elliott Ihm, Taves uses concepts such as 'ways of life' and 'big questions' relating to ontology, epistemology, axiology, praxeology and cosmology as ways of getting at these 'worldviews' (Taves, Asprem and Ihm 2018: 207–8). This desire to move away from distinctions between 'religion' and 'non-religion' towards the study of 'worldviews', 'cosmic belief systems' (Baker and Smith 2015), 'existential cultures' (Lee 2015) and so on is all well and good. Indeed, 'the way in which humans conceptualize their own existence and the nature of reality ... is intrinsically transcendent ... [and] cuts across religious and non-religious divides' (Lee, in Lee and Cotter 2018: 4). However, what about the unremarkable or the mundane? Studies which are guided by questions on 'what it means to be' (non-)religious or secular (e.g. Lee 2012a) or on what (non-)religious people believe (e.g. Day 2011) are bound from the start to produce models of religion and non-religion which focus on the profound, the transcendent, the meaningful. A focus upon 'big questions' – no matter what the critical, destabilizing intent – is doomed to play into the hands of vested interests which want to make (non-)religion all about addressing the ineffable question of life, the universe and everything pondered by the computer 'Deep Thought' in *The Hitchhikers Guide to the Galaxy* (Adams 1982). In these cases, we end up with typologies of 'existential culture' or, in the case of my own Master's project, four of five types of narrative which would all fall under the heading *Science and Meaning* above – 'naturalistic', 'philosophical', 'spiritual' and 'humanistic' (Cotter 2011b).[10] Given that these discourses appear as but one strand among eight in the contemporary Southside, and given that they were entirely absent in the PEP, this suggests that an unwitting reification of these discourses is at work in studies of the other-than-religious. Just like the Magratheans who constructed Deep Thought, these studies know what they are looking for but are still seemingly not asking the right question.

This reification is perhaps rooted in the significance placed upon these issues by people 'on the ground' – not to mention the whole academic industry of 'science and religion' studies. In other words, just because 'religion', 'non-religion', 'science' and 'meaning' *need not* be conceptualized as inherently connected, there is a prevalent and powerful discourse (in the contemporary 'West' at least) which connects these domains discursively: as scholars, we can study that discursive entanglement (Cotter and Alderman 2018).

Although we might wish to ask some critical questions of the underlying research, in their overview of the field of non-religion studies, Smith and Cragun write:

> Research has already shown the centrality of science, critical thinking, and skepticism to atheists and other nonreligious individuals … and how their religious counterparts tend to have less confidence in science … The nonreligious create systems of belief out of available cultural resources (e.g., normative structures, moral codes, scientific knowledge) and often in dialectic relationship with religion and its claims about the nature of the cosmos. (2019: 6)

Indeed, a prevalent view encountered by Lundmark and LeDrew among atheists online is that 'religion' is 'a failed science' (2019: 125), and the Canadian secularists studied by Jonathan Simmons saw themselves as engaged in an 'everyday project involving thinking like scientists, eliminating delusions and wishful thinking, and taking responsibility for educating others about the dangers of scientific misinformation and pseudoscience', with many being 'careful to distinguish themselves from naïve or dictionary atheists who did not share their respect for reason and science' (2018: 447).

In previous publications focusing upon my Master's typology (Cotter 2012, 2015), I explained the prevalence of these types of meaning-loaded discourses by working with Kim Knott's concept of the 'secular sacred' (2013). Holding that the 'sacred' is not 'a uniquely religious category' (Anttonen 2000: 274), Knott argues:

> Various things, places and people are set apart according to time and context. The boundaries that become the focus of sacred-making discourse and activities have the potential to erupt as sites of struggle but for much of the time lie dormant and, as such, invisible. (2013: 214)

For the sake of clarity, I shall resist the temptation to digress on a number of issues surrounding the usage of the nomenclature 'sacred' (Owen 2016). However, the fact that these discourses on *Science and Meaning* arose in the contemporary Southside, without prompting on my part, suggests that they are heavily implicated in the religion-related field as 'sites of struggle' and are much more likely to provoke the positioning of social actors in religion-related subject-positions when compared with the more a-religious discourses I shall now discuss. However, I think it is incumbent upon scholars to acknowledge the role of their guiding assumptions about religion and non-religion in the production of their conclusions. Acknowledging and attempting to understand a prevalent discursive entanglement between the religion-related field and fields of discourse on science, meaning-making and so on is a worthy project. Attempting to understand and map ways of life and responses to 'big questions' is another. But allowing one's interest in the latter to tarnish the former by obscuring the contingent, socially constructed nature of the so-called 'debate' is critically problematic, normative and ideologically loaded.

Religion-related discourse

In this chapter, I have introduced the major religion-related discourses encountered in the Southside – initially via Keith, and then in more depth. I then placed these discourses into their broader socio-historical context and reflected on some points of continuity and change, and on the role of the researcher – particularly in reifying meaning-laden models of (non-)religion. In this final section, I discuss some of the theoretical implications of the material discussed thus far. Some discourses are shown to be effectively a-religious, however particularity and contextuality may mitigate against this. Some of the discourses are shown to maintain their structure regardless of the discursive objects that populate them. Finally, I reflect on the relatively unmarked nature of the secular or non-religious in some of the discourses presented.

First of all, it can be argued that many of the discourses described above are effectively 'a-religious' in that they can generally be 'described and analysed without any reference to religious phenomena' (Quack 2014: 446). For example, the discourses on *Power* which concerned certain hierarchies and power relationships – the individual versus the state, the local versus external forces – can be understood as a-religious in this sense. Religion was, indeed, constructed as both a domain over which the state should exert control and a resource that could be co-opted by the state, but I contend that the key dynamic here is that 'the state' is being constructed as the regulator and legitimate user of resources. Religion is but one domain with which the state is perceived to interact and through which it regulates the behaviour of individual citizens. Religion, whatever it is, *need not be* entangled in this power relationship, but the thrust of my conversations with these Southsiders led to an intersection between the discursive fields of religion and politics, centred on the dominance of the state over the local and the individual. Similarly, the discourse on the local versus external forces is not inherently religion-related, but it is *contextually* entangled with the discourse of secularization in the Southside and with discourses on religion and conflict.

As a further example, looking at the discourses on *Civic Space*, some of these constructed the Southside as multicultural and heterogeneous. For the most part, this diversity was celebrated as good for the Southside and for the individual, with intolerance and extreme views discursively placed outside its boundaries. Other discourses inverted this positivity, seeing multiculturalism as oppressive political-correctness, and negatively assessing some of the manifestations of this multiculturalism. Others focused on strategies and tactics for managing this diversity, with a dominant strategic discourse of moderation marginalizing exclusivity claims and 'extreme' positions, being negotiated through entangled tactical discourses of indifference. This brief summary demonstrates once again that these discourses on *Civic Space* are not inherently religion-related: they concern the nature of (appropriate) interpersonal interaction in general, in the Southside and beyond. However, it is also clearly the case that these discourses are not only entangled in the religion-related field in a manner reflective of the Southside's 'local particularity' (T. Jenkins 1999; see Chapter 6) but, in the case of the discourses on multiculturalism, this entanglement runs much deeper.

This leads to my second point: much as this 'a-religious' description and analysis can occur at a theoretical level, the local particularity of many of these discourses (or the 'national particularity', in the case of the discourses on multiculturalism) means that it would be difficult and disingenuous to give an account of these discourses without making reference to religion. What we *can* say is that the religion-related field in the Southside was entangled with several other discourses that were theoretically a-religious but became religion-related due to the entanglement dictated by the specificities of my data, that is, the Southside of Edinburgh. For example, although aspects of the discourses on *Space and the Built Environment* were not inherently religion-related, such as the Southside's sedimented history and local versus external dynamic, other aspects were much more entangled. Indeed, it makes little sense to speak of a post-Christian hegemony, or a welfare view of 'religion', as not being religion-related. Religion seemed to remain a major fault line along which people articulated differences, and although many of the differences weren't inherently religion-related, the acknowledgement of diversity seemed to bring with it the assumption of religious diversity. Indeed, in academic, policy and popular discourse in the twenty-first-century UK, it is remarkably difficult to speak about cultural difference without invoking religion. It remains in the popular imaginary as a prominent arena for clashes of cultures (cf. Huntington 2011), despite this discourse arguably lacking an empirical basis (Sharify-Funk 2013).

Thus, we can conclude that the theoretically a-religious character of some discourses is rendered effectively meaningless in certain contexts.

Third, it can be argued that some of the discourses outlined above maintain their structure regardless of the objects that populate them. The scaffold remains the same, despite what is hung upon it. Returning, for example, to the discourses on *Power*, I noted above how the very category 'religion' and the notion of specific religions can be perceived as oppressive. Whilst there was a distinct bias in this data set towards constructing particular 'World Religions' as oppressive, there were also instances of a variety of 'non-religions' being constructed in a similar fashion. Religion-related terms were invested with significant power, especially when considered in terms of group identity. Whether individual social actors consider themselves insiders or outsiders to specific religion-related groups, the designation of a group as religion-related carries with it the potential for oppression – being oppressive as well as being oppressed – regardless of the specific terminology involved. Further, the metaphor of *Containment* was applied across the religion-related field, with subject positions being constructed as lenses for making sense of the world. In actors' relationships, it was marked *differences* or *changes* in religion-related beliefs, practices and identifications which were invested with meaning and not the specific configurations of these differences and changes. However, other discourses complicate this picture.

In the discourses of multiculturalism, the diversity that was being 'accommodated' by the Southside is discussed in terms of the 'other' sights, sounds, smells and – particularly in the case of the Mosque Kitchen – tastes experienced by social actors in the Southside's shared public spaces. As Vassenden and Andersson found in their research in Grønland, Oslo, in particular contexts religiosity can, in many ways, be 'hidden by whiteness' resulting in differences in 'interactional freedom and constraints, when compared to non-white religious persons' (2011: 590). In the Southside these dynamics extend beyond non-normative skin colour to non-normative clothing, language, food, practices and so on in such a manner as to construct the Southside once again as post-Christian and secular. Despite the theoretical interchangeableness of religion-related terms, in the Southside the normative position from which levels of multiculturalism are judged is one of white, Scottish, post-Christian secularity. Turning to the discourses of moderation, similar dynamics are in operation, whereby non-moderate, normative, religion-related discourses are demonized – be they Christian, Islamic, Atheist or Secularist. Indeed, as Knott, Poole and Taira argue, this correlates with a dominant view in the UK whereby both 'campaigning atheism and creationism are unwelcome' in public space

(2013: 110). In other words, the dominant model of 'appropriate' conduct in the civic spaces of the Southside is such that it seemingly applies equally to all subject positions within the religion-related field. However, in other cases, as with my point above concerning the a-religious character of these discourses, this interchangeability of discursive objects remains more theoretical than empirical. Discourses on secularization in the Southside, whilst theoretically concerning the loss and/or maintenance of religion-related power, are contextually inflected with Christianity. Thus, we return to 'local particularity' (see Chapter 6) and the importance of looking beyond the terminology in order to see the underlying structure of the discourses and avoid reifying (one section of) the religion-related field.

Finally, a pertinent question to ask of many of the discursive groups presented above – particularly *Living, Space and the Built Environment*, and *Social Identity* – is where is the non-religious and/or secular? Given that most of these discourses were populated by religious discursive objects, it might be tempting to fall back on naïve discourses on the insubstantial nature of 'secularity', 'non-religion' and so on (see Lee 2015: 49–69) and declare that because 'religion' has substance, it is what is felt, embodied, seen, encountered and assessed. However, interviewees were aware of instantiations of the non-religious, in the form of atheist bus adverts and irreverent material culture, and of a feeling of oppression in secular public space – a feeling whereby one is limited in one's ability to manifest one's religion-related identity (see Lee 2017b; Tomlins and Bullivant 2016). Further, there is indeed some truth to the notion that in the discourses on *Living*, it is 'lived religion' which is perceived as having substance. However, it is the position of the speaker, the presumed shared perspective within which our interviews took place, that is constructed as the 'neutral' secular space which provided the context for differentiating between religion and non-religion. Likewise, in the discourses on *Social Identity* the Southside was constructed as a neutral, secular (and post-Christian) space from which pronouncements could be made or exceptions to the rule noted. And the discourses on *Space and the Built Environment* made no reference to 'non-religion' or 'the secular', suggesting that these concepts go unmarked in a visual assessment of the Southside. Thus, the discourses I have sketched in this chapter further suggest that the 'non-religious' might be implicit in the subject position of those actors utilizing religion-related discourse, rather than explicitly articulated.

In conclusion, from the discussion above, we clearly stand to benefit from looking beyond the terminology and beyond the supposed 'religious' or 'non-religious' character of discourses. The discourses I have presented are utilized from a whole variety of religion-related subject positions. This allows us to see the underlying structure and to avoid reifying one section of the religion-related field. But further still, we should avoid reifying the *whole* religion-related field: in this *particular context*, certain discourses are entangled to varying degrees with contextual constructs of 'religion' and populated with fixed or varying discursive objects. In other contexts, the discourses might be 'religion-related' in wholly different ways, or religion might not be implicated at all.

In the next chapter, I turn my gaze on the problematic notion of 'identity' in relation to the non-religious. There, I develop my argument about the interchangeability of discursive objects and argue for setting aside the particularities of the religion-related 'identities', viewing them rather as 'operational acts of identification' (Bayart 2005).

5

Religion and non-religion as acts of identification

> [T]here is no such thing as identity, only operational acts of identification. The identities we talk about so pompously, as if they existed independently of those who express them, are made (and unmade) only through the mediation of such identificatory acts, in short, by their enunciation. (Bayart 2005: 92)

This chapter argues for setting aside the particularities of the religion-related 'identities' of individuals and communities, viewing them rather as 'operational acts of identification' (Bayart 2005). Through these relational acts of identification, social actors make use of discursive resources to contextually position themselves and others in relation to religion. Providing further support for the argument advanced in the preceding chapter, some of these contextual acts result in the positioning of phenomena as 'non-religious', in Lois Lee's sense of being 'primarily understood in relation to religion' but not being 'considered to be religious' (2015: 32). In other cases, the non-religious is implicit in the subject position of particular actors. In all cases, religion-related terms have the potential to be constructed as 'power categories', acting in dialectical interplay with other power categories such as 'politics', 'science' or 'nature' (Fitzgerald 2015b).

From identities to identifications

In Chapter 2 I argued that a major problem with substantive approaches to non-religion is the ease with which identity talk becomes ideal-typical. This is problematic because although the 'ideal type' was conceptualized by Weber such that it 'is only rarely encountered in historical reality' (cited in Bayart 2005: 34), it is almost invariably the case that its artificial and constructed nature becomes lost in translation, giving the false impression that individuals can be easily boxed off into one of a discrete number of types. Whilst such work is very valuable for macro-level analysis, it fundamentally breaks down at the level of the individual where heterogeneity, contextuality, 'indeterminism, incompletion, multiplicity and polyvalence' abound (Bayart 2005: 109): there is 'no such thing as a perfect or ideal-typical form' of difference to 'religion' (Lee 2015: 44).

Much has been written in recent years on how the logics of survey methodologies such as censuses can encourage individuals to claim certain identities which might not be claimed in other circumstances, or which do not simplistically map on to other aspects of individual belief, practice or values – particularly when the identities at focus are religion-related (Day 2011; Day and Lee 2014; Wallis 2014; Lee 2015). Indeed, Gervais and Najle (2018) have recently conducted some ground-breaking work utilizing the 'unmatched count technique' (cf. Dalton, Wimbush and Daily 1994; Raghavarao and Federer 1979) to propose that 'roughly one in four (26%) American adults may be atheists – 2.4–8.7 times as many as telephone polls' suggest (Gervais and Najle 2018: 8). They go on to argue that the 'disparity between self-report and indirectly measured atheism rates underscores the potent stigma faced by atheists (Edgell, Gerteis and Hartmann 2006; Gervais 2013), as even in an anonymous online survey, about a third of American atheists may be effectively "closeted"' (2018: 8). In short, self-reports are unreliable – particularly when related to religion – and the extent of this unreliability varies according to a host of contextual factors. Yet, in spite of these important critiques of survey methodologies, self-report and ideal types, the implicit assumption underlying much of this work is that identity is 'an internal quality only subsequently expressed for others to see, making social interaction the effect of prior and private sentiments' (McCutcheon 2017b: 2).

In *The Illusion of Cultural Identity* (2005), the French social theorist Jean-Francois Bayart – quoted in the epigraph to this chapter – argues that 'identities' are political, ideological and, ultimately, historical constructs (2005: ix). Throughout this book, Bayart convincingly builds his case that we should rather speak of 'acts of identification' and that 'an individual's act of identification is always contextual, multiple and relative' (2005: 92). According to Bayart, one individual might define themselves as a resident of a particular street, district, town, nation or continent, or by their gender, ethnicity, sexuality, religion, employment status, job title or health condition depending on with whom they are interacting (2005: 92). However, 'none of these "identities" exhausts the panoply of identities at an individual's disposal' (2005: 92–3). Moreover, approaches which (unintentionally) reify these so-called identities into natural, primordial, fixed and stable categories are critically flawed because, not being satisfied with erecting into an atemporal substance identities in continual mutation, [they conceal] the concrete operations by which an actor or a group of actors define themselves, at a specific historical moment, in given circumstances and for a limited time. (2005: 93)

These issues disappear when one abandons identity-talk and instead focuses upon identification.

By shifting from seemingly static identities to the more active claims and counterclaims surrounding them, our study then becomes the study of 'discrete strategies of identification and the situationally-specific techniques for fabricating the impression of authenticity, autonomy, and primordiality' (McCutcheon 2017b: 6). And thus, as I and many others have argued before, 'Religious, spiritual, secular, and non-religious identities are not stable, unitary formations' (Hoesly 2015: 9) but rather 'relational' categories (Quack 2014), which reflect 'a relationship to the Other as much as a relationship to the Self' (Bayart 2005: 96). As we further explore the narratives of Edinburgh's Southsiders, the identity claims and counterclaims discussed will be of interest not because of what they might tell us about some 'inner being' of the interlocutors involved, but for the boundaries that are being drawn and the power dynamics that are in play for these interlocutors in 'the settings to which they are inevitably subjugated' (McCutcheon 2017b: 7). As Craig Martin puts it:

unlike inanimate objects, humans respond to the concepts we use to organize ourselves into different groups; the identities we internalize literally make us who we are and alter our experiences of the world. (2017: 50)

'I don't necessarily discuss with them the fact that I'm Jewish'

Naomi is a 'retired' writer in her late sixties who self-described as a 'secular(ish) Jew' when she agreed to speak to me in October 2014 and declared herself to be 'a dedicated Southsider who considers it the most interesting neighbourhood in the city'. In her own words:

Edinburgh is really the city of my heart. I do come from ... the suburbs of New York, so I grew up there, so I have ... I have a fine sense of cities. And I've lived in London, I lived in Glasgow, and ... um, Edinburgh itself is a city I've always loved.

Having come and gone several times since first arriving in the city as a student she

> was extremely happy to move back about 14 years ago into the Southside proper, because I think it is an extremely interesting, multi-layered, properly urban area in this city which is a city of such historic richness, high romance, but deeply complicated socio-economic stories.

I shall now take you through a section of roughly three minutes from my conversation with Naomi, which is particularly rich in acts of identification and provides a useful mooring for the discussion that follows on the interpersonal, spatial, societal and conceptual dimensions of religion-related identification in the Southside. The extract begins two-thirds of the way through our conversation, following immediately upon a discussion in which Naomi described the feeling of a delicate balance in the Southside, whereby she feels able unproblematically to *be* a Jew. Although 'it's not like being a … Hasidic woman walking all around *Mea She'arim* … in Jerusalem', she begins to tell of particular spaces where her 'Jewishness' is activated by a visceral sense of meaningful connection to a historic Jewish community in the Southside.

> **Chris:** … yeah, so you're not necessarily walking around feeling <pause> particularly conscious of the fact that you are 'a Jew' as you're walking..
> **Naomi:** Indeed, no … in the Southside …
> **C:** Um …
> **N:** Except when I'm doing things like passing the little syn … the little cemetery.
> **C:** Yeah …
> **N:** Then I'm, you know, I kind of like to kind of, as I say, send a little message, but yeah …
> **C:** Yeah, so yeah there are particular points which …
> **N:** Yeah.
> **C:** Have that sort of embodied memory …
> **N:** Indeed. Yeah.
> **C:** Yeah. Okay, and… in terms of just, while we're still on it … in terms of interaction with, let's say, non-Jews, in the Southside… like, does it … does it ever come up? Is it something that comes up in conversations or interactions?
> **N:** Mmm not really so much about my Jewishness, I mean it's like obviously our corner shopkeeper's, you know, it's a really good corner shop that you try to get as much as you can there and not buy it in the supermarket <inaudible> um, you know, he's … he's … he's not obsessively religious, but I

know he did make the Hajj … um, and he, you know the guy who's the sort of … the boss guy, you know, his nephew who's in more often, I think, I've never really talked much about religion with him at all, but you know, with <name> we will, you know … 'Oh, it's coming up for Eid' or 'How you doin' on the Ramadan fast? And how's it going this year?' and, you know, that sort of thing … you know, there's that sort of casual thing. But I think I would probably … I don't necessarily discuss with them the fact that I'm Jewish, …¹ partly because it brings up "the whole Israel thing" … and as I say, I am not particularly a Zionist …I mean, I'm not a Zionist, I'm a … you know, I think Israel has a right to exist … but it, you know, I'm profoundly uncomfortable with it, so unless I were in a situation where there was an actual sort of inter-faith, sort of 'Hey, I'm Jewish', you know … because I think it becomes … people, you know, make assumptions and … I, you know, I think probably, you know, I'm not assuming that people would automatically go 'Oh well, you know, you must be Netanyahu's niece', but <pause> you know, it's just … it's not something I would necessarily be rushing around … and, you know, I was not brought up to wear a Jewish star, nor would it occur to me to do it. My … in fact, I remember my mother being quite appalled when people did that sort of thing. She felt it was kind of shoving your religion in people's faces. But I'm quite happy, say, to talk with my corner shop guy … because it's sort of something that's important to him, I think he really likes the fact that people are interested, but you know it's [also] an area where I know there is more cousinship between us, and that I can understand certain aspects of what it feels like to be, you know … you go home from your day of running the shop, and then there's going to be some big religious … you know, some family dinner because it's a big important religious festival [so I know what] that feels like … You know, but I, you know, I won't necessarily say, 'Ah, yes, this is … just like, you know, you're goin' home to break your Ramadan fast, well I'll tell ya, Yom Kippur, when we broke the fast, this is what we did … " you know, it's not that sort of relationship.

C: Yeah. But it's like, yeah, an empathy of some …

N: Yeah, yeah there's an empathy …

This extract begins with me somewhat awkwardly summarizing what I understand to be Naomi's position: her identification as Jewish isn't something that she is consciously made aware of in her day-to-day walks around the Southside. Her response – 'Indeed, no … in the Southside' – indicates that she has experience of being in other urban spaces where this aspect of her identity is brought more clearly into focus. Indeed, it turns out that the Jewish Cemetery on Sciennes House Place is just such a place, and by her account its effect on her is not purely intellectual. Indeed, she tells of journeys being interrupted by ritualized interactions with members of Southside Jewry from days gone by. In our discussion, I dub this 'embodied memory'.

Sticking with this train of thought, I was interested in the impact of Naomi's identification as Jewish upon her interactions with others – with non-Jews – in the Southside, with the underlying assumption that religion is, or at least might be, of such social significance as a boundary marker that it manifests itself in the mundanities of day-to-day life. Naomi's immediate response indicates that, although she is aware that she invests specific places in the Southside with religion-related meaning, this is not obviously the case in the rhythm of her regular interactions. As was the case for most of my interviewees, her go-to mental space to locate multicultural interaction is the stereotypically superficial and short-lived social and commercial transactions that occur in shops and restaurants between social actors who are deemed to represent different cultures, religions, nationalities and so on.

In this instance, she turns to a member of staff at her local corner shop, implying that he is Muslim – not only Muslim but 'obviously' Muslim – yet without feeling the need to explicitly use the word 'Muslim' itself: although this is implied shortly through her discussion of Islam-specific rituals, there is an underlying discourse shared between the two of us of corner shops being commonly owned and/or run by individuals from the Indian subcontinent and who can relatively safely, in the Southside at least, be assumed to have some connection with Islam. This shopkeeper is designated as 'not obsessively religious' – the implication being that this is a good thing and that were he 'obsessively religious', this would be evident from their day-to-day interactions – although his Islamic identity is deemed to be more than nominal due to his having participated in the Hajj, and Naomi being privy to this knowledge. Because Naomi can place the shopkeeper within an Islamic container, she feels that she has enough cultural capital to engage in conversation with him about this. The fact that she invokes the distinction between the shopkeeper and his nephew suggests that she feels that she can more easily talk about religion with someone who is closer to her age and that the younger individual is less likely to be, or is at least less obviously, religious.

Naomi then continues to describe her interactions with this shopkeeper as a 'casual thing'. He is apparently happy to discuss aspects of his religion with Naomi, who is equally happy to engage in this discussion, yet not to reciprocate with similar information about 'the fact that I'm Jewish'. In this scenario, the implication is that the shopkeeper has instigated these conversations through some form of public display of his religion, whilst Naomi desires to keeps hers private as she considers it contentious – at least in interaction with a 'Muslim' – due to its connection with the ongoing conflict in Israel-Palestine, and thus it might cause issues. There is no pressure here for Naomi to divulge information she does not wish to – these are casual, convivial interactions, and their very superficiality is what makes them safe and unthreatening.

Naomi's uneasiness with declaring her religious identification is connected to a feeling that 'people [will] … make assumptions' that she is a 'Zionist'. Clearly, for her, 'Zionist' is a bad word – or at least has the potential to be interpreted in a negative manner by others. She appreciates that the label might apply to her – she does, after all, think that 'Israel has a right to exist' – but she is 'profoundly uncomfortable with it'. The wider discourse surrounding the State of Israel and her perceptions of how others engage with it mean that, despite her overwhelmingly positive view of the freedoms granted to her (and to all) in the Southside, this is still an oppressive space where she cannot simply be her authentic self. The label 'Jew' carries discursive baggage and the threat of negative social consequences. Indeed, later in the interview Naomi quite plainly states: 'I am Jewish, but, you know, … I worry, because, to a lot of people, Jew means a lot of things that it doesn't mean to all of us' (i.e. all 'Jews'). Thus, she remains guarded about embodying and announcing her 'Jewishness'. Indeed, this is how she was 'brought up', and she seems to share her mother's distaste for those who publicly 'wear' their religion, castigating this as 'shoving your religion in people's faces' – an assault and invasion of privacy and personal space that is inappropriate for the public square. This guardedness is exemplary of a form of 'tactical cosmopolitanism', whereby 'pragmatic considerations of achieving practical goals' are balanced by restricting one's 'openness' with others (Wessendorf 2014b: 69) and by selective (and protective) self-exclusion (Landau and Freemantle 2010: 387).

Towards the end of this extract, Naomi focuses largely upon the unspoken empathy that she feels with this shopkeeper. Due to some unspecified indicators, Naomi infers that religion is 'something that's important to him' and thinks that 'he really likes the fact that people are interested' (implying, therefore, that interest in such matters is not the norm in the Southside). She describes a feeling of 'cousinship' with this shopkeeper, of understanding 'certain aspects of what it feels like' to engage in analogous, highly ritualistic religious practices in a local context where one is in a minority and where participation in 'big important religious festival[s]' sits uneasily alongside a hegemonic (post-) Christian calendar. Interestingly, this feeling is not explicitly articulated in their interactions. Indeed, it may be entirely of Naomi's construction. But although it is not seen as the 'sort of relationship' where such articulations might occur, these brief moments of convivial connection are clearly invested with significance and meaning.

This lengthy discussion of a relatively small section of discursive data not only shines further light on my analytical process but provides a map for the rest of the chapter. We have encountered discourses on spatial hegemony, local identity, embodiment, emotion, experience, ritual, the community (living and dead), multiculturalism and conviviality, moderation, conflict, in-groups and out-groups, civic space, youth, performance, indifference, anonymity and politics. We've seen Naomi construct an identity as a 'secular(ish) Jew' which would fly in the face of standard survey measures. We've seen her subjective, embodied experience in specific spaces challenge ideal-typical constructions of Jewishness and that her identifications vary dependent upon context and with whom she is interacting. And we've seen religion-related identifications being implicated in processes of othering and boundary maintenance. I'll take each of these points in the sections that follow, before concluding with a discussion of the ways in which religion-related identifications in the Southside are constructed as *identities* – as containers with all the attendant issues discussed at the beginning of this chapter, and what this says to notions of the 'non-religious' or the 'secular'.

Subjectivity and religion-related identification

We've just seen Naomi's narrative chart a course through subjects relating to individual choice and autonomy, aversion and discomfort surrounding the notion of religion, (in)appropriate contexts for religion-related conversation and on embodied experience. This section expands upon each of these points, focusing upon the tension between the individual's sense of self and the religion-related identifications at their disposal.

Turning first to individual choice and autonomy, in my conversations I regularly encountered echoes of Rational Choice Theory (RCT),[2] whereby the idealized individual was constructed as an autonomous social actor in the religion-related field, picking and choosing how they position themselves within that field based upon seemingly idiosyncratic criteria: 'I always thought that a man has a choice whether to follow this religion, or that religion' (Amir). Where others (individuals or groups) were perceived to limit the individual actor's autonomy in this regard, these limiters were frequently dubbed intolerant or exemplars of 'bad (non)religion'. The focus might be upon the way in which religion in general spreads by being 'drilled in' (Fred) to people at a young age, or more upon specific religions, with Ivan criticizing the Jehovah's Witnesses for being 'very tight [with] no room for manoeuvre', and Aisha recalling past encounters where her identity as a Muslim woman elicited responses akin to 'she's a woman and she's gonna be oppressed and forced to wear things, and, you know, chained to the kitchen sink'. The very term 'religion' can be understood to oppress, with Keith effectively banning conversations on the topic in his pub because 'it leads to arguments', and many who identified with established religions (like Naomi above) feeling an aversion to being described as religious, seeing religion as a 'toxic brand' (Woodhead in Elgot 2014; cf. Lee 2015: 5):

> I don't consider myself 'religious', that seems <pause> no I don't. <hushed> I go to church but that doesn't necessarily make me very religious, I've never seen it like that. (Ella)

However, as we shall soon see, groups were also perceived as complementary to the individual's religion-related journey, providing resources, comfort, meaning and a context within which to interpret material and make decisions.

These discourses on religion as a choice were further supported when interviewees highlighted a sensed conflict between their identification and a sense of duty or reflected on whether religion was a choice or a 'state of being', a way in which one was brought up, 'hard-wired into my DNA' (Naomi). This dynamic was strengthened when non-religious interviewees implied that while the non-religious are free to make their own decisions in matters relating to religion, the religious are not. Conversely, when some of my religious interviewees reflected on this view, they asserted that the non-religious merely *like to think* of themselves as free. These discourses on the autonomy of the individual were complicated further through the common cliché that religion is inherently personal, a matter between the individual and their 'god', and thus also something which is private, not anyone else's business and certainly not a topic of polite conversation (Walsh 2017).

Perhaps unsurprisingly, a related cliché rehearsed by my informants was that religion is primarily about belief (McCloud 2017) – 'I found myself having to argue quite a lot, both with atheists and with other Christians, about whether my beliefs fitted into either category' (Aoife) – and hence, again, a notionally private matter for the individual. Simultaneously, informants were highly aware of the performative aspects of belief:

I'm a Catholic because I'm baptized and confirmed a Catholic, I went to Catholic school, I'm part of that culture and my ancestors were part of the culture ... and you know, just because I don't believe in God, that can't be taken away. (David)

Paradoxically, then, the 'totally private' beliefs of the individual are subject to scrutiny by others – implicit or explicit, within or outside one's own community. This belief-oriented model of the relationship between religion and the individual was further nuanced by the construction of a variety of belief-based dichotomies or spectra: from normal to credulous, proper, practicing or extreme belief. In other words, although the 'religion' and the 'belief' might be the same in theory, in practice every individual is different. And once again we see how 'identities' are negotiated, ascribed, adopted and enforced; the identities we internalize literally make us who we are and alter our experiences of the world (C. Martin 2017: 50).

My next point concerns individuals' relationships with ideal-typical constructions of societally dominant religion-related identifications. In some instances, Southsiders posited a hypothetical, idealized (non-)religious individual as a kind of foil – 'I haven't met many "real" Buddhists' (John), 'I would still define myself as a pretty secular or secular-ish Jew' (Naomi) and so on – or, occasionally, with negative connotations, the implication being, once again, that those others who 'really live up to the name' are too extreme in their dedication to the identification, reflecting a prominent theme in contemporary atheist discourse and a general distaste for the 'deeply religious' in contemporary UK society (Clements 2012: 421). Significantly, this also applies to the 'deeply non-religious'; for example, 'I'd say I'm an atheist, but I'm open-minded' (Sebastian, cf. Cotter 2017a). More often, however, these discourses concerned the paradoxically normative deviation of individuals from presumed norms of consistency in identification and ideal-typical behaviour.

Many Southsiders acknowledged fluidity in their identification with certain religion-related terms, painting their identifications as tactical,[3] contextual discursive acts. For some, this fluidity was portrayed as pragmatic and situational. For example, Courtney described considering herself an atheist who appreciates some aspects associated with the humanist label, while 'secularist and non-religious seem like answers I'd put down on a census' (Cotter 2015: 179). For others, this situational identification was much more relationally charged, with Iona taking care to remain 'really sensitive with people who actually are religious' and who might use it 'as a way to cope', and Séverine fondly saying, 'I'm not gonna have an argument with a very old lady ... I don't think I'm an atheist for my grandmother' (Cotter 2015: 179). Some expressed a profound discomfort with labels in general (the feeling that one's 'identity' is inadequately represented by particular identifications) and with situations in which one feels forced into making declarative statements:

> Um, <pause> and maybe that's lazy <laughs> um, but there's part of me that actually just doesn't want to … to actually have … 'I am this' you know? Partly because I … and it also feels like it actually then excludes … 'I am this, I am not that'. (Stacey)

In many cases, this 'mismatch' was traced to a perceived divide between identities as 'lived' or 'everyday' and the official or dominant discursive baggage attached to them, as discussed above.

On the other hand, many (of the same) Southsiders spoke of their fluid identifications as indicative of something much more existential. Think of Niamh in the introduction to this book, who 'swing[s] from not really knowing if there's a God or not, to being adamant there isn't, to finding myself praying when I hit rock bottom'. Or of Scott, who acknowledged a shift from an 'extreme' position that viewed agnostics as 'not just somebody who doesn't know but somebody who doesn't care' to one where 'I'd be more happy to say that I'm open to doubt, and that's what agnosticism is trying to get at' (Cotter 2015: 179). This 'attribution bias' (Amarasingam 2010), this general willingness to impart fluidity and individuality to oneself and to others sharing one's identifications (one's 'in-group'), was somewhat less evidenced in interviewees' discussions of others. Muslims, for example, were more readily portrayed by non-Muslims as being much more likely to live up to the ideal-typical Muslim norm, presumably because Muslim-like behaviour (abiding by dietary and alcohol restrictions, 'veiling', etc.) is much more visible to non-Muslims in the Southside than that of 'normal Christians' or 'secular' individuals.

This leads to my final point on subjectivity and religion-related identification, which concerns how individuals identify religion in the Southside (usually the religion of 'others'), as well as individuals' subjective embodied experiences of said religion. In addition to the built environment (see the next section, and Chapter 6), religion was frequently identified in the Southside through its inhabitants. Given that religion was understood, for the most part, to imply Christianity – and most 'Christians' in the Southside are not perceived to stand out from the crowd, due to its post-Christian character (discussed below) – most religion was seemingly invisible. Yet where it was identified in the Southside's inhabitants was in unusual dress and in visible practices such as participation in communal acts of worship, the observing of festivals and food taboos or enrolling in a religious school. The Southside sits comfortably in wider scholarly constructions of cities as 'prime arenas in which the public presence of religion – through, for instance, modes of dress, buildings, sounds, rituals and performances – is displayed and discussed' (Knott, Krech and Meyer 2016: 125). Indeed, as Hjelm argues, 'what counts in the public visibility of religion is practice, not belief. Beliefs are not very interesting per se … The practices putatively arising from particular beliefs are' (2014b: 218).

Unsurprisingly, it was Islam that stood out the most in terms of visibly different dress, although allusions were also made to the stereotypical Church of Scotland 'Sunday best' (Brenda) and to the visible presence of clergy from the Orthodox Community of St Andrew in Edinburgh (Naomi), which is located on Meadow Lane in the Southside. Furthermore, the Central Mosque was singled out by many as a place of visible religious activity, in conjunction with somewhat wistful allusions to similarly visible activity being an historical staple of the Southside, and the UK more broadly, on a Sunday morning. Arguably, the visibility of attendance at the Central Mosque is due to the clash between Friday prayers and the hegemonic post-Christian calendar – that is, the attendance of hundreds of people at the mosque on Friday lunchtimes is much more visible to other residents and users of the Southside, due to its occurrence during the 'normal' working week. A challenge to 'liberal secular principles' if ever there was one (Fitzgerald 2015b: 306).

Reflecting further on the history of religion's visibility in the Southside, it is worth noting that the dynamics surrounding Islam in this context can be viewed as a contemporary instantiation of dynamics that historically surrounded Catholicism. Longer-term residents recalled divisions between Protestants and Catholics in the Southside being similarly embodied and pertinent, with children attending different schools, the smell of steak emanating from certain residences on Fridays and particular surnames identifying individuals as 'different'. Over time these differences have become less visible or meaningful, and new differences – new 'out groups' – have arrived on the scene. Thus, it isn't essentially religious difference that is embodied in this manner, so much as difference in general. Informants attested to encountering this difference in the soundscapes of the Southside – particularly in the languages that were spoken – and in the shops, restaurants and eateries of Nicolson Street and its surroundings.

By way of contrast, whilst 'other' religions in the Southside, with which most interviewees had limited personal experience, were discussed primarily in terms of sights, sounds and smells, religions that were subjectively more familiar were frequently discussed in terms of emotions and embodied experience. I understand that sights, sounds and smells are embodied in the sense that they are experienced by embodied individuals, but my distinction here is between discourses that focus on the external (the triggers for experiences) and the internal (the experiences themselves). We'll hear more about this in the next section, but interviewees spoke of certain places triggering feelings and emotions identified with religion or spirituality, of buildings acting upon users of the spaces of the Southside and of locations or objects triggering embodied memories. Personal encounters with religion – positive, negative or banal – were spoken of in terms of emotional content and feelings, not with intellectualized notions and theological discourse. Some spoke of enjoying the experiences associated with religion and spirituality without feeling especially connected to a tradition and/ or without subscribing to the substantive content. And connected to this, and to those discourses surrounding 'other' religions, was the notion that changes in subjective beliefs were unproblematic in social interaction, but that (attendant) changes in behaviour and practice – which can be observed by others – are thus disruptive to the hegemonic order and can have profound impacts upon individual lives. Particular identifications *should be* accompanied by certain behaviours and practices. Yet at the same time, many individuals discussed how engagement in practices, by themselves or others, is not *in reality* an accurate measure of their full, or even partial, implication in the identification(s) associated with those practices and the range of connected baggage that might entail. Thus, identifications come with prescriptive assumptions, yet, at the same time, individuals and groups utilizing the same concepts 'may literally see, taste, smell, and inhabit different worlds' (C. Martin 2017: 50).

In this section, we have seen how identifications are intensely political and far from stable or unitary. They are navigated, exert power, are felt and experienced and are implicated in in-group and out-group dynamics. We now turn to some of the more explicitly spatial dynamics surrounding religion-related identifications in the Southside.

Spatial identifications and contestations

Edinburgh is full of these stony fingers, Christian steeples poking up … the odd minaret just showing we've maybe moved on a little. (Naomi)

Jan Blommaert argues that physical spaces are also social, cultural and political spaces: they influence patterns of social behaviour, always belong to someone, are filled with history and are 'space[s] of power controlled by, as well as controlling, people' (2013: 3). This section concerns such dynamics, focusing on the entanglement of perceived manifestations of religion (but not, seemingly, non-religion) in the built environment with the identity or character of the Southside and those actors associated with it. These discourses constitute some of the discourses on *Space and the Built Environment* and are also intimately bound up with the discourses on *Power*, as they relate to the power that buildings deemed 'religious' were perceived to exert over the locality. I introduced these discourses in Chapter 4, where I demonstrated how the Southside is imbued with a lingering Christian character for many of my informants – there are 'traces of the Christian past in [this] urban space' (Knott, Krech and Meyer 2016: 129). The statement above from Naomi contributes to my case and serves to neatly illustrate a key dynamic whereby religious buildings in the Southside are perceived as making spatial claims on territory by dominating the skyline. Not only do these symbolically serve as contested markers of belonging[4] but they also act as potent indicators of religious diversity in a manner similar to the dominant view encountered by Kong in Singapore, whereby the diverse array of religious buildings was seen as 'evidence' of 'tolerance and acceptance' (1993: 33).[5] Yet despite this, Christianity retains its hegemonic position. In Fred's words,

> multicultural is a word that I've used quite a lot obviously, but at the same time you're still, it's still quite obvious about its Christian roots ... There's still quite a lot of kind of an idea of, eh, historically it being quite Christian based and it, it still is these days.

Non-Christian buildings – where acknowledged at all – seemed particularly worthy of comment, with an underlying discourse of the threat of Islam 'taking over' certain parts of the Southside (and Edinburgh more widely). Indeed, the 'appearance of mosques in Glasgow, Edinburgh and Dundee may be the most striking visual sign of change in Scotland's religious culture' (Bruce 2014a: 3). For example, when discussing the image of a halal butcher in Nicolson Square, Brian hesitantly stated 'that, to me, I think could almost be perceived as being the last straw for that square. And I say that because <pause> of the Islamification of, of that square'. While such attitudes are reflective of a UK-wide anxiety about Islam (see, for example, Gilliat-Ray in Wells and Watson 2005: 268; Bluck et al. 2012: 117–18), the manner in which these dynamics generally played out was intimately tied to the particular identifications of the interlocutors concerned:

Naomi also saw the area as intimately bound up with Jewish history; Fiona, as highly secular; John, through his relationships with the former churches; Aisha perceived the churches to all be defunct *unless* there were some further evidence of their ongoing use, such as a 'Trypraying' banner (see Figure 3.3); and Ella viewed the area through the lens of her childhood, lamenting the disappearance of particular churches not as religious buildings but as buildings long gone that belonged to the Southside. In other words, certain buildings or types of buildings in the Southside were bound up in particular discourses on religion, dependent on the particular lens through which the individuals in question viewed them: upon the *act of identification* taking place.

Taking up this subjective element, other related discourses concerned the more visceral aspects of my informants' interactions with religion in the Southside, how they *feel* when they interact with elements of the built environment that they deem to be religious. These feelings were once again multifarious, ranging from feelings of threat and intimidation (whether associated with *all* religious spaces or merely *others'* religious spaces), via feelings of majesty, awe and transcendence, to feelings of togetherness and belonging, or of exclusion, that were traced to the community associated with a space, synchronically and diachronically, rather than to the space itself. And, of course, feeling *nothing*. As a particularly powerful illustration of the complex web of feelings associated with such buildings, Brian said of the Community Centre (see Figure 3.2):

> that building to me is threatening, it's intimidating, it's inspiring, it's, uh, grand, it's beautiful, uh, it's gothic, it's pointing accusingly at the sky, uh, it's also reaching up to the sky, reaching up to a deity that's being perceived to be up there.

Most frequently, these perceived manifestations of religion in the built environment were associated with (former) houses of worship, but they were also associated with less obviously religious sites, including graveyards, the Labyrinth in George Square and public houses. For instance, Julian described experiencing similar feelings in *specific* churches – 'I don't find that in every church I go into' – and in his Southside back garden. However, despite this clear range in the specificities of the feelings involved, and the spaces considered religious, each informant operated with a working model for identifying religion in the built environment; associated this model with remembered, embodied and emotional experiences; and was able to utilize this model as a lens through which to retrospectively analyse their experiences in the Southside (cf. Mumford 2015). For example, when I asked Aoife whether she could think of any 'particular points or moments' in the Southside 'that maybe make you feel more, say, agnostic than' other aspects of her 'identity', she answered that religion hasn't particularly shaped my experience of the Southside. There are a lot of areas, for instance that community centre that I've walked past pretty much every day that I've lived there … um, I notice the buildings … especially because some of them are really stunning buildings … [but] I never actually went to one, so I can't say what it's like for me going to church in Southside coz I never have. Um, the only real time that I've noticed religious feeling is around Christmas, and especially Christmas carol services and that kind of thing. Because although I don't necessarily identify as Christian anymore, I still love Christmas carols. And I still absolutely love carols by candlelight. So, I do still notice that, and I still attend that, and I think it's … really fun to go to. But … it isn't a huge part of what I've done while I've been in Southside.

As Birgit Meyer argues, perceptions are 'always subject to cultural framing' and 'people learn to direct their attention, tuning out certain stimuli while emphasizing and developing a sensibility toward others, generating certain emotions in the process' (in B. Meyer et al. 2014: 217). The 'cultural framing' in the Southside includes the language of religion, which is attached by some to elements of the built environment that 'do more than merely represent' but that 'interplay with bodily sensations' (Beekers and Tamimi Arab 2016: 152; see also B. Meyer 2015: 20). Put simply, 'religion' and 'religious' were meaningful terms for understanding embodied experience in the Southside, and certain embodied experiences triggered certain acts of identification.

Social identifications

In the preceding sections I set the scene regarding individual subjectivity and religion-related identifications, and some of the spatial dynamics surrounding them. In this section, I turn to the social and interpersonal, with discussion focusing on three different levels of society – the micro, the meso and the macro. In this context, this means the interpersonal, the Southside and the Scottish/UK national.

At the micro level, I acknowledged in the previous chapter that it is no real surprise that a connection between 'family' and 'religion' was frequently made. Interviewees were generally asked a question such as the following I asked of David: 'so maybe if you could just tell me a bit about your, we'll call it your "religious journey" for want … of a better term?' Such questioning in turn tended to produce autobiographical responses that began with family, with David responding, 'Well I, yeah I would consider myself an atheist now … my mum comes from an Irish Catholic family, and so I … went to church from probably from a baby', etc. Yet, despite the convention of autobiographical narratives beginning with family, many of my informants elaborated that issues arise when there is a mismatch between family members concerning matters relating to religion.

Some described particular issues that have arisen due to changes in identification, with Eileen sorrowfully saying, 'I'm quite sad that neither of my sons go to church, but then that's their … you know, that's their life now', and Aisha quipping that 'I told my [secular] parents I wanted to be a Muslim at sixteen … as you can imagine, that didn't go down well'. Others spoke of arguments concerning religion, or – as we saw above – of mitigating their opinions out of concern for family members,[6] with prime examples of both coming from Peter when I asked him about a crucifix displayed on his wall:

> I've got two of these crosses and, em, I will give, I mean I've got two nieces, I've got no children, and they're both, you know, they're both secular, they're both brought up by my sister. They're beautiful, they're wonderful girls. And I'll give one each, because they loved their grandparents … and that's the sort of thing that actually is a difficulty with me and my sister. She hates these expressions of that, that sort of religion … I kind of feel as though if I give these two things it will be secretly at some stage when I'm with my two nieces, I don't want my sister to know because I feel my sister would be upset.

Here Peter vividly demonstrates the emotion and pain induced through mismatched religious identifications, the desire to transmit traditions down the generation and the lengths that some individuals will go to keep the peace through situational acts of identification – just as Keith attends Catholic services with his wife and her family (see Chapter 4).

At the meso level, I have already discussed the prevalent secularization narrative constructing the Southside as normatively secular, with religion being backgrounded as a minority concern alongside a narrative of decline from a past state of 'ubiquitous religiosity' (Naomi). The very fact that this secularization is constructed as the result of a decline in *Christianity* means that the Southside is imbued with a Christian flavour. Prompted by the 'trypraying' advert (see Figure 3.3), Peter described the Southside as

> a kind of post-Christian, or a kind of Christian society, full of Christian symbolism, it's all over the place – so you see the churches, you see those things, and you see those things all the time – but there's nothing that's actively Christian.

It is 'post-Christian' not in the sense that Christianity 'has become irrelevant per se' but that 'its effects are diffuse and indirect' (Lee 2015: 30). We've seen that Naomi views the contemporary space of the Southside as being claimed by 'stony fingers, Christian steeples', and Alistair recalled the Southside of his childhood, where a particular form of Christianity was perceived to dominate: 'you just weren't allowed to go out [on a Sunday], because if you went out to play football the police used to chase you.' Here, (Protestant) Christianity is granted hegemonic – that is, 'dominant' (C. Martin 2010: 161) – status, being seen as embedded in local and national rituals, in institutions such as scouts and schools, in the very fabric and skyline of the Southside itself. Indeed, the 'skyline itself is an important indicator both of past history and present developments' (Davie 2014: 615), and 'the overwhelming presence of Christian buildings' in the UK creates expectations and in some senses 'impinges on the secular' (Davie 2015: 72, 78).

The particularly Protestant flavour to this hegemony seems to reflect an internalization of the relative marginalization of Roman Catholicism in Scottish history in the modern period, due in no small part to Catholicism's historical connection to Irish immigration (see Bruce 2014a: 41–79). However, according to the 2011 census results for the area roughly corresponding to the Southside (see Table 3.1), Roman Catholics currently make up around 35 per cent of the Southside's self-identifying 'Christians' (a proportion almost identical to those self-identifying as 'Church of Scotland'). In addition, the number of self-identified Catholics in Scotland increased slightly between 2001 and 2011, in contrast to the 10 per cent decline in the numbers identifying with the Church of Scotland (Bruce 2014a: 234–5). Islam received particular attention in the narratives of Southsiders, with Muslims being referred to as a distinct out-group – a 'they' – even if, for example, the annual Islam Festival[7] at the Central Mosque was viewed as 'a good thing, [as] they're not ... hiding it away from people, making it more ... scary than it is ... not that it's scary, but you know ...' (Lily). Much tension seems to reside in how 'local' certain groups are considered to be, with allusions to the liminal position of not just Catholics but Episcopalians and generalized other non-local religions: 'I'm very glad we're living in Scotland and not being run over by everything else, so there's liable to be wars, you know, internal conflict ... we have less of that in Scotland' (Samantha). Blame was also laid at the feet of segregated education or a general human tendency to dislike difference. How one positions oneself, or is positioned, in relation to these specific constructions of 'religion' and 'Christianity' will have enormous impact upon one's acts of identification, how and when these occur, and if one even feels one is identifying at all.

Many of these dynamics also play out at the macro level – here, the level of the UK state. The discourse of irrelevance associated with the secularization narrative reflects a dominant trope in the UK media, whereby the left-wing press tend to cast Britain 'as secular and plural, with an accompanying discourse of Christian decline and irrelevance' (Knott, Poole and Taira 2013: 174). Similar discourses are evident in the world of (stand-up) comedy, which can be seen as a useful barometer for a dominant 'left-leaning' constituency in contemporary Britain (cf. McKearney 2011; Cotter, Aechtner and Quack 2012). The seemingly inoffensive, unproblematic, banal or simply not comment-worthy nature of many of the perceived manifestations of Christianity in the Southside scans with Sullivan's observations on the 'naturalization' of 'religion' (read 'Christianity') in the United States, which is increasingly seen as a 'natural, and largely benign – if varied – aspect of the human condition' (2009: 2). We have seen how those interviewees who positioned themselves as in some way connected to Protestantism, or as 'secular' – invested or uninvested, active or inactive – felt unthreatened by placing themselves in, or being placed in, these categories: 'I think that's absolutely fine, I don't have a problem with that' (Fiona). After all, when one identifies as part of a majority, one need not feel threatened by this act of identification.[8] For instance, although Lily acknowledges a general reticence in Scotland for people to say, '"Yes, I'm a ... I'm a Christian" unless they're ... a born-again Christian', she acknowledges that because she has 'grown up being Church of Scotland and things like that', she doesn't feel that she must make this kind of statement. She is part of the norm, whereas those who primarily identified with a minority religion felt quite differently.

As a cultural marker, Christianity 'continues to frame the borders of inclusion and exclusion' in UK contexts (Wells and Watson 2005: 268). Those who are positioned in the majority might view Christianity as a positive social force, a benign curiosity or a laughable non-problem yet feel threatened by mere perceived manifestations of Islam: 'if Muslims advertised on public things such as buses, there'd be quite an uproar ... you know? Saying, "oh, look at these Muslims trying to convert us all to Islam"' (Aisha). On the other hand, those in minority positions can perceive state apparatus and local dynamics to be denying diversity in their respective communities – diversity that *is* granted to Protestant Christianity – and indeed can feel that they have something in common with *all* religious minorities, regardless of identification, in contrast to the hegemonic norm. This feeling of threat permeates the UK, due to the 'public and collective nature of Islam' as a 'non-European' religion (Poole 2012: 187). More broadly, though, a common theme above is that religion has the potential to serve as a boundary marker, whether between 'religion' and the 'secular' world, or between different groups – as exemplified by Aisha's comments on churches:

> I myself have never walked into a church. So part of it may also just be a feeling of just feeling like ... because you're not part of that faith, kind of like that hesitant to go in and just ask, or just see what it's about, and maybe that feeling like you wouldn't be welcome there because you don't follow the faith.

The Southside is thus implicated in macro-level discourses on religion as a potent source of both unity and division, demonstrated no more clearly than in an amusing exchange with Sebastian, who, when discussing David Cameron's remarks on the UK as a 'Christian country', delighted in motioning to the list of religion-related identifications we had discussed earlier in the interview:

> **S:** ... no we're not a Christian country, you know. This is our country <motions to list>. Oh <realization>, this is our country!
>
> **C:** The list.
>
> **S:** Pointing to the list <laughs>.

Here one divisive discourse of Christian hegemony is contrasted with a multiculturalist discourse of 'unity in diversity', emphasizing the complex entanglement of the religion-related field with notions of community in the Southside. These themes of othering and boundary maintenance, through acts of identification, lead us nicely to my final section on concepts and containment.

Concepts and containment

In Chapter 4, I noted how the very category 'religion' and the notion of specific 'religions' can be perceived as oppressive by my Southsiders. Whilst there was a distinct bias in this data set towards constructing particular 'World Religions' as oppressive, there were also instances of a variety of non-religions being constructed in a similar fashion. Here, religion-related terms are invested with significant power, especially when considered in terms of group identity. Whether individual social actors consider themselves insiders or outsiders to specific religion-related groups, the designation of a group as 'religion-related' carries with it the potential for oppression – being oppressive as well as being oppressed. Once again, the utilization of religion-related concepts in acts of identification *matters*.

In Chapter 6, I begin my analysis by introducing readers to Ella – whose voice has already been peppered throughout the above. In the extract I discuss, the appearance of the Southside Community Centre (the former Nicolson Street Church, see Figure 3.2) is one of the elements at focus. Ella laments that 'it looks too much like a church' and that because of this 'it could put some people off' and isn't as inviting as it could be. As we shall see, one implication is that former church buildings are confusing and infused with their former role, implicated in discourses on church as 'not for us', and that Ella sees the exclusivity claims that are associated with religious buildings as inappropriate for a building that purports to serve the (whole) community. Here, the identification of a building as religious is bound up in problematic processes of othering and boundary maintenance. This is compounded further when Ella continues, telling me that the building's appearance certainly put the 'new man' from 'the Mosque' (i.e. a local Muslim leader) off, because 'he thought this was a church'. Here, the 'new man' from the Mosque is constructed as only being interested in the building because he thought it was a church and being 'put off' by discovering its current function. As we shall see, Ella's problem is thus not with churches or religious buildings – far from it: her problem is with ambiguity, and with this ambiguity getting in the way of the Community Centre fulfilling its purpose for the whole community. *In this context*, the potential for this building to be entangled in the religion-related field, and identified as (inappropriately) Christian, has become a barrier and source of division.

These dynamics of boundary maintenance are evinced nowhere clearer than in the discourses on *Containment*, which concern the interaction between various constructions of 'religion', particular social actors and the metaphor of containment. These discourses construct religion as a container, as a context within which action happens, within which social actors move, where their movements are constrained, which strongly influences social interaction and which cannot be abandoned lightly. Furthermore, religion is constructed as one container among many, acting in combination and competition with other contextually relevant containers such as culture, education, gender and sexuality, which similarly influence and constrain social action.

The metaphor of containment was extensively invoked throughout my body of data, through a variety of mutually reinforcing discourses. Religion was frequently described as analogous to a context in which social actors interacted with and made sense of the world. For example, Moira stated, 'I always say "I'm trying to live a Christian lifestyle"'; David's Catholicism is justified 'because I feel like I'm part of that heritage'; and John builds his own model of religion through his critique of Freethinking, asking, 'If you're a Freethinker, where does your authority come from? Where does your guide for living come from?'. Religion is something within which one can be brought up – or not – a tradition stretching back through time and made manifest through the broader context in which one finds oneself – indeed, it forms and informs that context. Many individuals related positively to these notions, finding (or hypothesizing that others might find) grounding, meaning, continuity and a positive lineage in religion or describing religion in terms of comfort, safety, contentment and freedom. For example, Peter 'justified' the crucifix he had subtly displayed in his living room by stating that this image tells him 'I'm a victim. I'm with you. I have nothing to do with grandness or anything like that.' Many others related more negatively to religion, focusing on the (potentially) restrictive nature of the container, conceptualizing institutions as 'hierarchical massive historical traditional lumbering structures' (Stacey) and feeling constrained or misrepresented by religion-related terms – viewing them as 'having to do with external, dogmatic authority set over the individual' (Vincett and Woodhead 2009: 320). Indeed, think of the way Keith (Chapter 4) portrayed his wife's engagement with Catholicism and the sense of obligation she (and by extension he) feels both to the tradition and to her mother. The metaphor of containment provides the link between these varied discourses, regardless of whether this containment is conceptualized positively, negatively or more neutrally. And thus religion-related identifications in this context are entangled with complex systems of othering and boundary maintenance.

As was indicated above, however, the positioning of social actors in religion-related containers also raises the possibility of these containers interacting with others, whether these are explicitly understood in religious terms or as religion-related by virtue of the interactions. An especially good example of the interaction between containers explicitly related to religion is the notion of (de-)conversion (Hood and Chen 2013), which tended to be conceived as moving out of/into a container and potentially into/from another. If these containers were perceived to overlap, sharing a significant portion of dimensions in common, this change would conceivably be less problematic. I am here reminded anecdotally of my parents' frequent light-hearted quips that my father led my mother astray when she 'converted' from her familial Presbyterianism to his familial Anglicanism. However, other 'conversions' – such as Aisha's (from 'secular Scot' to 'Muslim'), David's (from 'active' to 'lapsed Catholic') or Naomi's (from the centre to the periphery of 'Judaism', and back again) – were loaded with much more trauma, if not with less meaning. That these conversions involved identifications that are more marked in the Southside (i.e. viewed as different from the hegemonic norm) is discursively significant. Any change in a social actor's habitus is going to leave a lasting impression, yet some of these changes were invested with much greater significance than others.

In many cases, this significance was rooted in the entanglement of explicitly religion-related containers with other forms of containment. Immigration acted as a locus for these discussions in relation to the Southside, being visibly linked to the changing religious character of the area, with many individuals being at pains to emphasize what a 'good thing' this was for the Southside (implying that the pervading view may not be quite so positive). Indeed, I frequently encountered unselfconscious allusions to an idealized historic time when 'Scottish society' and 'Christianity' used to map onto each other almost identically. At a more individual level, religion was viewed as a particularly gendered and heteronormative container, with resulting misalignments meaning that some felt the need to reassess their relationship to religion in the light of these competing 'sacreds' (Knott 2013).

So, once again, *identification matters*. Yet, in this section we have seen that whilst identifications are fluid and situational, religion-related identifications are discursively constructed as socially significant, varyingly porous containers, acting in combination and competition with other contextually relevant containers which similarly influence and constrain social action.

Conclusion

In this chapter, I began with an extract from my interview with Naomi and proceeded through four sections which emphasized the importance and utility of moving from conceiving 'identities' as static categories to viewing them rather as acts of identification. We saw how the subjective, embodied and emotional experiences of individuals pushed against the application of bounded categories, how acts of identification are spatial and relational and how agency flows both ways, with individuals being contained and constrained by the discursive repertoires at their disposal. In sum, we have seen how 'we need to "take seriously the historicity of human subjects – which includes not just agents but also the settings to which they are inevitably subjugated' (McCutcheon 2017b: 7).

Much as my own identifications as 'Irish', 'Northern Irish', 'Scottish' or (less often) 'British' meaningfully fluctuate temporally and between contexts, interlocutors, questions, spaces and more (Cotter 2017b), so too we see in the Southside that religion-related identifications are characterized by 'indeterminism, incompletion, multiplicity and polyvalence' (Bayart 2005: 109), depending less on our perceived membership of a community or culture 'than with respect to the communities and cultures with which we have relations' (Bayart 2005: 95). Identifying or being identified – or not – as religious or non-religious are profoundly contextual discursive acts, entangled in webs of discourses that are impacted by subjective, spatial, relational and conceptual factors. This chapter has argued for shifting our approach from studying social actors *as* 'religious' or 'non-religious' to the ongoing process through which we as social actors 'manage that continually shifting set of similarities and differences that simultaneously unite/estrange us to/from all others – thereby creating different selves and different identities' (McCutcheon 2017a: 157). Doing so provides us with a richer and more critically sound grasp of the machinations, agendas and vicissitudes at play in the religion-related field in any context, and – at a time when global politics has become highly polarized around such matters – makes an important critical intervention to destabilize the highly problematic 'illusion of cultural identity' (Bayart 2005: 252).

In the next chapter, I develop this argument by shifting focus from the interlocutors to the Southside itself, which is shown to be 'more than a mere context or backdrop' (Knott 2009: 159), to actively participate in the construction of religion and non-religion by affecting the agency of local inhabitants.

Local particularity

This chapter, in conversation with locality-based studies in Birmingham (Stringer 2013a) and Comberton (T. Jenkins 1999), as well as the national-level discourses explicitly addressed in Chapter 4, argues that particular configurations of 'religion' and 'non-religion' are heavily influenced by 'local particularity' (T. Jenkins 1999). Factors that are specific to the Southside – its post-Christian built environment, a semi-settled/transient population, the prevalence of convivial social interaction, a local versus external dynamic and so on – are shown to be written into the structure of the religion-related field, leading to the conclusion that locality actively participates in the construction of religion and non-religion by affecting the agency of local inhabitants.

Locality

A key concept in this chapter is 'locality', which I introduced in Chapter 3 as a framework for organizing my discursive analysis. There, I drew on Kim Knott's work to define a locality as a material or discursive space that is meaningful for the social actors within it, 'important for individual and group identity' and is also amenable to academic study due to its size and relative internal coherence (1998: 283–4). I argued that viewing localities as discursive fields facilitates a social constructivist approach to group and individual identifications (see Chapter 5) and helps us to avoid reifying contested religion-related categories, whilst simultaneously providing a relatively bounded and coherent context within which to conduct analysis. In order to more fully assess the role that the Southside has played in the production of religion-related discourse, this chapter places the present study into conversation with other locality-based studies. I begin by briefly introducing studies by Martin Stringer (2013a) and Timothy Jenkins (1999), which act as my main comparative cases. I make these introductions at this point in order to encourage the reader to begin considering the impact of locality upon religion-related discourse. Indeed, I have already made passing reference in the preceding chapters to Jenkins's concept of 'local particularity', which now moves from the wings to centre stage.

Highgate, Handsworth and Comberton

In Martin Stringer's *Discourses on Religious Diversity* (2013a), and in further elaborations (2013b, 2014), he paints a picture of some of the prevalent everyday discourses on religious diversity which he and his doctoral students encountered over several years working in cities including Birmingham, Manchester and London, bringing a large body of variously 'circumstantial data' (Stringer 2013a: 2) into conversation with new and innovatively gathered material (Stringer 2013b) and broader academic literature from anthropology and urban studies. It is worth noting that Stringer downplays interview data due to a desire to access unprompted, everyday discourses, and as such the voices of the people of Birmingham and elsewhere are somewhat absent from his text, resulting in a book which purports to be analysing discourse yet engages in comparatively little formal discursive analysis. Despite these differences in methodological and substantive focus – 'discourses on religious diversity' as opposed to 'religion-related discourse' – Stringer's work shares much in common with my own, and his book offers a highly relevant contemporary source for comparative material. Specifically, my comparison focuses upon his presentation of the discourses on religious diversity in the Birmingham districts of Highgate and Handsworth.

As presented by Stringer, Highgate is an inner-city residential area that is clearly defined geographically, 'relatively simple' in terms of religious diversity and has had a fairly stable population since the 1970s – something which is 'unusual for an inner-urban area of this kind' (2013a: 40). The area is dominated by the towers of St Alban's Anglican church and of the Central Mosque (these forming the locus of discussion in the third chapter of his book), although it also includes an active but visually unobtrusive Baptist church and a Roman Catholic church on its periphery. According to Stringer's reckoning of the 2001 census figures, less than half of the area's population identified as 'White', with roughly 45 per cent identifying as 'Christian', 27 per cent as 'Muslim' and 22 per cent being placed in 'None or not stated' (2013a: 41). However, due to disparities between boundaries in census areas and what Stringer reckons to be Highgate 'proper', he estimates that the non-religious population could be anything from one-third to 50 per cent (2013a: 44).

In the grand scheme of the UK, Highgate might therefore seem to exemplify high levels of diversity. However, this pales in comparison to the district of Handsworth, which Stringer conceptualizes using the notion of 'super-diversity' (Vertovec 2007), which is 'obvious and celebrated through the stores of the Soho Road' (Stringer 2013a: 56). The Soho Road – the main artery of Handsworth – has received increased attention in recent years (Hingley 2011) due to the clustering of 'religious and community spaces reflecting considerable diversity' (Stringer 2013a: 54) in a manner which Stringer judges to be much more fluid and integrated than the 'ethnoracial enclaves' encountered, for example, by Livezey in Chicago (Stringer 2013a: 53–5; cf. Livezey 2000). In Stringer's reading of the 2001 census figures, Handsworth's population identifies as roughly 32 per cent 'Christian', 29 per cent 'Muslim', 12 per cent 'Sikh' and 8 per cent 'Hindu', with 17 per cent being placed in 'None' and 'Not stated' (2013a: 59). A relatively high proportion of the area's residents (35 per cent) were born outside of the European Union, and around 20 per cent of residents identified as 'White British' (2013a: 58). The (super-)diversity of the area is surrounded by a variety of competing discourses, being seen as 'something to be proud of' (2013a: 63) by many of the residents, while the 'Handsworth of popular discourse … is characterized by its reputation for the level of racism and riots that were associated with the area' (2013a: 64) in 1981, 1985, 1991, 1995 and more recently in August 2011 (2013a: 57–8).

As presented by Stringer, and as we shall see below, Highgate and Handsworth act as useful contemporary comparative localities for my work in the Southside, sharing much in common with it in terms of the discursive dynamics at play, yet beneficially differing in their 'local particularity' (T. Jenkins 1999: 77) and notably higher measures of (super-)diversity. It is with this notion of local particularity – the 'local ways of doing things and of thinking, ways of organising continuity and coping with misfortune which, while they are not in fact unique to any particular locality are tied in to the actors' perceptions to the experience of that locality' (1999: 77) – that we move to my final comparative case study, as presented in Timothy Jenkins's *Religion in English Everyday Life* (1999).

The key chapter here, 'The Country Church – The Case of St. Mary's, Comberton' (1999: 41–73), provides a stimulating examination of the 'stereotype of the country church' as both flourishing and in crisis and decay, demonstrating that discourses surrounding the notion of 'the village' are, in this context, intimately entangled with discourses on 'the country church' (1999: 43–5). Comberton lies four miles south of Cambridge, and its population grew from a relatively stable 300–600 individuals in the decades up to the 1950s to over

2,300 by the time of Jenkins's study in the 1990s (1999: 45, 49). This population explosion has seen a change in the social composition of the village (1999: 60) that is recognized by all residents (1999: 50), resulting in an 'economy of fantasies' surrounding an opposition between 'villager' and 'incomer'. The village church, which has been located on the same site in some form since 1100, is caught up in this 'economy of fantasies', whereby

> each model of the village perceives Comberton in terms of villager and incomer, but … in each case the distinction means different things. While from above the class divide, the difference can appear to rest upon differing life styles, aspirations and use of opportunities (for instance), from below, it appears to be about power, privilege and those things to which one is subjected. (1999: 57)

Although the nature of Jenkins's text is such that he doesn't provide percentage breakdowns of the population in terms of 'religious identification'[1] and other characteristics, it is safe to say that Comberton would be placed towards the more homogeneous end of an imagined continuum of diversity, with the Southside and Highgate respectively being placed further towards the heterogeneous end and Handsworth acting almost as a synonym for 'diversity'. These differences in levels of diversity and in local particularity, combined with a discursive thrust and an interest in the 'everyday', make Jenkins's presentation of Comberton, and the discursive entanglements of St Mary's, a further intriguing comparative case study for my work on the Southside of Edinburgh.

'It looks too much like a church'

As has been my practice in preceding chapters, I begin presentation of the Southside with the voice of one of the Southside's residents. The section of interview presented here is a portion of roughly three minutes from my interview with Ella, recorded at the Southside Community Centre in May 2014. Ella is in her mid-seventies, identifies as a 'Roman Catholic' – or rather, as she jokingly states, 'we're roamin', roaming Catholics, I go anywhere … I go all over the place … My husband's in a choir and it sings in different places so wherever they're singing we go'. Although she currently lives by the seaside in Portobello, a half-hour bus journey away from the Southside, she describes her relationship to the area as follows:

> Yes, well to me the Southside as, em, <name> used to say … 'Do you really get sick when you're outwith the Southside? Do you really feel ill?' … And in a way I sorta do … I really love the Southside, and I'm not here now, and I would love

to get back … I was brought up here. My father was born and brought, brought up in the same stair actually. My grandparents stayed in that stair. My great grandparents stayed in that stair. Eh, so it goes back to the nineteenth century.

This extract begins about twenty minutes into the interview, and we have just begun the photo elicitation exercise and are discussing the image of the very building where our interview was taking place (see Figure 3.2). She responds to a question that I asked each interviewee after initially asking them to describe to me what was going on in each picture:

C: Yeah, um, I guess one way I can ask about these images is sort of why do you think, knowing what I'm studying, why I might have included that as part of the interview?

E: Well, I wonder whether you think it should still be a church, or whether it, it … to me, em, I think they should change the front of it because … and make it into a, a Community Centre, em, <hushed> it looks too much like a church … Okay, I don't care [that] it's a listed building, I really don't care, I don't know why it's listed to be honest, but that's my personal opinion. But I think you could change the front. I think you could leave the gothic pinnacles and everything but they could change the front and make it more inviting.

C: Mmm. So this sort of …

E: It could put some people off.

C: Yeah.

Ella's initial response indicates a tacit assumption that someone who is interested in the study of religion is likely to have an invested, conservative, Christian agenda – 'I wonder whether you think it should still be a church' – and conflating religion with Christianity. Furthermore, this statement implies that this building is no longer a church – it may be a *former* church building, but its function has changed. Its identity comes from its current function, from the use to which it is put.

Ella continues to focus upon the Community Centre's appearance, claiming that 'it looks too much like a church' and that because of this 'it could put some people off' and isn't as inviting as it could be. Her hushed tone combined with her mitigating 'to me' and 'that's my personal opinion' suggest that she is aware that this might be perceived as a controversial opinion. This could be due to a perception that others might consider interfering with a church building, or the notion that a church building might somehow be uninviting, to be in some way sacrilegious. The implication, however, is that former church buildings are confusing and infused with their former role, implicated in discourses on 'church' as 'not for us', and that Ella sees the exclusivity claims that are associated with religious buildings as inappropriate for a building that purports to serve the whole community. Moreover, there is some negativity here directed towards the 'they' that *could* do something about the building's uninviting appearance but have, instead, granted it 'listed' status. These outsiders are blamed, presumably through a lack of local knowledge, for reinforcing boundaries and divisions. Although we can tell from other points in Ella's interview that she is very invested in the preservation of local heritage, her views here clearly indicate that this should not come at too high a cost – her desire for preservation is functional and community-focused and not solely directed towards the built infrastructure of the Southside.

Ella then turns to what she sees as a paradigmatic example of the confusion surrounding the building's identity:

E: It certainly put the, uh, the uh, <pause> what do you, what's the, one of the, uh, from the Mosque … the new man came up …

C: Okay?

E: And he came in here coz he thought this was a church. He went looking for the priest. Now that says something that that still looks just like a, like a church …

C: Yeah.

E: Which might stop some people coming in.

She grapples for the word 'Imam' or equivalent and recounts a story of how 'the new man … came in here coz he thought this was a church. He was looking for the priest'. Whether or not there is any truth to this story, there is a lot going on here. First, this is a story that has circulated among users of the Community Centre, suggesting that the appearance of a 'Muslim' leader was considered an unusual occurrence. Not only was this unusual but it is explained away by his apparent interest in connecting with another *religious* community, and not with 'the community' in general. Here we can detect perceptions of the visible 'otherness' of Islam in the Southside and perhaps an underlying discourse on religion not being particularly relevant to or interested in the wider community. Second, an underlying implication is that if even a religious leader thought that this building was still functioning as a religious building, then there must be something very religious about its current appearance. Not only does this invest certain individuals with authority over, and expertise in, the whole religion-related field but it also adds nuance to Ella's notion that the building might 'put some people off'. Here, the 'new man' from the Mosque is constructed as only being interested in the building because he thought it was a church and being 'put off' by discovering its current function. Ella's problem is thus not with churches or religious buildings – far from it: her problem is with ambiguity, and with this ambiguity getting in the way of the Community Centre fulfilling its purpose for the whole community. *In this context*, religion has become a barrier and source of division.

Next, I make an empathetic interruption of Ella's narrative:

> C: Mmm. Well, yeah, just like, yeah when I was here a few weeks ago and you were discussing the whole foyer and …
>
> E: Yeah.
>
> C: And there's something about the, the, the grills and everything and the … it just looks quite prison-like as well, they're not …
>
> E: Mmm hmm. I would, I would completely change it.

My interjection concerning the foyer and the grills, referring to a previous gathering at the Community Centre, serves two main purposes. First, it can be read as a means of empathizing with Ella, showing her that I share her view, that I am not one of 'them' and also recalling a shared experience as a means of enhancing rapport and my own legitimacy. Second, it seemingly comes from a desire to add nuance to the discussion: it's not that this building is uninviting simply because it looks like a church but also because it is seemingly particularly grim, fortified and uninviting apart from its former function. This is not insignificant, in that it once again places some of the blame for this unfortunate appearance upon the City Council (see Chapter 4) and upon the 'powers that be' who have listed the building and limited the ability of the local team to do their jobs more effectively.

At this point, I turn my discussion back to what I had not-so-implicitly wished us to be discussing:

> C: Mmm. But sort of thinking then around that into the, the broader, broader issue there of, of church buildings being re-used for, for other purposes, so … what, what do you think about that? There are other examples, and …
>
> E: They're only a building. They're only bricks and mortar, you know? Em, but I don't, I … well, I think if they took it down and put up … the Appleton Tower … If they brought that down and put up … the Appleton Tower I would not be pleased. That is better than the Appleton Tower.

Ella's immediate and candid response that churches are 'only a building' indicates that this is a premeditated thought and that she sees nothing inherently sacred about a church any more than any other building. Presumably, how a building is used is more important to her. In her further comments, we once again see the ominous, hypothetical 'they' being constructed as thoughtlessly interfering with the built environment of the Southside and potentially tearing down this structure to erect something inappropriate (like the Appleton Tower).[2] Once again, it is external forces that are granted the agency in this hypothetical scenario, but we also gather that Ella considers preservation of heritage to be quite a good thing. Presumably, however, if a better or more useful building was constructed in the place of the Community Centre, she would be happy.

In the final section presented here, I raise the spectre of an analogous incident in the Southside, where the former building of Hope Park United Presbyterian Church (1867) was demolished in 1948, and a tower block erected in 1972 as part of the expansion of the University of Edinburgh's Royal (Dick) School of Veterinary Studies:[3]

> **C:** Mmm. Like what they did at the, the Dick Vet … wasn't there a church on the corner there?
>
> **E:** It was a beautiful church …
>
> **C:** Yeah.
>
> **E:** Yeah, it was a, it was a lovely church, it really was. It was, it was quite outstanding where it was, you know, with the, the sort of Melville Drive and all the trees and everything and this church on the corner. I always thought it was a sort of red stone church but that might be my imagination colouring it, but it had steps at the front up to the, the front door, because I always ran up the steps and down the other side, I remember. And I did the same with the Dick Vet steps, I'd have to run up and down. I never walked right along.
>
> **C:** I love, I love it when you have those sort of little memories of things …
>
> **E:** <Laughs>

Immediately, my invocation triggers pleasant and vivid memories for Ella. Not only does she remember the building in its surroundings but she internalizes and re-experiences this memory through her recollections of running up and down the church steps. Although she admits that her imagination may be providing some of the specifics of this memory, clearly the destruction of this former Southside landmark is bound up in memories and embodied experiences that are quite distinct from its status as a religious building.

In summary, in this short extract we encounter discourses on Christian hegemony and on the power invested in certain buildings, individuals and malevolent external agents. We have seen buildings entangled in discourses on community engagement, charity, heritage, utility, claims to territory and essences (religious or otherwise). And we have heard how material spaces can be welcoming; erect boundaries; and produce visceral, ambiguous or indifferent reactions. In the sections that follow, we explore these dynamics in more detail, focusing on the discourses on utility and heritage, before taking a broader look at local particularity and the built environment, and entanglements with the religion-related field.

Utility and heritage

A major theme throughout my conversation with Ella was on the (former) church buildings in the Southside and their place within an 'urban heritage economy' (Knott, Krech and Meyer 2016: 127). This shall prove highly relevant when I turn to the comparative exercise and exploration of the Southside's local particularity below.

Ella's evocative and romanticized description of running up and down the steps of Hope Park United Presbyterian Church is suggestive of the tone here. My Southsiders were unanimous in the view that the historic churches of the Southside are beautiful buildings that are embedded in the (hi)story of the area and thus, by virtue of these two attributes, worthy of preservation. As Ivan demonstrates, this is quite apart from their perceived status as (former) religious buildings: 'I don't always look at them as places that I associate with faith or spirituality or anything like that, I just view them as local landmarks. And making sure they're in use can be a really important thing.' This echoes Knott, Krech and Meyer's observation that this 'heritage presence rarely renders the theological or ritual particularities of religious traditions, but it does foreground the place of religion in the history of cities' (2016: 127). Indeed, as we have seen in Ella's invocation of the infamous 'Appleton Tower', the Southside's churches were symbolic for many of an idealized past where buildings were built to last and have character, as opposed to modern 'architectural abominations' (Naomi). Significantly, the (former) churches that were granted this 'beautiful' and 'historic' status were those that *looked like churches*, that is, like 'a rocket with two afterburners' (Peter). Other veritable churches, such as the *True Jesus Church* (which has occupied a former tenement block on Gifford Park since 1976),[4] or the *Salvation Army* premises on East Adam Street (which was opened in 1987), didn't feature in anyone's 'religious map' of the Southside, with the exception of John, who mentioned the Salvation Army premises as a geographical marker in his map of the territory covered by 'Newington Churches Together'. It is not insignificant that John, being a church leader, was the only interviewee to mention this.

The two most prominent buildings associated with 'other' religions in the local imaginary – the synagogue and the mosque – were not constructed in quite the same manner. The synagogue is much less visible due to both its design and its location on Salisbury Road (a relatively quiet, one-way, residential street). However, when it was mentioned at all, it was either simply acknowledged or constructed as an important part of the Southside's history: 'to me the synagogue always has been [part of the Southside]' (Julian). The Central Mosque, on the other hand, whilst occasionally being mentioned off-handedly, features much more prominently in the imaginary of the Southside, being variously described as 'new' (Peter), 'in your face' (Aisha), 'obvious' (Eileen) and associated with (potential) controversy or the local institution of the Mosque Kitchen.

Related to this universal desire for church buildings in the Southside to be preserved is another cluster of discourses on their perceived usefulness for the broader community. For instance, when reflecting on the image of the Southside Community Centre (Figure 3.2), all interviewees expressed positive views towards the fact that this particular (former) church and many others like it were being used by the community – even if the 'church-like' appearance might 'put some people off', as Ella suggested – and through this use were being preserved as part of the Southside's architectural heritage. This reuse as a community centre was seen as 'a great idea because it's sorta still based on what it was built for' (Keith), reflecting broader discourses on churches as resources which are, and *should be,* resources for the whole community, and on 'proper' Christianity as something which is oriented towards 'good works'. Such notions echo Davie's analysis of a correlation between long-term establishment of national churches and a 'welfare-view of religion' (2000b; cf. Schenk, Burchardt and Wohlrab-Sahr 2015: 6; Woodhead 2012a). One interviewee wryly stated that 'it's better used as it is now than as a church' (Richard). Others invoked a clear hierarchy of (in) appropriate potential uses, some for moral or religious reasons – 'if you then take what was a religious place and [some]where people went to worship God and change it into something like a club, I'm … not so comfortable with that, … it's my religious view … you know, like the consumption of alcohol and things is forbidden within Islam' (Aisha) – and still others for more 'practical' reasons – 'this building was used as a carpet storage centre at one point and I didn't like the thought of that, but now it's *a useful place*' (Eileen, emphasis my own). Whatever the specifics of the discourses invoked, a common theme among these Southsiders was that these buildings should be for the whole community, regardless of (non-)religious identification. Seemingly they can best fulfil this function in the contemporary, multicultural and multireligious Southside either through no longer being exclusively occupied by a single religious group (or any religious group at all) or through broadening their remit and opening their doors to serve the whole Southside community: '[That] their buildings remain central to many communities without, without the religious aspect is, em, is a good thing' (Ivan).

Although we can already sense that underlying these discourses on heritage and utility there 'may lie deep differences about how religious sites should be maintained and for what purpose' (Knott, Krech and Meyer 2016: 127), it is significant that these differences do not dominate in the Southside. But what else is significant about this locality, religion-related discourses and the built environment?

Local particularity and the built environment

The Southside, as I have already discussed above and in Chapters 3, 4 and 5, is imbued for my informants with a 'post-Christian' character, with a significant number of visible church buildings for what is a relatively small area of the city, many of which are no longer being used for 'religious' purposes. The area is also rich with history, but this history is for the most part quite hidden amongst the urban sprawl and is spoken of nostalgically by my informants whilst being perceived to be under threat from a variety of malevolent agents such as the City Council and the University of Edinburgh (which, ironically, owns and maintains many of the more 'historic' spaces in the Southside). With this context in mind, it is unsurprising that my Southsiders should be so invested in preserving former church buildings as heritage. These buildings act as symbols of an idealized past in the face of more recent architectural developments: as connections to a past that is otherwise hidden in the sedimented layers of the Southside story. As these are historic sites, and a significant proportion of the few existing large indoor spaces in this built-up area, Southsiders feel justified in their sense of ownership over these buildings, seeing them as their right; ergo, the desire that they be 'useful' in some way.

That the Southside's churches are implicated in these discourses on heritage and utility contributes to the general tendency for active Christian congregations in the Southside to fall somewhat under the radar. Yet simultaneously, the sheer dominance of church steeples in the skyline is internalized and felt as spatial claims to territory by Christianity – albeit *historically*. As far as the 'other' religions are concerned, the historical presence of the synagogue on Salisbury Road has allowed it, in many respects, to sink into the unproblematic background alongside the historical churches. This contrasts markedly with the recently perceived arrival of 'Islam' in the built environment of the Southside, instantiated by the mosque and various 'ethnic' shops. That this 'community' has not been granted 'historic' status in the Southside means that the built infrastructure associated with Islam is perceived by many as a threat to the identity of the Southside, and this, combined with broader discourses on the 'problem' of Islam, has perpetuated discourses on the 'Islamification' of the Southside (see Chapter 5). It is significant that this same threat was not as evident in Handsworth or Highgate, which each have more than five times the proportion of resident 'Muslims' as the Southside. It is also worth noting that 'non-religion', 'the secular' and other concepts were not invoked in these discourses. Indeed, it seems to be that these go unmarked in a (remembered) visual assessment of the Southside – a point which contributed to my argument in Chapter 4.

In Chapter 5, I discussed in detail the various spatial contestations where the religion-related field was entangled in constructions of Southside identity. In Highgate, Handsworth and Comberton, the built environment was similarly one of the key areas in which religion was located by residents, yet in each case, the discursive dynamics surrounding these buildings were quite different. Turning first to Highgate, Stringer describes a situation whereby religion is primarily perceived through the built environment, by what he estimates to be a majority of 'non-religious' residents, and is generally constructed as foreign and in negative terms (2013a: 44–5). Much as there is a distinction in the Southside between local and external forces, there is a distinction in Highgate between buildings that are 'for us', that is, for the community, and those which are not. As far as the buildings of St Alban's and the Central Mosque are concerned, the dominant discourse tends to (a) 'link the two together and use the same language about both' and (b) hold that 'neither community, neither building, neither religion is "of us"' (2013a: 50). On the other hand, the Baptist church, which doesn't *look like* a religious building, is constructed as being for the community due to high levels of perceived engagement (Stringer 2013a: 46). Thus there is a discursive knot between the communities that use the buildings, the buildings' appearance and their perceived embeddedness in the locality that leads to the construction of certain buildings as 'religious' and thus not 'for us' (2013a: 44–8). The Central Mosque and St Alban's are 'representational spaces' in Highgate discourse, in that they are associated with 'preconceived ideological understanding[s] of religion' that lead to their classification as 'religious' and 'therefore to ... a negative attitude to "religion"' (2013a: 52; cf. Knott 2005: 38–40). This is markedly different from the situation amongst my informants, where a much greater number of former church buildings are generally viewed as important historical sites that should be for the whole community, where the 'invisible' religious buildings are precisely that and where the mosque is singled out for different treatment.

The situation is also markedly different in Handsworth, with its 'sheer multiplicity of religions' (Stringer 2013a: 63). The dominant perception here is that this is an area with religious populations that are resident and active, as opposed to the outsiders who are perceived to use the religious buildings in Highgate (2013a: 69). This 'super-diverse' context facilitates a sense of pride in the diversity of the area, which is accompanied by a general lack of interest or literacy in the specifics of the religions in question (2013a: 63, 67, 69). In this context, 'sheer multiplicity' facilitates the incorporation of religion into the positive image of the area in a very immediate sense. This contrasts with the generally negative discourse in Highgate, where religion was associated with two buildings that were not utilized by the local community and the more nostalgic, historical and utilitarian discourse that dominates in the Southside.

Finally, we turn to the other end of the diversity spectrum to the situation in Jenkins's presentation of Comberton, where we find the church and the vicar constructed as having obligations to the village as a resource, a right and a rich patron (1999: 57, 63, 65, 69). As mentioned above, this church is bound up in the dichotomy between villagers and incomers: villagers don't participate in the parish council as a rule, yet expect the patronage of the church; incomers, on the other hand, are aware of their position and do participate (1999: 57, 69). The villagers resent St Mary's as a 'religious' institution (1999: 63) yet expect it to act unequivocally as a social institution (1999: 69). Thus, we have a situation where the discourses on utility, heritage and local identity that are evident in the Southside are also evident in Comberton, but to much more pronounced degree. In Comberton there is a single church, which has a much lengthier historical presence in a much more 'closed' community – it is little wonder that the 'villagers' feel a sense of ownership over this building and that the 'incomers' recognize its symbolic power and are inclined to greater participation.

To conclude this brief discussion of the place of the Southside in the discourses on *Space and the Built Environment*, it is clear that although the general dynamics of the discourses seem to be mirrored across these contexts, it is the particularity of the Southside that gives these local discourses their form and content. Some of this local particularity is specifically religion-related in the minds of my informants, such as the number of churches and other 'religious' buildings, while other aspects, such as the sedimented history of the Southside or the local versus external dynamics, are not. But do we see local particularity playing such a role in other discursive groupings?

Local particularity and religion-related discourse in the Southside

In my discussion of the discourses on *Living*, I drew attention to a cluster of discourses on the meaningfulness of practice. These discourses were somewhat abstract, referring to 'religion in general', and are thus not particularly tied to the Southside. This contrasts with the situation in Comberton, whereby the 'egalitarian' view of the 'incomers' demands participation in the church, whilst the 'conservative' view of the 'villagers' expects patronage: the incomers hold to a model that invests practice with significantly more meaning (T. Jenkins 1999: 69). Jenkins also tells of how 'the vicar is criticized for not participating more in village affairs' – that 'in the villagers' minds, the vicar is not doing what he should' (1999: 62). Here we have a religious figurehead being criticized for not practising that religion in the way that is locally expected, for not practising enough. Jenkins also notes that 'were the vicar to respond to these criticisms, another set would be formulated: he has nothing better to do than call on people, he does not mind his own business, he exudes a false bonhomie, and so forth' (1999: 62). Thus, we see similar discourses being given a Comberton twist.

Other discourses on *Living* focused upon embodiment and further emphasize the importance of the Southside's local particularity. In Handsworth, religion is similarly perceived through the embodied actions of others, particularly through dress and visual images (Stringer 2013a: 70), yet, while the Southside seems to be imbued with a post-Christian hegemony, in Handsworth the norm is 'an acceptance of the diversity of the neighbourhood and hence of religious diversity as a fact of life' (2013a: 69). Here, Islam does not stand out because it is seen as simply one religion among many. This generally 'positive' attitude also meant that 'there was much more overt religious language and religious reference within conversations in this neighbourhood' than in the Southside or in Highgate (2013a: 69). In Highgate, activity associated with the churches *and* the mosque 'does not really register' with the 'non-religious' populace (2013a: 44), and this contrasts markedly with the position of Islam in the Southside. Stringer's explanation for this is that due to the mosque's location on the periphery of Highgate, 'the people of the neighbourhood … tended to exclude the Mosque itself, as a building, from what they consider to be Highgate proper, and so recognize its continued "otherness" without specifically rejecting the religion it represents' (Stringer 2013a: 47).

As far as other discourses are concerned, the discourses on *Social Identity* which focused upon the supposed social (ir-)relevance of religion echoed similar findings to Stringer's in Highgate and Handsworth. Although the specifics are not necessarily clear-cut, these discourses can be placed along a continuum addressing 'the question of whether the discourse is essentially positive or essentially negative' (2013a: 33). Furthermore, the resentment many Southsiders felt towards being made to discuss religious matters was encountered by Jenkins in Comberton (1999: 63). The discourses on *Power* were bound up in, and contributed to the construction of, the post-Christian character of the Southside and included discourses on the local versus the external which related to dynamics particular to Edinburgh City Council and the University of Edinburgh that cannot be abstracted from this local context. The discourses on *Civic Space* involved dominant discourses on multiculturalism and moderation, which, although effectively national discourses, were indelibly imbued with the Southside in the way they were tactically subverted by my informants. Without the spatial configurations and power relationships particular to the Southside, different shifts between religion-related containers would prove problematic, the discourses on the decline of the local community would not necessarily be entangled in discourses of secularization and diversity would be conceptualized in alternative configurations. On the other hand, the discourses on *Science and Meaning*, for example, or those surrounding the purported meaningfulness of certain practices can be relatively easily abstracted from the Southside. However, as this chapter has emphasized, even those discourses which appear to transcend local particularity are inflected by their social and historical context. There is no *sui generis* discourse on religion.

Context, context, context

In Chapter 4, I presented a variety of contemporary discourses on religion that predominate in the UK, in which 'religion' is constructed as a minority interest, entangled in a variety of controversial and traumatic events in the state narrative, and associated (negatively) with a broad range of social issues. Dominant tropes include the reification of a conflict between science and religion, the construction of a dichotomy between good/moderate/liberal religion and bad/immoderate/illiberal religion and the valorising of the autonomous, rational individual consumer. In this chapter, we have seen how the discourses on religion in the Southside are entangled in these broader, national discourses – and others on the urban heritage economy, a welfare view of religion, anxiety about Islam, and so on – as well as in the subjective biographies of individual Southsiders. Whilst locality provides an effective means through which to approach religion-related discourse, localized discourses clearly do not operate in isolation. As outlined by Wijsen, drawing on Fairclough,

> discourse analysts distinguish between different dimensions of one and the same practice and look at them from different perspectives: the individual dimension or micro perspective, the institutional dimension or meso perspective, and the societal dimension or macro perspective. (2013b: 72)

Whilst the focus of this chapter has remained upon the micro-level discourses of Southsiders in a localized discursive field, these Southsiders clearly employed meso- and macro-level discourses throughout our conversations. The preceding analysis suggests that a fruitful avenue for future studies might be to focus on the inter-relationship between discourses at different levels in order to more fully map the religion-related field and the discursive agency of social actors and of localities. Yet this has not been my purpose in this context.

Regardless of the *degree* to which the discourses I encountered were produced by the Southside, the essential conclusion from the above is that they are *products of this locality*. Viewing the Southside as a coherent discursive field has provided a relatively bounded and coherent context for the analysis of religion-related discourse, which both feeds into broader societal conversations around religion and illustrates the benefits of thoroughly contextualizing one's data in its local, as well as broader, socio-historical context. Through comparisons with Highgate, Handsworth and Comberton, I have shown the Southside – and locality in general – to be much 'more than a mere context or backdrop' in which discourses are manifested (Knott 2009: 159), but an inextricable constituent part of those discourses. Factors that are specific to the Southside – its post-Christian built environment, a semi-settled/transient population, particular histories relating to Judaism and Islam, the prevalence of convivial social interaction, a local versus external dynamic, tactics of indifference and the tendency for interviewees and interviewer to construct it as a neutral, secular space – inflect the ways in which religion is constructed in this context, and result in specific religious or non-religious subject positions being taken up by the interlocutors involved. The Southside actively participates in the construction of 'religion' and 'non-religion' by affecting the agency of local inhabitants.

Localities are contexts where abstract discourses 'become outworked as tangible, sedimented social relations through collective imaginaries and the production of community normativities ... and forms of regulation' (Valentine and Sadgrove 2013: 1982). Indeed, such is the nature of all discursive fields, which invariably define the situation for their occupants (von Stuckrad 2010a: 5). Thus, whilst choosing locality as a 'container' for my discursive analysis brought an element of 'coherence and conceptual manageability' (Knott 1998: 283), it also represented the artificial containment of a fluid field of discourse on my part. By placing boundaries on the field, my own organizing rubric impacts upon and, in some ways, *constructs* the field itself. And so, too, for all studies of religion and related categories.

'Being religious' or 'being non-religious' in different contexts means different things. We've seen here at least part of what it means in the Southside, and this emphasizes the importance of thoroughly contextualizing one's data in its local, as well as broader socio-historical context, particularly in this contested area of study. In the next chapter, we push this analysis to the limit by looking at the so-called 'indifference' to religion. What is it? How can we find it? And in researching it, how much are we involved in its production?

The power of indifference

> I just don't have any interest either way, but I wouldn't want to understate
> how uninterested I am [in religion]. There still hasn't been a word invented
> for people like me, whose main experience when presented with this issue
> is an overwhelming, mind-blowing, intergalactic sense of having more
> interesting things to think about. (Goldacre in A. Z. Williams 2011)

In this opening quotation, physician and science writer forcefully articulates a
position which Lois Lee has dubbed 'engaged indifferentism', whereby 'disinterest
in religion … [is presented as] the core aspect of an individual's "religious" identity
and is something they are invested in and committed to' (2014: 474). Such a
perspective presents a problem for studies of religion and non-religion in that it is
clearly related to both categories yet involves the speaker positioning themselves
in neither. This entire book has been pushing readers to critically reflect on the
constructed binary of 'religion' and 'non-religion', and the effects of context upon
the boundary between these supposed opposites. In this chapter, I place this front
and centre as we scrutinize a phenomenon that seemingly exists in the conceptual
No Man's Land between these two constructs: 'indifference' to religion. I begin
by discussing some definitions of indifference to religion and a brief overview of
the academic discussion on the subject, before asking why it is of interest to the
critical project, what problems are associated with its study to date and how one
might approach it in a more critically sound manner. I then place this discussion
into conversation with my work in the Southside, taking a discursive approach to
argue, amongst other things, that the *performance* of indifference can serve as a
tactic for coping with contextually meaningful difference.

Defining indifference

The *Collins English Thesaurus* provides three synonyms for 'indifference',[1] each
of which touches on an area of relevance to religion-related indifference. First,

a negatively inflected sense of disregard, detachment, coolness, lack of interest/attention and so on. Second, the similarly negative notion of irrelevance, insignificance, triviality or unimportance. And third, the more positive sense of objectivity, equity, neutrality or impartiality. In each of these senses, it is important to note the paradox whereby the very definition of the word indifference contains evaluative language that is, itself, *not indifferent* (see Catto 2017).

In the introduction to their edited volume on *Religious Indifference* (2017b), Johannes Quack and Cora Schuh outline two prevalent types evinced in scholarly considerations of the topic, both of which are distinct from 'ignorance'. First, 'considered' or 'evaluative' indifference, which is 'an elaborate position and assessments of religion being neither – or equally – good nor bad and thus indifferent' (2017a: 16). Second, 'unconsidered indifference', which is 'a more implicit and habitualised stance' that the matters under consideration are irrelevant (2017a: 16). These distinctions are then augmented by divisions into 'absolute' indifference – for 'those who do not care about religion at all, that is, a label for absent (non)religiosity' (2017a: 17) – and 'relative' indifference to certain aspects of religiosity. Furthermore, it matters whether we are speaking about 'indifference to religiosity' (as seen in the behaviour of social actors) or 'indifference to religion' as 'a social institution with different (public and private) manifestations' (2017a: 17). Quack and Schuh demonstrate how the concept is imbued with Christian baggage, retaining associations with the notion of 'adiaphoron' – that which is morally neutral, and to which one can remain indifferent – and remaining to this day associated with 'philosophical nihilism, moral and value relativism, pragmatism, cynic hedonism, subjectivism, egoism, narcissism, and consumerism' in authoritative Catholic discourse (2017a: 5; cf. Tiefensee 2011). Indifference is also tangled with secularization theory as a potential indicator that secularization has taken place (Bréchon 2017; Siegers 2017), or with secularization understood as a precondition for indifference (Quack and Schuh 2017a: 7), and can even be seen as a characteristic of interpersonal relations in modern society as distinguished from kinship-based societies (Quack and Schuh 2017a: 9; Simmel 1903).

Thus, the notion of religious indifference is bound up in a host of evaluative discourses surrounding the position of religion in contemporary society, and the subject positions that might be taken in relation to it.

Why be interested in indifference?

In her contribution to Quack and Schuh's volume, Lois Lee asks, 'why, if humans are indifferent to any number of things, [should] indifference to religion …

be interesting' (2017a: 103)? What is it about constituencies that appear to have remarkably little investment in the concept of religion or who explicitly articulate stances of indifference that might make them interesting to the scholar of religion and/or non-religion? There are two main answers to these questions.

First, we must consider the power-plays and contestations surrounding those deemed indifferent. James Beckford argues that 'indifference and hostility to both the particular and the generic meanings attributed to religion are no less interesting from a social scientific point of view' than the 'frontier skirmishes' and 'border patrols' that are 'constant features of the social process of constructing, defending, attacking, reforming and replacing ideas and institutions that claim to represent "real" religion' (Beckford 2003: 197–8). Whilst the explicitly 'non-religious' might have various direct relationships with religion – criticism, competition, copy, cooperation and so on (Quack and Schuh 2017a: 12) – the indifferent are less directly related but are 'contested, scrutinised and co-constituted from both religious as well as more explicit nonreligious positions' (2017a: 3). Thus, the 'absence of direct relationship may be rendered remarkable by others', perhaps because these others have reason to presume the existence of such a relationship or because religion is considered to be ubiquitous in a particular context (2017a: 12). Therefore, rather than saying that this presumed population is inherently of interest to the critical study of (non-)religion, we can say that it is interesting because of the contestations surrounding it – the ways in which it is *deemed remarkable by others*.

Second, the notion of 'religious indifference' cuts right to the core of the scholarly endeavour and provides 'an occasion for exploring the assumptions required to produce social scientific knowledge' (Blankholm 2017: 254). In a thought-provoking text exploring the possibilities of using fiction to open indifference to scholarly inquiry, Joseph Blankholm argues that indifference 'marks the limit beyond which scholarly inquiry … cannot proceed' but also tantalizes by offering us 'the unknown, and perhaps, the unknowable' (2017: 254). He continues:

> Religious indifference demands of us that we ask what it is we are doing, why we are doing it, and what will be different once we have done it. It is a fiction that thrusts us back upon our fictions, calls our attention to our entanglements, and delimits the boundary of our inquiries. … Do we inscribe it, or do we allow it to remain indifferent? Regardless of whether we give chase, we ought to pause for a moment to wonder what we intend to do with religious indifference once we catch it. We should also worry more than a little about what might happen if it catches us. (2017: 255)

Clearly, indifference has a lot to tell us about our terms of reference and, more importantly, about the very point of our scholarly endeavours. Studying it does, however – as Blankholm has illustrated – come with its own problems.

Problems with studying indifference

The first major problem with studying indifference is analogous to Heisenberg's Uncertainty Principle in quantum mechanics, where the very act of measuring the position of a quantum particle changes the momentum of that particle, meaning that knowledge of either position or momentum changes the value of the other. In a similar manner, the social scientist interested in exploring a supposed state of 'unconsidered' indifference might irrevocably alter the very phenomenon under scrutiny through conducting their research, for example, 'by engaging interviewees in discussions about religion and by thereby suggesting the topic to them' (Quack and Schuh 2017a: 12). Positions of 'genuine indifference might have to be given up in situational opposition to lures and claims of the religious (or nonreligious)', which raises the questions: Do these situational positionings lead to anything more stable? When? And how are we to recognize this (Schuh and Quack 2017: 268)?

A second problem concerns the contextuality of indifference. Reflecting on the possibility of indifference on both sides of the Atlantic, Samuel Bagg and David Voas note that 'Americans, forced to choose, would commit strongly to a tradition, but the British, not made to think twice about their religious choices, passively accepted the benign, tolerant national default, and moved on with the rest of their lives' (2010: 104). 'Lapsing' into indifference in the former context is much more likely to have a profound impact upon one's social network, sense of identity and so on, whereas the effects in the latter are likely much less traumatic. Indeed, as we have seen in previous chapters, it appears that there is a certain social desirability in the UK towards *appearing* to be indifferent. As Schuh and Quack argue, it is only in contexts 'where religion is societally unimportant' that 'indifference is possible without a more widespread disengagement from society' (2017: 264). They continue:

> This is true in terms of religion as a resource, an objectified social category, or a contested claim-maker in the public political realm. In any case, the indifferent – if they do no assert their indifference or the secularity of the state – inhabit a difficult position, finding themselves at the margins of cultural communities or potentially deprived of recognition and influence. (2017: 264)

Just as with religion and non-religion, being indifferent to these constructs, and how this indifference might be made manifest, is highly contextual. Indeed, it is worth thinking on just how post-Protestant the concept is.

Third, we ought to consider once again the problem of reification discussed in Chapter 2, understood here as the 'apprehension of the products of human activity as if they were something else than human products – such as facts of nature, results of cosmic laws, or manifestations of divine will' (Berger and Luckmann 1966: 89). Returning to Lee's question above, what about other fields in which indifference might play a role? Certainly political indifference, apathy or disenchantment is a major concern to those in the political sciences and to those who are engaged in, or experience the effects of, politics in its many and varied forms (Dahl et al. 2018; Dassonneville and Hooghe 2018; Mackenzie 2018), but it is difficult to think of many other cogent examples. By constructing indifference to any phenomenon such as 'religion' as a 'problem' that needs scholarly attention, we reify religion, and thus we are playing into the hands of those who construct religion as a normal, inherent, *sui generis* aspect of human social life, society and so on. Might this be because scholars who are so accustomed to studying religion see supposed indifference to their object of study as a threat? If the categories of religion and non-religion are critically problematic, then supposed 'indifference' to these constructs is even more so.

A fourth and related problem concerns the construction of indifference as a kind of ideal-typical 'state of being' or position related to religion (cf. Bagg and Voas 2010: 99; Bruce 1996: 58, 2002: 42; Dalferth 2010: 324; Lee 2014: 474–6; Voas 2009: 161–2; Zuckerman 2010: 104–9). Consider, for example, the epigraph to this chapter from Ben Goldacre. Such explicit, *contextual*, declarations of indifference with their over-lexicalization suggest emotional, intellectual and other forms of investment in the concept of religion: '[s]imply put, people who identify as "indifferent to religion" are *not* indifferent to religion' (Lee 2012a: 160). As I have previously argued,

> What we can say is that when confronted with 'religion' in this context, Goldacre utilized an emotional discursive repertoire to place himself in a (seemingly desirable) position of indifference, with the specifics of said repertoire making it problematic to describe this statement *as* indifferent. (Cotter 2017a: 46)

As hinted at above, although we might be able to conceptualize 'settled periods' (Schuh, Burchardt and Wohlrab-Sahr 2012: 359) of indifference between moments of controversy (Knott 2005: 218), explicit instances of 'evaluative indifference' are profoundly contextual, and do not scan with labelling individuals, states or societies as 'indifferent' per se. Going further, settled periods of 'disinterested indifference' are likely a misnomer, given that indifference seemingly 'requires at least some awareness of religion and therefore taking some position' (Lee 2012b: 131). I discuss this at greater length in Cotter (2017a), but the point of my argument 'is that given the inherent relationality of the concept of indifference, and the variety of nuanced relationships that can be encapsulated by this single term', we should avoid constructing it ideal-typically 'and instead embrace this relationality, and the contextuality that comes with it' (2017a: 47–8). This critique reiterates my objections to ideal typical approaches discussed in Chapter 2, but this is not to say that conceiving of indifference as an ideal type of relation to religion would not yield some potentially useful insights nor, as we shall see below, that stances, expressions or discourses of indifference are not meaningful for those social actors involved.

A final problem that I also discuss in Cotter (2017a) concerns where indifference is to be placed in relation to the categories 'religion' and 'non-religion'. It is relatively common to find indifference to religion being considered a form of non-religiosity: 'profound cases of nonreligious attachment and normativity' (Lee 2012a: 114), for example (see also Bagg and Voas 2010: 99; Habgood 2000: 6; Lee 2012b: 131; Meulemann 2004: 48). However, it is important to note that it is common for religious social actors to display indifference towards other religions (Beckford 2003: 84; Stringer 2013: 69–70) or towards aspects associated with their own religion-related identification (Hervieu-Léger 2000: 168; Voas 2009: 162; Lee 2017a; Klug 2017). Furthermore, positions of indifference might relate to the entire religion-related field: 'a society that is indifferent to manifestations of religion … ought, therefore, to be just as indifferent to manifestations of "nonreligion"' (Bullivant 2012: 100; cf. Bagg and Voas 2010: 107–8). Taking up the baton, Lee argues that indifference

> stands in relation not only to religion but to nonreligion too, because the irrelevance of positioning oneself as religious must necessarily extend to positioning oneself as religion's other; therefore understanding indifference as a form of nonreligion is, in my view, problematic. (2017a: 105)

From a critical perspective this is also problematic, because considering indifference to be non-religious once again 'reifies "religion" by placing perspectives that are "indifferent" to the whole "religion-related" conversation into an oppositional stance towards just the [supposedly] "religious" parts of it' (Cotter 2017a: 50).

To summarize, the study of religious indifference is entangled with several problems for the researcher, many of which are problems associated with the study of religion turned up to eleven. Through the very act of engaging in research, scholars may preclude the possibility of encountering 'true' indifference, run the risk of constructing an unrepresentative ideal type from contextual expressions of so-called indifference and, in the process, may further contribute to the reification of a *sui generis* religion. However, given that the study of this apparent boundary case has much to contribute to the theorization of 'religion', 'non-religion' and related categories, how might we approach it in a critically sound manner?

Approaching indifference

As anthropologists they are, Quack and Schuh naturally suggest that 'Participant observation is probably best suited to gradually assess degrees of certainty and assertiveness as well as degrees of being involved with the question in the first place' (2017a: 18). It is likely to be quite difficult to convince funding organizations to support research with this explicit aim, and, thus, research involving participant observation is likely to yield results of relevance to indifference – to any phenomenon – only as a bonus. An innovative way of addressing this issue is to use fictionalized narratives as a means of exploring indifference. Just as Ethan Quillen utilized the novels of Ian McEwan as a means to 'understand how Atheists define themselves by dialectical communication' (2015b), so Joseph Blankholm (2017) offers some tantalizing reflections on the inscrutability of indifference through an examination of Herman Melville's titular character in *Bartleby, the Scrivener: A Story of Wall-Street* (1853). Fiction provides a means whereby we can potentially access and assess narratives that, by virtue of their construction by human beings and their apparent relatability for other human beings, may be taken as 'real' contributions to the contextual discourses on whatever topic is at hand.

However, for those of us who have engaged in projects utilizing qualitative interviews in the Southside of Edinburgh, luckily Quack and Schuh continue:

> An underlying attitude of disinterestedness, however, can also be seen in the analyses of interviews. Would the indifferent maybe shrug their shoulders and say something like 'hmpf'? Would they search for words and a position? Would they merely reproduce perfunctory platitudes, reflect about not having thought about these issues prior to the interview, or would they maybe say anything at random thereby signalling that affirming or dismissing answers to religion-related questions are not as decisive as the underlying attitude of disinterest? (2017a: 18)

This all sounds very much like examining the themes appealed to by the informant and the linguistic, grammatical and argumentative tropes they utilize. In other words, this sounds very much like the three-level Discourse Analysis I outlined in Chapter 3, drawing particularly on Stephanie Garling's work (2013), which formed the basis for my analysis of religion-related discourse in the Southside. Although not engaging in discursive analysis per se, Lee (2017a) points to some of the exciting possibilities for examining indifference 'in between the lines' of an informant's narrative. She points out that self-presentation as indifferent 'might contrast with in-depth knowledge of friends and family members' religious views and cultural attachments', or, alternatively, self-proclaimed enthusiasm for religion-related matters might be combined with 'a lack of knowledge about religiosity, spirituality and nonreligiosity in discussion of relationships and situations in their everyday lived lives' (2017a: 109). Such 'internal triangulation' (2017a: 109) is of vital importance to discursive analysis of interview data of relevance to indifference, and it is to this approach and to my data that I now turn.

Indifferent discourses and discourses of indifference in Edinburgh's Southside

Throughout this book, I have adopted a relational model of 'religion' and 'non-religion', seeing them as constituent parts of contextual religion-related discursive fields (see Chapter 3).[2] If 'indifference' is conceptualized as a type of religion-related discourse, it can be incorporated into this model without any need to position it as religious or non-religious. Such discourses could be made manifest in several ways. For example, following Quack and Schuh's lead, we can conceive of discourses which are not related to religion and where the absence of such a relationship is 'rendered remarkable by others' (2017a: 12). Such discourses might be dubbed 'indifferent discourses' in that there is seemingly no reference to religion-related themes, and this absence is judged to be relevant by particular actors (such as the researcher). More explicitly, and of more relevance to the discussion which follows, I propose referring to 'discourses of indifference' which are located where explicit claims to indifference, or evaluations, equivocations and so on are encountered that are demonstrably religion-related but which suggest no strong opinions or significant investment for the interlocutors involved. I now turn to some empirical examples which demonstrate the power of such discourses of indifference in the religion-related field.

Situational indifference

Turning first to my Master's project among non-religious students at the University of Edinburgh (although questions of discourse and indifference were not on my radar when engaging in this study), it was clear that 'being non-religious' did not play a major part in many of these students' lives. However, I also noted that this seeming lack of emphasis did not imply that this aspect of their lives was *un*important. Every student that participated in my study was asked to respond openly and in their own way to the question 'who are you?' and to list ideas, places, people, concepts, stories and so on that were of greatest importance to them. Each student attested to multiple entanglements in their models of self, with the majority citing their personal relationships, their sense of self, their pursuit of knowledge and/or 'virtues' such as kindness, love or compassion as the most important things in their life, and describing themselves primarily as students, as individuals or by listing dispositional characteristics. Most claimed that their non-religiosity only came to the fore when challenged by specific situations, such as the following questionnaire respondents:

- 'Not often. Only in discussions of religion'
- 'When I'm reading the paper and the subject of religion comes up'
- 'When some Christians try to evangelise fowk [*sic*] outside the library'

I have previously suggested that an explanation for this seemingly low salience of religion-related identification is related to the difficulty New Atheists seem to face in differentiating and selling a coherent 'positive' agenda: many of their stances 'strike a chord with the current [Western political] atmosphere[;] ... their concerns are — diffused throughout society' (Cotter 2011a: 95–6; cf. McAnulla, Kettell and Schulzke 2018). No student referred to feeling like an embattled minority; in fact, the opposite occurred, with students describing a societal attitude of tolerance, non-discrimination and indifference regarding (non-) religion. Even Courtney, from California, said, 'nobody cares if I'm an atheist, at least where I come from, literally nobody cares ... it's not a big issue, um, your religious beliefs'. This observation proves very significant when turning to my contemporary Southside data.

Throughout the remainder of this chapter, we will hear from several Southsiders, but particularly from Aoife, Fiona and Richard.[3] Each of these individuals cannot be unproblematically labelled as 'indifferent to religion' due to the fact that they have each identified with traditionally 'religious' signifiers in the past (Anglican-Presbyterian, Church of Scotland and Roman Catholic-Quaker, respectively) and that they identified primarily in non-religious terms when speaking to me. Throughout our conversations they each expressed considered, and at points remarkably impassioned, positions related to aspects of religion, positive and negative. At other times they positioned themselves as indifferent to (different aspects of) religion.

Due to the photo elicitation segment of these interviews, all interviewees discussed a material instantiation of religion-related discourse in the Southside: the 'trypraying' advert on the side of a local bus (see Figure 3.3). Richard remarked that these adverts make him laugh, because 'it's such a waste of money and time and, well you can try if you like but it doesn't actually do any good'. However, he also vocalized the sound of rushing wind as he stated, 'it sort of <whoosh> goes over my head', and he didn't think such public displays should prove offensive for anybody. Fiona reacted positively to the image, considering it 'brilliant' and 'very clever ... from an advertising perspective', while adding the caveat that 'it wouldn't probably influence me but ... I don't think it's a bad thing'. Aoife's reaction was more negative and was echoed by other interviewees, who saw the campaign as 'devalu[ing] what humanity can do for itself', and as 'very dismissive' of the extent of the problems faced by some people. We can already see several entangled discourses emerging surrounding this image.

Although I cannot escape acknowledging that the context of the interviews will have likely contributed to this, all three Southsiders interacted with the image as a religious image. They recognized it as containing a message of theological and ritual import and positioned themselves outside a constituency who might find the performance of prayer to a supernatural force to have any relevance. In this manner, each positioned themselves as somewhat indifferent to the perceived message. However, Aoife and Richard also evaluated the potential social impact of this image, with Aoife considering it particularly harmful and Richard, although acknowledging temporal and financial costs, viewing it largely as an amusing and harmless curiosity. Richard's attitude exemplifies a prevalent 'discourse of indifference', whereby, for example, the British 'left-wing' press tend to cast the UK 'as secular and plural, with an accompanying discourse of Christian decline and irrelevance' (Knott, Poole and Taira 2013: 174). This discourse explicitly engages with religion (here, Christianity), placing it beyond the realm of phenomena to be given serious attention, and into a benign – if mildly amusing – category that can be viewed with indifference.

Fiona's commentary largely focused on the aesthetics of the image: 'I think it's very clever. I think from, eh, an advertising perspective, I mean, it's brilliant copy.

It's a great strapline, I think it's fantastic.' These discourses on 'brilliant copy' and the utility of 'great strapline[s]' are clearly engaged with the fields of advertising and marketing yet are indifferent discourses with respect to religion. However, they clearly intersect with the religious field in this instance. Going further, both Richard and Aoife expressed views invoking a broader multiculturalist discourse (see Chapter 4). Aoife placed the advert alongside similar 'religion-related' campaigns, stating, 'I don't necessarily think it's any worse than certain bus adverts that atheists have put up as well', yet emphasized that 'it is good that people of any faith are interested in outreach of some kind'. These comments allude to similar reservations in the UK media, a 'dominant discourse in which some versions of atheism and secularism are conceptualized as unwanted and a potential threat to society' (Knott, Poole and Taira 2013: 116).[4] Richard noted that the image 'doesn't offend me, … it's not getting at people, … it's not one of these "We're right, you're wrong" type of statements'. Here, he invokes a discourse of indifference, whereby moderate expressions of religion that do not impose upon users of public space can be viewed with indifference. Conversely, public expressions of 'strong' or 'abnormal' religion – when judged against the hegemonic moderate Christian-secular norm – are problematic. Aoife's celebration of 'religious outreach' invokes this discourse through inversion: here, a presumption that 'people of any faith' will be indifferent towards public life is challenged by the advert, and Aoife deems this of benefit and relevance to the wider (secular) populace.

Although we cannot infer what other discourses may have been invoked had I pressed these interviewees on the issue, clearly this image is situationally implicated in a broad range of contextual discourses on religion, some of which could be described as 'indifferent discourses' and others as 'discourses of indifference'. Discussion now focuses on the latter, expanding on the above in two broad strokes: on strategic versus tactical indifference and on indifference at the centre and the periphery.

Indifference at the centre and the periphery

In the same photo elicitation exercise discussed above, each interviewee was presented with a photograph of the Southside Community Centre (Figure 3.2), which now occupies the building of the former Nicolson Street Church. The congregation that met in the church merged with two other congregations in 1969 (Pinkerton 2012: 32), and the Community Centre opened in 1986 (Palmer 2007), the building having served as a saleroom in the interim. Most of my interviewees struggled to recognize where the centre was located, despite its location directly opposite a popular supermarket on the Southside's busiest thoroughfare, a place that is very familiar to Southside residents. Upon being told where it was, Fiona acknowledged that she did recognize it, although she 'would have carried up and down past it for many a long year'. Her statements construct the presence of churches as unremarkable elements in a typical Scottish background. She continued, suggesting that because Nicolson Street is such a 'shopping parade, you wouldn't really expect a big church to be there' but then immediately began to re-examine things, conceding that 'there's actually quite a lot of churches up there reused. … Yeah, there's a heck of a lot of churches there'. These comments not only echo the background and normative character of an unobtrusive Christianity but they also place Christianity outside the hustle and bustle of the vibrant modern city, locating it in rural, traditional or historical urban contexts.

The spatial metaphor of centre-periphery can help us comprehend the discursive dynamics or 'knowledge-power strategies' (Knott 2008: 55) in operation here. Many of the illustrative discursive fragments above, and throughout this book, place Christianity as an historically central component of the Southside's built environment. However, it was Fiona's perception of this historical centrality that led her to place Christianity on the periphery. According to her account, this physical manifestation of Christianity does not intrude upon her everyday experience of the Southside. However, when prompted in the interview to consider this building, and to consider it as religion-related, when it was brought back to the centre of Fiona's construction of the Southside from the peripheral status to which it been assigned, its presence – and with it, the presence of other such (former) churches – stimulated expressions of surprise. These churches are 'matter out of place' (Douglas 1966) in her construction of Nicolson Street as a busy and important local site of secular capitalism. Here we see a paradox whereby Christianity occupies a peripheral position in many of my informants' mental models of the Southside, whilst simultaneously retaining a central position in the historical imaginary and physical environment. In other words, it is simultaneously *not* 'matter out of place'. This centrality is the very thing that allows Christianity to be assigned to the periphery and, thus, to (potentially) be viewed (locally) with indifference. It is little coincidence, then, that the nearby Edinburgh Central Mosque was not treated with such indifference by my Southsiders: clearly indifference acts to mask the hegemonic status of certain representations of Christianity in the Southside as 'normal', instituting 'a regime of privilege that benefits [this] group over others' (C. Martin

2010: 161). Those forms of Christianity that are 'historical' and 'traditional' are relatively 'unmarked' in the Southside – unmarked, that is, until events trigger a situational, religion-related interpretation. This is a privilege of the powerful and illustrates the potential power masked by 'indifferent' status. This also brings us back to the discussion of the 'trypraying' advert above: this advert was able to fly under the radar in the Southside, or be brushed off as largely harmless, precisely because of the central, historical status of the tradition associated with it. Certain forms of Christianity – and, presumably, other suitably 'moderate' religion-related expressions (see below) – get a free pass in secular civic space and can be treated with indifference.

Returning to Southsiders' reactions to the photograph of the Community Centre, when Aoife was reflecting on the visibility of church buildings in general, she stated that she definitely 'notices the [church] buildings … [in the Southside], especially because some of them are really stunning buildings … but I don't necessarily think about them … in any active way'. This despite failing to place this particular (former) church. This alludes to an 'indifferent discourse' of aesthetic appreciation which is once again quite distinct from any religion-related connotations. However, in this case she explicitly articulates indifference to religion, meaning that the statement crosses a boundary and expresses something about the place of Christianity. All of my interviewees expressed positive views towards this particular (former) church, and many others like it, being used by the community and towards their preservation as part of Edinburgh's 'secular cultural heritage' (Burchardt 2017). These notions conceptualize Christianity as integral to the Southside's history and reflect broader discourses which centre 'proper' Christianity (and, indeed, religion) on 'good works' in the *whole community* and which construct churches as resources which *should be* for the whole community. Indeed, Richard acerbically stated that 'it's better used as it is now than as a church' yet added that 'if people wanted to go in there and have a … service of some sort, [that's] fine'. This invokes a discourse constructing certain religious practices as benign, harmless curiosities.[5]

Strategic and tactical indifference

A final insight from the Southside involves a useful distinction between strategic and tactical indifference. In making this distinction, I am drawing on Michael de Certeau's model of strategies and tactics in *The Practice of Everyday Life* (1984). De Certeau defines a 'strategy' as the 'calculation (or manipulation) of power relationships that becomes possible as soon as a subject with will and power …

can be isolated' (1984: 35–6). It is a 'prerogative of the powerful' that presumes a vantage point with time, space and panoptical vision (Woodhead 2012b: 7). Tactics, by contrast, are 'calculated action[s] determined by the absence of a proper locus' that are utilized in the space of the 'other' (de Certeau 1984: 36–7). In this space, dominated by contextually relevant hegemonic powers, the dominated actor does not have the option of general strategizing or taking stock of their opponent but 'operates in isolated actions, blow by blow' (de Certeau 1984: 37). Strategies are the domain of the powerful, who benefit from foresight and planning (think, for example, of the coach of a sports team), while tactics tend to be more reactive and improvised, occurring on the field of battle as opposed to in the war room (for example, a sports team engaged in play).

It is in the discourses on *Civic Space* that we most clearly encounter the interplay between strategic and tactical discourses of indifference in the Southside. Of particular relevance here is the concept of 'conviviality', which has been developed in recent years in studies of urban diversity to describe 'a low-intensity but nevertheless very real (and important) level of social cohesion characterized by the avoidance of conflict and a "live and let live" attitude' (Blommaert 2014: 16) and focused on 'the many small connections we make with others that may just make us feel happier or part of a population as a citizen' (Fincher 2003: 57).[6] For example, while Fiona was quite willing to have religion-related conversation in our interview, these were apparently things that she 'wouldn't be articulating' in her everyday life. Although she 'might know the odd person who is religious … we don't have too much of a conversation about it', and she couldn't recall any specific encounters with religion or (non-) religious people where her perspective would come to the fore. Similarly, Aoife commented that religion-related conversations aren't 'necessarily any more prominent than conversations about existential philosophers and conversations about politics … and whatever else. So, it … isn't a huge part of what I've done while I've been in Southside'.

Regardless of the factual basis of such statements, given these individuals' demonstrable and sometimes strong opinions on, for example, 'faith schooling' (Fiona), L. Ron Hubbard's 'nonsense' (Richard) or David Cameron's comments concerning the UK as a 'Christian country' (Aoife),[7] I contend that such *tactical* claims to indifference are entangled with a dominant,[8] *strategic* discourse evident throughout the Southside and beyond (and alluded to above and throughout this book). This is a liberal secularist discourse extolling religion-related moderation and conviviality in interpersonal interaction and demonizing militancy or extremism: to quote Samantha, 'I'm definitely not a fundamentalist'. This discourse is detailed by Fitzgerald – with good religion staying out of politics and bad religion taking a critical stand against 'liberal secular principles' (2015b: 306; also Casanova 2009: 139).

Holding – or, more importantly, expressing – 'strong opinions' was dubbed by many as inherently problematic, although this view was frequently articulated alongside the notion that it is not the substance of the message that matters, so much as the manner in which it is expressed. Immoderate assertions of exclusivity were dubbed 'extremism', and whilst tendencies to extremism were generally viewed as an inherently human problem, some viewed religion or being religious as potent correlates with such extremism. Nevertheless, others railed against this popular exhortation to moderation, holding that one should be unafraid to speak one's mind if one's message is worth hearing: 'I ... I ... but I, you know, political correctness I kind of view as a kind of extremism' (Julian). Mortimer and Prideaux have described this dynamic as originating in a 'secular sacred boundary around the concept of inclusivity' (2018: 72) in the contemporary UK, rooted in a (cynical?) 'desire to project publicly an inclusive attitude towards those with different beliefs' (2018: 77).

This portrait scans with Stephen Bullivant's observations concerning Pope Benedict XVI's visit to the UK in 2010. Bullivant suggested that 'people had ... "internalized" the *perceived* indifference not only of the nation as a whole, but of people like themselves' (2012: 104). It also further evidences Bagg and Voas's description of declarations of faith as 'unusual' among a UK populace who 'pride themselves on their self-proclaimed "moderation"' (2010: 94; cf. Beckford 1999: 34; Davie 2015: 179). The 'perceived indifference' acknowledged by Bullivant is part of a tactical discourse deployed in the face of the pervasive, powerful and strategic discourse of moderation (i.e. strategic indifference) that demonizes those who take 'religion too seriously' (Bruce 1995: 3), encourages Britons to keep quiet 'on the subject unless formally prompted' (Knott, Poole and Taira 2013: 120) and discourages 'the open expression of religion in many public arenas' (Woodhead 2012a: 25). Strategic indifference can be illustrated by the supposed neutrality of an ideal-typical 'secular state', which 'is not merely tolerant but defines itself as neutral with respect to the option between religious and non-religious ways of life', restricting its own and its citizens' interactions with religion, and 'systematically distinguish[ing] the self-description of religious groups and traditions in their own imagery, conceptuality, or semantics' (Dalferth 2010: 334). Can a powerful strategic discourse which effectively quashes open expression of difference be understood to be *merely* indifferent?

It is important to acknowledge that tactical indifference is not the only possible response to this strategic discourse of moderation. One need only think of moderation's 'other' – extremism – to see that this is not the case. Also, what of ridicule and chastisement, as in the case of *Charlie Hebdo* (Temperman and Koltay 2017)? There were certainly acknowledgements in my data of *others* engaging in ridicule and extreme behaviour, of interviewees being on the receiving end of some of this, or at least witnessing it, and there are also hints of ridicule in some statements. These 'exceptions to the rule' raise questions as to why alternative tactics did not emerge in my data. Some methodological reasons for this might be that, for reasons discussed in Chapter 3, I did not have access to groups who could be described as particularly marginalized in the Southside. These alternative tactics are also caught up in the dominant discourse of moderation and so are othered: indifference is a more 'acceptable' response, in this context, when speaking about the positives of an area to a stranger,[9] and it also befits the genre of the conversation (a formal interview). Sociologically, the discourses above also attest to the relative, perceived invisibility of religion in the Southside – with, therefore, the concomitant invisibility of 'bad religion' against which to more forcefully articulate one's position.

More important, however, is the nature of the 'community' in the Southside (as discussed in Chapter 3). Although there is a significant core population, the area is marked by transience, with students coming and going and the area serving as an intermediate stage in young families' moves up the property ladder towards the leafy suburbs. As such, although there are significant numbers of people who might be classified as 'ethnic' or 'religious' minorities, the constant flux of the area and the dominance of the student industry mitigate against the segregation of the Southside into different 'communities', and thus diminish the attendant mobilization of resentment that might be expected in other areas of the city that might be 'split along one central, typically ethnic or religious, fault line' (Hewstone et al. 2007: 108). In the very different context of Hackney in London, Wessendorf (2014b: 44) prefers to avoid talk of indifference because 'difference is acknowledged and people are aware of the manifold cultural differences around them' (i.e. they are *not indifferent*). However, based on the observations above, I argue that the *performance* of indifference is a prominent tactic for 'dealing with diversity' (van Leeuwen 2010: 639) in the Southside, in the face of a dominant strategic discourse of indifference (moderation), rather than necessarily implying an ideal-typical state of being indifferent.

Indifference can also be fruitfully performed in the face of more subjective, micro-level power dynamics. For example, Aoife attests to presenting a veneer of indifference and not 'rocking the boat' when she is with her family:

it's somewhat difficult, I haven't necessarily … I actually haven't told my family that I no longer see myself as Christian, and I probably wouldn't ever tell my grandparents, but I think being Christian was a huge part of what shaped me, … [and] I still see huge value in it for other people and for where I came from, but it's just not who I am.

This tactical presentation of indifference is entangled with the importance she believes her family places upon Christianity, her apprehensiveness regarding the potential effects that taking a more actively non-religious stance would have. Such negotiations are by no means exclusively religion-related and will undoubtedly be familiar to many readers. Yet, when they are religion-related, they implicate religion in broader discourses on the family and echo findings from my Master's project in which, in many instances, an 'emphasis on the family takes precedence over (non)religious identification, and is associated with an image of "religion" – positive or negative – which is closely linked to intimate relationships' (2015: 186).

Conclusion

It has been my aim in this chapter to emphasize that the very notion of 'indifference to religion' is problematic from a critical perspective, because of the impact of the researcher upon its construction, the reification of the religion to which this presumed constituency is supposedly indifferent and a tendency towards ideal-typical deployment of the concept. However, I also emphasized that the idea of indifference provides an excellent opportunity to reflect on power-plays and contestations surrounding the notions of (non-)religion, and the very limits of the scholarly endeavour.

I began this chapter with a quotation from the physician and science writer Ben Goldacre, in which he forcefully articulates a position which Lee has dubbed 'engaged indifferentism' (2014: 474). A discursive approach, distinguishing between 'indifferent discourses' and 'discourses of indifference', allows us to avoid constructing 'indifferentism' as an ideal-typical position, whilst also making space for such a position to be situationally occupied and spoken from. Although I cannot speak to Goldacre's specific case, my analysis of religion-related discourse in the Southside suggests that, in some instances, the *performance* of indifference is a tactic for coping with contextually meaningful difference. In such cases, tactical indifference can conceal positive and negative attitudes, particularly in the face of dominant strategic venerations of indifference. In the religion-related field in the Southside, discourses of indifference are entangled with, and mask, the hegemony of Christianity and contribute to the maintenance of what Fitzgerald would call 'liberal secular principles' (2015: 306).

These conclusions combine to strengthen calls for critically engaged studies of religion and non-religion to incorporate religion-related subject positions, such as positions of indifference, without disingenuously labelling them as 'religious' or 'non-religious'. Rather than asking whether a social actor is 'indifferent to religion' or not, we should ask – drawing on Craig Martin (2017: 156) – *who* is identified, by *whom,* as indifferent to *what* and with what *social effects*? When we do so, 'indifference' becomes not so much a problem to be dealt with, as a productive means to further unmask the ideological function of religion and related categories – in society at large, and as perpetuated by the academy.

Epilogue: There is no data for non-religion

I began this book by positioning myself firmly within the critical strand of Religious Studies, arguing that 'there are no disinterested, external positions' (Knott 2005: 125) from which to examine 'religion' (whatever that might be), but rather, scholars perpetuate and shape the 'discipline of religion' (McCutcheon 2003). At the heart of this critical strand is Jonathan Z. Smith's famous statement that

> while there is a staggering amount of data, of phenomena, of human experiences and expressions that might be characterized in one culture or another, by one criterion or another, as religious – *there is no data for religion*. Religion is solely the creation of the scholar's study. It is created for the scholar's analytic purposes by his [*sic*] imaginative acts of comparison and generalization. Religion has no independent existence apart from the academy. (1982: xi)

The six-word italicized phrase 'there is no data for religion' has been dubbed 'the most frequently cited sentence in theoretical/methodological discussions in the field of religious studies during the last two [now, nearly four] decades' (Benavides 2003: 895) and can easily be taken out of context and critiqued in the face of the data 'out there' that is so obviously 'religious' (e.g. Hedges 2016).

To be fair, as Kathryn Lofton observes, 'there is something dazzlingly absurd about such a claim', which 'could seem utterly idiotic, argumentatively important, or perfectly axiomatic, depending on your own relationship to religion as a problem for humanistic inquiry' (2014: 536). In my reading, Smith is not arguing that scholars should therefore cease all empirical work on social phenomena deemed 'religious', nor that they should abandon the category altogether, nor that 'religion' is uniquely problematic when compared to some of the other categories that are 'created for the scholar's analytic purposes'. I argue that a key element in Smith's argument lies in the sentences immediately following this oft-cited passage. Smith continues:

> For this reason, the student of religion, and most particularly the historian of religion, must be relentlessly self-conscious. Indeed, this self-consciousness constitutes his [*sic*] primary expertise, his foremost object of study. (1982: xi)

It was in this spirit of relentless self-consciousness that I undertook this project in order to critically engage with, reframe and to some degree rehabilitate the burgeoning body of contemporary research on 'non-religion' – a term that is definitively 'the creation of the scholar's study'.

I began in Chapter 1 with a broad survey of the field of non-religion studies with reference to the UK context. I first built the case that non-religion is worthy of study because it seemingly serves as the boundary of the study of religion and allows us (a) to assess claims to the universality of religion, (b) to explore real-world contestations involving some key non-religious identifiers and (c) to continue and develop the highly pertinent questioning of the problematic religion/non-religion and religion/secular binaries. I proceeded through a discussion of the key vocabulary populating the field, some important statistics and demographics, some key non-religious manifestations and some central issues animating existing scholarship. Although I set critical issues to one side in this chapter, I also demonstrated that surveys are problematic, that context is key and that ideologies, agendas and political climates animate the production and presentation of notionally objective scholarship. I showed that terminology matters and will never satisfy everyone, that intersectional approaches have much to offer, that speaking of the non-religious as a coherent group – or even as a group at all – is problematic at best and that asking who wins and loses by the demarcation and labelling of certain phenomena as religious or not can be much more interesting than assessing the validity of such acts of classification.

Chapter 2 began my theoretical argument in earnest, with a critical assessment of four dominant approaches to the 'non-religious', which I dubbed 'subtractionist', 'context specific', 'substantial' and 'discursive'. Subtractionist approaches were critiqued for operating within a framework that is dominated by secularization theory and focused upon religion as something substantial and interesting, as opposed to the insubstantial, empty, baseline norm that remains when religion is removed from the equation. Context-specific approaches were assessed more positively, yet their rootedness in particular contexts makes it very difficult for scholarly comparisons to take place, or for these studies to contribute directly to contemporary debates on category formation within the critical study of religion. Substantial approaches were praised for providing in-depth qualitative and quantitative studies relating to a neglected population yet critiqued on three levels. First, I argued that these approaches are problematically implicated in the World Religions Paradigm and its associated baggage. Second, I argued that the plethora of new and idiosyncratic terms that has accompanied these approaches makes fruitful collaboration between scholars more difficult. Finally, I demonstrated that substantial approaches to non-religion seem unable to shed 'religion' and thus seem doomed to be tarred with the same critical brush. I concluded that discursive approaches provide a fruitful way forward for the critical study of non-religion, combined with a discursive adaptation of Johannes Quack's concept of a 'religion-related field' (2014). Through a discursive re-reading of my Master's project, I then outlined the key questions that would motivate the rest of the book: Would it be possible to flesh out the insights from my Master's project with more rigour, based on the analysis of a broader set of discursive data? Could my approach be expanded to include the voices of those who are ostensibly religious and non-religious, those who are 'indifferent' to religion and those who are in-between? What would this say to academic constructions of non-religion? Are religion-related discourses dependent upon specific configurations of discursive objects? What are these points of meaningful intersection, and just how contextual are they?

In Chapter 3 I argued that the critical agenda outlined thus far could be well-served by working empirically with religion-related discourses employed in social interaction by non-elite social actors who (strategically or tactically) place themselves, and are placed by others, in a variety of positions within a contextual religion-related field. I utilized 'locality' as a framework for organizing my discursive analysis, arguing that viewing localities as discursive fields facilitates a social constructivist approach to group and individual identifications and helps us to avoid reifying contested religion-related categories, whilst simultaneously providing a relatively bounded and coherent context within which to conduct analysis. I then introduced the Southside as my chosen field site, and my data sources: the *Peoples of Edinburgh Project* (PEP), new interviews and ethnographic observation and interviews from my prior research. After outlining the specifics of my interview techniques and my iterative analytical process of coding and triangulation between data sources, the four chapters that followed presented the fruits of my empirical project, leading to the following core conclusions.

Conclusions

First, in mapping the religion-related field of discourse in the Southside, I showed that it encompasses a wide variety of discourses and is significantly entangled with other discursive fields. In some cases, these discourses were effectively a-religious, in that they could be 'described and analysed without any reference to religious phenomena' (Quack 2014: 446), and were quite loosely entangled with the religion-related field. However, despite this theoretical a-religiosity, many of these discourses were contextually entangled with the religion-related field, rendering the apparent a-religiosity meaningless. For example, discourses on multiculturalism in the twenty-first-century UK are such that talk of 'cultural difference' is almost inevitably religion-related, despite being theoretically a-religious. Going further, some other discourses – on, say, post-Christian hegemony, or religion and welfare – could not be described without recourse to contextual constructions of religion. These observations demonstrate the importance of looking beyond the surface of discourses in order to understand the tightness of their entanglement in the religion-related field and the significance of the acts of positioning taking place by relevant actors. They temper the temptation to reify the religion-related field simply because of certain entanglements and focus our attention instead on the nature of these entanglements.

Second, turning specifically to the relational category of non-religion, my analysis of the religion-related discourses in Edinburgh's Southside demonstrated that it makes no sense to refer to the discourses as 'religious' or 'non-religious'. What can be said is that these are resources that are utilized by social actors to contextually position themselves and others in relation to religion. Some of these contextual acts result in the positioning of phenomena as non-religious, in Lois Lee's sense of being 'primarily understood in relation to religion' but not being 'considered to be religious' (2015: 32). However, in many of the discourses in the Southside – particularly *Living, Space and the Built Environment,* and *Social Identity* – 'non-religion' or 'the secular' were seemingly much less visible than religion. My data showed that we should not fall back on naïve notions of insubstantial secularity, non-religion, etc. (see Lee 2015: 49–69) but that the non-religious might be implicit in the subject position of those actors utilizing religion-related discourse, rather than explicitly articulated.

Moreover, in Chapter 5 I emphasized the importance and utility of moving from conceiving religion-related 'identities' as static categories and viewing them rather as acts of identification: as the contextual acts of positioning mentioned above. We saw in the Southside that religion-related identifications are characterized by 'indeterminism, incompletion, multiplicity and polyvalence' (Bayart 2005: 109), depending less on our perceived membership of a community or culture 'than with respect to the communities and cultures with which we have relations' (2005: 95). Identifying oneself or others as (non-) religious – or not – is a profoundly contextual discursive act, entangled in webs of discourses that are impacted by subjective, spatial, relational and conceptual factors. Some discourses, such as those surrounding the built environment, utility and heritage, were clearly entangled with the religion-related field, but this entanglement was relatively uncontroversial and peripheral to their central themes. In my presentation of these discourses, we do not really see a 'non-religious' position being constructed, adopted or spoken from. Seemingly, it is not so important to be 'non-religious' when confronted with 'banal religion'. However, other discourses, such as those on *Containment, Relationships,* and *Science and Meaning,* were entangled in a much more contentious and disruptive fashion. In these discourses, the religion-related field is invested with power, and this investment carries with it the potential for oppression and being oppressed. Here, the non-religious subject position becomes much more meaningful (as do all related positions). Each of these discourses involves contextually normative configurations of religion-related categories – such as religion and science as competing epistemological frameworks, or transmission of religion from parents to children – meaning that the discourses function by positioning phenomena relative to this standard model. Quite simply, being positioned as religious or non-religious means more in certain circumstances than it does in others. Thus I argue for a shift in approach from studying social actors *as* 'religious' or 'non-religious' to the ongoing process through which social actors 'manage that continually shifting set of similarities and differences that simultaneously unite/ estrange us to/from all others – thereby creating different selves and different identities' (McCutcheon 2017a: 157).

Third, in Chapter 7 I honed in on the critically problematic notion of 'indifference' to religion, beginning with a quotation from physician and science writer Ben Goldacre, in which he forcefully articulates a position of 'engaged indifferentism' (Lee 2014: 474). This perspective is problematic in that it is clearly related to both religion and non-religion yet involves the speaker positioning themselves in neither category. My analysis of religion-related discourse in the Southside suggested that, in some instances, the *performance* of indifference is a tactic for coping with contextually meaningful difference. In such cases, indifference can conceal positive and negative attitudes, particularly in the face of a dominant discourse of moderation. In the Southside, discourses of indifference are entangled with and mask the hegemony of Christianity and contribute to the maintenance of 'liberal secular principles' (Fitzgerald 2015b: 306). These conclusions combine to strengthen calls for studies of religion and non-religion to incorporate a range of positions which can act as productive means to further demystify the ideological functions of these categories in the academy and wider society.

Finally, my analysis demonstrated that the particular entanglements and configurations of discursive objects in the religion-related field are heavily influenced by 'local particularity' (T. Jenkins 1999: 77). Factors that were specific to the Southside – its post-Christian built environment, a semi-settled/transient population, the prevalence of convivial social interaction, the local versus external dynamic, etc. – were written into the structure of the religion-related discursive field, meaning that its influence extended beyond merely providing the discursive objects, the hooks on which to hang some independently existing discourses. This local particularity was also 'temporal particularity' in that the contemporary Southside attested to a number of discursive shifts from the time of the PEP, including the rise and fall of multiculturalism discourse, increasing state control of religion, greater visibility of critics of religion and a general cynicism surrounding entanglements of religion with power, capitalism and more. This leads to the conclusion that locality is 'more than a mere context or backdrop' (Knott 2009: 159) for the religion-related field but actively participates in its construction by affecting the agency of local inhabitants (Knott 2005: 129), resulting in specific 'religious' or 'non-religious' subject positions being taken up. An alternative methodological approach in another conceptual space would have produced a different map of the religion-related field. This further emphasizes the importance of being relentlessly self-conscious about the limits we have set on our vision and how these impact our conclusions.

   With these core conclusions in mind, how can we move forward with the study of non-religion and its place in contemporary Religious Studies?

Moving forward

A consistent theme throughout this book has been that the logics of research projects both limit the scope and influence the content of any conclusions that can be made. Indeed, one of my major critiques focused upon studies which are guided by questions on 'what it means to be' (non-)religious or secular, what (non-)religious people believe or how people answer the 'Big Questions' (Taves, Asprem and Ihm 2018). In Chapter 4, I argued that such studies, no matter their good intentions, are bound from the start to produce models of religion and non-religion which focus on the profound, the transcendent or the meaningful and are doomed to play into the hands of vested interests. Readers will also be aware that my own project is not immune to related critiques. Although I have tried to remain reflexive throughout, my conclusions are unavoidably limited by my project's discursive nature and by methodological factors.

By utilizing discourse and locality as my framework for approaching non-religion, I have left many potential aspects unexplored – including, but not limited to, material culture, psychology, cognition, ritual and embodiment – and could potentially be charged with producing quite an intellectualized account of the religion-related field. These limitations I fully acknowledge and hope that my work can be seen as one approach amongst many in the arsenal of the critical study of religion. That being said, it is worth emphasizing that discourse is 'a *social practice*' (Hjelm 2014a: 6, emphasis in original) in itself and that much of what my informants spoke about centred on identity formation, the built environment, embodiment, emotion and more. Thus, my study sits alongside and complements other studies focusing on these areas and provides a useful bridge for triangulation between different theoretical and methodological approaches.

From an intersectional perspective (see Chapter 1), it goes without saying that the discourses I have presented in this book were employed by the participants in each study. The interviewees in the PEP were selected as representatives of minority communities with links to homelands outside the UK. My own study prioritized individuals who were invested in the Southside, giving the discourses a somewhat different, but similarly 'celebratory' flavour. The contemporary interviews – although augmented by my Master's project amongst University of Edinburgh students – were skewed towards older Southsiders, meaning that some generational particularities might have been overlooked. Also, as discussed in Chapter 3, I did not have access to groups who could be described as marginalized in the Southside, meaning that social class is a factor that is largely absent from my analysis (on this, see C. G. Brown 2017). And despite speaking to almost as many women as I did men, gender – which, as we know, significantly impacts upon social actors' engagements with the religion-related field – remains largely absent in my analysis. Indeed, I cannot escape the charge that the very interviews I conducted were gendered, due to my own subject position as a white male and my privileged position as the interviewer.

Furthermore, the discourses that have been mapped in this book were not naturally occurring but were produced mainly in the context of interviews, and were thus influenced by my pragmatic pre-determination of topics likely to encourage religion-related discourse and the localized boundaries I constructed around the field. Much as in the PEP, interviewees were at times clearly being led by the interviewer, and it is clear from some responses that interviewees had not necessarily noticed things or thought about them (in relation to religion) before the interview. Also, the very genre of these conversations – formal interviews –

arguably led to the production of 'acceptable' discourses. Indeed, the fact that in the final months of writing up my doctoral dissertation I became embroiled in a heated argument in a Southside pub with some strangers who were loudly expressing anti-Muslim sentiments was a particularly stark reminder that the strategic discourse of moderation does not dominate in all Southside spaces. However, the discourses that I have mapped have not come from nowhere: even if the interviewees had not thought about issues before, or were mollifying their responses, they were still drawing on the religion-related discursive repertoire available to them in the Southside. Future research would undoubtedly benefit from bringing in a more focused ethnographic element, whether online or offline, in order to explore discourses which emerge in more anonymous settings or the kinds of statements individuals are more prone to use in social situations where they are more likely to feel comfortable or less guarded. Yet this study has also demonstrated the utility and analytical advantages of utilizing data sets such as the PEP, in which religion was not a central concern, with which the researcher was not directly involved and which can be more easily placed in historical context with the benefit of hindsight.

In this book, I have demonstrated that religion-related discourse is a discursive repertoire that has the potential to be activated to a variety of ends when social actors are confronted with related or entangled fields of discourse, regardless of their religion-related subject position. Indeed, this was precisely the reason that my study – although grounded in critical reflection and elaboration upon 'non-religion studies' – incorporated social actors from such a broad range of religion-related subject positions. Now that I have mapped some of the significant entanglements of the religion-related field and suggested that some might be entangled in such a manner as to make the positioning of phenomena as 'non-religious' more meaningful and indeed likely, future research might proceed with the intention of researching these entangled discourses, in order to map the other discursive repertoires that can be brought into play and, in the process, assess the relative significance of the religion-related field.

I have also further facilitated the academic recognition of the legitimate position of those in society who wish, for whatever reason, to distance themselves from religion, whilst simultaneously avoiding pigeon-holing (to our analytical disadvantage) social actors as definitively 'religious', 'non-religious', 'indifferent' and so on. This recognition ties in with a broader disciplinary acknowledgement that the identifications of social actors are fluid and complex. My approach blurs the boundary between religion and non-religion, demonstrating that they are dynamic subject positions, and phenomena can occupy both positions at the same time, or neither, depending on who is doing the positioning and what issues are at stake. By conceptualizing such acts of positioning discursively, we see that from moment to moment social actors are not necessarily operating with a coherent or fixed understanding of what religion is, nor are they necessarily invoking a discursive repertoire that relates to religion at all. Rather, they assign specific phenomena or encounters to particular fields of discourse (where 'religion' is one potential but not necessary field) and engage with them by negotiating a repertoire of contextually relevant entangled discourses. Understanding this is an important corrective to naïve ideal-typical approaches, particularly in public discourse, which deny the 'situational' (Stringer 2008) nature of religion-related discourse and its 'local particularity' (T. Jenkins 1999: 77).

I have argued forcefully for an approach that looks beyond the supposed 'religious' or 'non-religious' character of particular discourses. I have intentionally not taken a position on what 'non-religion' is, or claimed that anyone is 'non-religious', or that this would have any meaning in their day-to-day lives. What I have done is emphasize that religion exerts enormous power in certain contexts in contemporary society and that therefore certain positions are placed into conversation with religion and might contextually considered to be 'non-religious'. This approach avoids reifying 'religion' as in some way unique, whilst also fully incorporating religion-related subject positions – including the 'non-religious' – into the academic study of religion. Timothy Fitzgerald has criticized empirical studies of non-religion, stating that 'Surely the only topic here that makes sense as an object of study is the discourse [on "religion" and "non-religion"] itself?' (2015a: 264 fn. 22) This book has built a strong case for conducting empirical work ostensibly under the rubric of this binary but also with the explicit aim of contributing to Fitzgerald's critical project. It is my hope that it can act as a bridge between two increasingly entrenched positions in the contemporary study of religion-related phenomena – one that is interested in understanding 'religion in the real world' and the other in understanding the discursive processes by which that statement makes sense (Cotter et al. 2016: 98).

My friend and colleague David G. Robertson has recently found himself asking the question, 'Am I a Religious Studies Scholar?' He writes:

> As scholars we like to think that we simply become interested in certain things, but in truth we create and defend disciplines. And we do this to a large degree through what we deign to include in the category. Identifying something as (a) religion- with or without some qualifier like 'Indigenous' or 'New' stuck in front of it to remind us that it's not one of the Big Five – legitimizes it.… The

terminology which defines the field – if only implicitly – protects its members from criticism, makes the category a subject of which serious talk is permitted. So when we name our discipline as 'Religious Studies' and not, say, 'the bizarre ideas of some foreigners', we are constructing the very object that we ought to be committed to critiquing. (2017: 18)

I understand that my empirical interest in non-religion might be charged with a similar act of construction and reification. However, the preceding chapters of this volume should be enough to emphasize that I am in clear agreement with Robertson's sentiment. I no more want to construct non-religion as a substantial phenomenon than I wish to perpetuate the problematic category of 'religion', nor the mystifying 'industry known as religious studies' (Fitzgerald 2000b: 8), in which I have pitched my scholarly tent. The field is currently going through a transition, whereby the compound phrase 'religion and non-religion' is seeing increased deployment in calls for papers, the titles of conferences and panel sessions and in the titles of scholarly books (cf. J. L. Cox and Possamai 2016b). This has been a useful rhetorical move for the field and is testament to the growing body of scholarship in this area. However, my closing admonition is that it is now time for us to move on from this cumbersome phrasing and fully embrace the position whereby the critical study of 'religion' includes all phenomena which are discursively placed in a meaningful relationship of difference to this constructed category. Just as with its 'semantically parasitic' other (Fitzgerald 2007a: 52), and to adapt Jonathan Z. Smith's famous phrase, *there is no data for non-religion*. But provided we can remain 'relentlessly self-conscious' in our approach, this need not be a problem.

Appendix 1: 2014 interviewee demographics

	Gender	Age	Religion	Job	Nationality
Julian	M	65–74	Church of Scotland	(Former) Company Director	Scottish
Ivan	M	35–44	Agnostic/ (Former) Jehovah's Witness	Communications Officer	Scottish
Peter	M	65–74	(Former) Catholic	(Former) Professor	Polish
Richard	M	79	Quaker/ None	(Former) Technical Author	Scottish/ Italian
Ella	F	75	Catholic	(Former) Secretary	Scottish
Alastair & Moira	M & F	65–74	Church of Scotland	Postal Worker/Civil Servant	Scottish
David	M	25–34	Agnostic/ Atheist/ Catholic	Lecturer	English
Samantha & William	F & M	65–74	Episcopalian	Company Director/ Dentist	Scottish
Brenda	F	76	Agnostic	(Former) Teacher	English
Eileen	F	Mid-70s	Episcopalian	(Former) Nurse	Scottish
Fiona	F	55–64	Atheist	Teacher	Scottish
Aoife	F	25–34	Atheist/ Agnostic/ (Former) Church of England	Administration	English
Stacey	F	Mid-50s	Pagan/ Unaffiliated Christian	Therapist	English
Aisha	F	21	Muslim	Student	Scottish
Naomi	F	65–74	(Secular) Jew	Author	Scottish/ American
Keith	M	45	Non-religious	Pub Landlord	Scottish
John	M	55–64	Evangelical Christian	Church Leader/ Insurance Salesman	English

	Gender	Age	Religion	Job	Nationality
Amir	M	35–44	Muslim (Former Christian)	IT Consultant	Syrian
Sebastian	M	25–34	Buddhist	Software Developer	Scottish/German
Walter	M	55–64	Atheist	(Former) Insurance Broker	Scottish
Lily	F	64	Church of Scotland	IT	Scottish
Brian	M	61	Atheist	Business Owner/Lecturer	Australian
Fred	M	24	Atheist/Agnostic	Social Care	Scottish

Appendix 2: 2014 interview schedule

Basic demographics

- Age, Gender, Religion, Ethnicity, Nationality
- Job
- (Relationship to the Southside? Work, Home, Socializing, etc.)

Southside (**10 mins**)

- What is the Southside for you? What area of the city is that referring to? Street names, etc. What is your relationship to the Southside? How much do you know of the history, etc.?

Free Listing Exercise (emphasize not positive or negative)

- Characteristics of the Southside – e.g. my flat – cosy, bright, cluttered, book-laden, incense

Mapping Task

- (Regular) interactions with the Southside; most significant buildings; landmarks; eyesores; have you ever been in?

Photo elicitation 1 (Zoo, Al Raheem, Trypraying) (**10 mins**)

- How would you describe what is going on here? What do you think about that? How does that make you feel? What does that tell you about Edinburgh? Do you think that is typical for any Scottish city? Etc.

'Religion' (**20–25 mins**)

Free Listing Exercise (emphasize not positive or negative)

What is the first thing that comes to mind when I say the word 'religion'?

- For example, 'sport' – teams, competitive, watching in the pub, rules, uniforms, fans, danger, excitement, tribes
- Features, characteristics, emotions, experiences, etc. of (ideal) religion

Identification Exercise

Do you consider any of the following labels to apply to you? You can select multiple labels or none at all. Make some sort of mark, etc.

- Agnostic, Anglican, Atheist, Baha'i, Buddhist, Christian, Episcopalian, Evangelical, Freethinker, Hindu, Humanist, Jain, Jew, Materialist, Muslim, Orthodox, Non-religious, Pagan, Pentecostal, Presbyterian, Protestant, Rationalist, Religious, Roman Catholic, Sceptic, Secular, Secularist, Sikh, Spiritual, Spiritualist, Zoroastrian, Other (write in).

Follow-ups:

- How do you define them etc.? Are you a typical _____? How frequently, and in what situations, do you find yourself identifying with these labels? What about some of the others? What makes you a _____? What characteristics do you share with others?
- What does this term(s) *mean* to you? What use is it? Why do you identify with it? Could you rank them in order of importance? Where did the term come from?
- Are you a member of any institutions relating to these labels? Why (not)? Etc.
- Approximately when did you first start to identify with this term/these terms?
- Is this term/are these terms something which you share in common with your family? Has this always been the case? Role of aunts, uncles, grandparents? Differing 'effects' upon siblings? Movement away from home?
- Long-lasting friends, acquaintances: How many of them would also identify with this label/these labels? How important do you feel that these labels are in your choosing of friends? Have you ever lost a friend because of issues surrounding these and similar labels? How do you know someone is/isn't 'religious'?
- Thinking of all of these terms – Where do they come up in daily life? Where do you hear them?
- Make sure to bring up 'others' – spiritual, atheist, non-religious, Christian, religious …

- What do you put your faith in?
- What would you consider to be your most valuable beliefs?
- Are there any other similar terms that you …?

Religion and the Southside (**10 mins**)

Mapping Task

- Religion in the Southside; places typically ascribed with 'religious' or 'spiritual' significance; why; have you ever been in there, etc.
- How would you describe 'religion' in the Southside? Do you know much about it? Integration? Diverse? In your face?
- How do the various cards fit? Do you know others who identify with different labels? How would you describe the Southside? Could you do this exercise again but thinking about the Southside in general? Etc.

2011 Scottish Census religion question (**5 mins**)

Answer + Discuss

- Did you answer? Would you answer? Why do you think this question is on the census? Can you foresee any issues people may have with answering this?

Further photo elicitation task (**if time, 10 mins**)

Discuss what it was that I was looking for, etc.

Notes

Introduction

1 A peculiarly Scottish designation (J. L. Cox and Sutcliffe 2006).
2 Mohammed's narrative was recorded and made publicly available by the Lived Religion Project: http://livedreligionproject.com/because-im-brown-and-my-first-name-is-mohammed-im-still-a-victim-of-islamophobia-even-though-im-not-muslim (Accessed 22 April 2019).
3 https://edge.ua.edu/identity/ (Accessed 9 July 2018).
4 https://edge.ua.edu/identity/ (Accessed 9 July 2018).

Chapter 1

1 For example, Vernon (1968), Hadaway and Roof (1979), Tamney et al. (1989), Baker and Smith (2009a, b), Pasquale (2007), Voas (2009), Lim et al. (2010), Cragun et al. (2012) and Wallis (2014), among others.
2 For example, Bullivant (2008), Zuckerman (2010, 2011), Cotter (2011b, 2015), Catto and Eccles (2013), Chervallil-Contractor et al. (2013), Hassall and Bushfield (2014), Silver et al. (2014), Baker and Smith (2015), P. Beyer (2015), Eccles and Catto (2015), Lee (2015), Mann (2015), Manning (2015) and Zuckerman, Galen and Pasquale (2016), among others.
3 Towards, for example, notions of 'implicit religion' (Bailey 1998), believing without belonging (Davie 1994), or 'vicarious religion' (Davie 2007, 2008).
4 On the 'resurgence of religion' (Blanes and Oustinova-Stjepanovic 2015) see, for example, Berger (1999) on 'desecularization', Davie (2010) on 'resacralization' or Gane (2002) on 're-enchantment'.
5 See, for example, Hall (1997), Orsi (2005) or McGuire (2008).
6 See Fitzgerald (2007a: 38, 268, 296).
7 https://research.kent.ac.uk/understandingunbelief/events/current-events/cultures-of-unbelief/ (Accessed 22 April 2019).
8 https://nsrn.net/bibliography/ (Accessed 27 June 2019).
9 Despite the main title of their 2016 book being *The Nonreligious*, Zuckerman, Galen and Pasquale prefer the term 'secular' as a catch-all term for the phenomena that interest them. They acknowledge that the term is problematic in its scope, many

variants and ambiguity (2016: 18) but think that there are benefits to the 'wide net' cast by the term (2016: 21), at least in its adjectival form, by distinguishing between political, public, popular and personal forms (2016: 23). However, the sense of 'otherness' as opposed to 'overt differentiation' (2016: 18; cf. Lee 2015) implicit in most understandings of 'secular' – combined with my position within critical religious studies – make 'non-religion' a more workable rhetorical umbrella term for my work in this book.

10   https://www.ukpopulation.org/northern-ireland-population/ (Accessed 27 June 2019).

11   However, some recent research by BBC News Arabic might show that the tide is shifting. Using data from 25,000 respondents across 10 countries in the Middle East and North Africa, they conclude, 'Since 2013, the number of people across the region identifying as "not religious" has risen from 8 per cent to 13%. The rise is greatest in the under 30s, among whom 18 % identify as not religious, according to the research' (BBC News Online 2019).

12   https://www.ons.gov.uk/peoplepopulationandcommunity/culturalidentity/religion/ adhocs/009830religionbylocalauthoritygreatbritain2011to2018#main (Accessed 11 May 2019).

13   https://unitedchurchofbacon.org/our-beliefs/ (Accessed 10 June 2019).

14   https://www.sundayassembly.com/story (Accessed 12 June 2019).

15   Amsterdam Declaration of the World Humanist Congress (2002): http://www. plymouth-humanists.org.uk/index.php/amsterdam-declaration-2002 (Accessed 12 June 2019).

16   https://humanists.international/policy/iheu-minimum-statement-on-humanism/ (Accessed 12 June 2019).

17   https://www.ipsos.com/ipsos-mori/en-uk/humanist-beliefs (Accessed 12 June 2019).

18   https://humanism.org.uk/humanism/how-humanist-are-you/ (Accessed 12 June 2019).

19   The only exception was the sixth nation, China, where 7 per cent of 'agnostics' and 16 per cent of 'atheists' picked the label 'humanist'. This may have been due to translation issues.

20   For more on this, listen to Flynn and Coleman (2014).

21   https://www.civilsociety.co.uk/news/british-humanist-association-changes-its-name-to-humanists-uk.html#sthash.Tk1W6nXX.dpuf (Accessed 13 June 2019).

22   But see also Fitzgerald (2003, 2007a), Horii (2018) and Reader (2004).

Chapter 2

1   Although I have utilized the non-hyphenated 'nonreligion' in previous work, my current preference is to utilize 'non-religion' in order to emphasize the relational

nature of this category and that I do not wish to reify 'nonreligion' as a substantive phenomenon (see below). Where I cite the work of others, I shall preserve their preferred (non-)hyphenation.

2　There are, of course, a number of prominent sociological (Demerath and Thiessen 1966; Vernon 1968; Demerath 1969; Campbell 1971) and historical (Budd 1977; Thrower 1979, 1980, 2000; Berman 1988) exceptions to the rule.

3　It is important to note that, as we shall see below, multiple approaches can be taken within a single study.

4　I had originally referred to these approaches as 'radically contextual' until a reviewer kindly pointed out that radical contextualism has a particular meaning in cultural studies, exemplified in the work of Lawrence Grossberg. This reformulation suffices to get my meaning across without getting into unnecessary additional debates.

5　For a valiant attempt at this approach, readers are directed to Reza Gholami's excellent *Secularism and Identity: Non-Islamiosity in the Iranian Diaspora* (2015).

6　See references in Chapter 1 note 1.

7　See references in Chapter 1 note 2.

8　For more on this see, for example, J. Z. Smith (1978, 1998), McCutcheon (1997), Fitzgerald (2000b, 2007a, b), Masuzawa (2005), Nongbri (2013) and Cotter and Robertson (2016a).

9　See also Burr (1995: 2–5), Gergen (1999: 47–50) and Hjelm (2014a: 1–16).

10　With a few notable exceptions, for example Towler (1984).

11　Not unique to 'religion' of course, but to all concepts.

12　See Wijsen (2013) for a brief overview of Discourse Analysis in the contemporary study of religion.

13　See Bourdieu (1990, 1998) and Foucault (1979, 1989) for more on these concepts, which are secondary to my purpose at this point.

Chapter 3

1　Here, it is worth reiterating a point from the previous chapter. Lois Lee is my main interlocutor in the substantive study of non-religion, and whilst her work contains much of value in empirical and methodological material, and detailed attempts to theorize and provide a vocabulary for an emerging field of study, it is also problematic from a critical religion perspective.

2　See, for example, Engler (2011b), Enkvist and Nilson (2016), Olson et al. (2013) and Stausberg (2010).

3　I prefer 'orienting metaphor', 'framework' and so on over a prevalent alternative term – 'lens' – as this mitigates Craig Martin's valid criticism that lens 'invites us to consider objects of study as existing "out there" in the world, independently of our vision. On this view, things exist independently of our construction of them, and different theoretical lenses permit differently useful perspectives on those things' (2016: n.p.).

4   This summary draws significantly upon a previous publication (Cotter 2015: 173–4).

5   Other 'religious' and 'spiritual' phenomena have 'always' had a presence in Scotland (see S. J. Brown 2010: 138–42), but the narrative associated with hegemonic 'Christianity' suffices in this brief illustration.

6   See Chapter 1 for more on these ceremonies.

7   http://www.scotlandscensus.gov.uk/ods-web/standard-outputs.html (Accessed 29 September 2016).

8   Since 1583, but particularly since the late eighteenth and early nineteenth centuries (Anderson, Lynch and Phillipson 2003).

9   And perhaps even more recently. I happened to live directly opposite Archer's Hall in July 2016 and witnessed this event first-hand.

10 For example, the Young Greens, Scottish Nationalist Association, Humanist Society, Catholic Students Union and Yoga Society.

11 http://southsidecommunitycentre.co.uk/ (Accessed 29 September 2016).

12 http://www.edinburgh.gov.uk/directory_record/304093/nelson_hall_community_centre (Accessed 29 September 2016).

13 http://content.yudu.com/Library/A2t7ea/TheMeadowsDirectoryA/resources/index. htm?referrerUrl=http%3A%2F%2Fwww.themeadowsdirectory.com%2Flibrary, p. 36 (Accessed 29 September 2016).

14 http://www.thecausey.org/ (Accessed 29 September 2016).

15 http://www.edinburghnp.org.uk/neighbourhood-partnerships/south-central/ (Accessed 29 September 2016).

16 http://www.braidwoodcentre.org.uk/cms/ (Accessed 29 September 2016).

17 http://www.edinburgh.gov.uk/directory_record/304102/south_bridge_resource_centre (Accessed 29 September 2016).

18 This is a non-denominational Christian initiative, describing itself as 'for those who are not religious and don't do church'. One of the major outputs of this initiative is advertising on public buses around the UK with the simple slogan 'trypraying'. Support for this initiative is voluntary and on a church-by-church basis. Many of the churches in Edinburgh have supported this initiative financially and by placing similar banners outside their buildings. See http://www.trypraying.co.uk/ and http://www.thereishope.co.uk/for more information (Accessed 16 May 2015).

19 See Appendix 2 for my interview schedule.

20 NVivo is software that supports qualitative research and is particularly suited to the organization and analysis of unstructured data like interview transcripts. It provides a space to organize and manage material efficiently, as well as serving a secondary function as a transcription tool.

Chapter 4

1 The University of Edinburgh occupies a precarious place within the conversations I participated in, appearing at many points as an integral part of the Southside, a source of pride, history and connection to the area, and at others as a blight, destroying architectural heritage and encouraging an influx of transient, loud, dirty and disrespectful students.

2 See, for example, W. Brown et al. (2015), Commission on Integration and Cohesion (2007), Levey and Modood (2008), Modood (2007, 2014), Modood and May (2001), Valentine and Sadgrove (2013), Vertovec (2007), Wells and Watson (2005) and Wessendorf (2014a, b).

3 Similar analysis has been offered by Bruce (2014a: 119–35), Fitzgerald (2015a, b), Hjelm (2014b), C. Martin (2010), Modood (2007), Swain (2016) and others.

4 This notion is problematic for many reasons – particularly because it assumes an air of 'authentic' as opposed to the presumably inauthentic and 'dead' institutional or traditional forms of religion. Further, 'lived religion scholars… seldom accept without qualification the statements of participants in physically violent movements or activities that these scholars consider unacceptable' (Ramey 2015: 4).

5 See McCutcheon (2015) on 'the complete inverse'.

6 My use of 'The 4Ms' is not only a convenient designation but a direct play on 'The 3Ms', an ecumenical church grouping in Marchmont, Morningside and Merchiston. These are three districts in Edinburgh that are on the periphery of what would generally be considered 'the Southside', and the grouping is roughly analogous to 'Newington Churches Together', which performs a similar role at the centre of the Southside.

7 Vincett and Olson also found these topics organically coming to the fore in their interviews with young people in Glasgow (2012: 199).

8 See Hervieu-Léger (see 2000: 17, 99–100), Harrison (2010) and Burnett (2012).

9 It is worth noting that many of these references were to humanist funerals. In some instances, the only mention of funerals and death was when the term 'humanism' was specifically discussed. This term itself was generally conceptualized first and foremost in relation to funerals and weddings, and in most cases little else (see, for example, Copeman and Quack 2015; Engelke 2015a).

10 An argument could certainly be made for also including the fifth type ('familial') under this heading.

Chapter 5

1 Where '…' has been inserted in this paragraph, it is indicative of redacted affirmations such as 'Yeah' and 'Mmm' from the interviewer, which were unnecessary obstructions to the flow of Naomi's narrative in this context.

2   See Stark and Bainbridge (1985, 1987) and Stark and Finke (2000).

3   See Chapter 7 for a detailed discussion on 'strategies' and 'tactics' (de Certeau 1984).

4   See also Beekers and Tamimi Arab on the Fatih Mosque in Amsterdam and the hopes of some that it would join the ranks alongside other 'important symbols with regard to dominant narratives about Dutch identity' (2016: 157).

5   See also Gale (2004) on Birmingham, UK.

6   See also, Cotter (2015: 185–6).

7   To coincide with the *Edinburgh International Festival*, *Edinburgh Festival Fringe* and other festivals that take place in the city in August, the Central Mosque runs an *Islam Festival*, with an exhibition, events and activities each year.

8   See, for example, Barth (1998: 31–2) on majority-minority dynamics in social interactions between different ethnic groups, or Vassenden and Andersson on the contextual 'faith information control' possessed by an individual 'in regard to how s/he is, and whether or not s/he wants to be, seen as religious' and its relationship to whiteness/non-whiteness in Grønland, Oslo (2011: 577 ff.).

Chapter 6

1   Indeed, this question wasn't asked on the census at the time of publication.

2   The Appleton Tower is one of the University of Edinburgh's most prominent buildings in the Southside and a prime example of 1960s post-war architecture. It is widely renowned as the university's 'ugliest' building (*Edinburgh Evening News* 2015) and tied to an embarrassingly premature demolition of tenements on Crichton Street and Marshall Street, which, due to lack of funds, resulted in a large 'gap site' for over forty years (Fenton 2002).

3   At the intersection of Hope Park Terrace, Melville Drive and Summerhall Crescent. See http://www.ed.ac.uk/vet/about/history and Wright (2011: 23).

4   http://www.tjc.us/library/DetailLibrary.aspx?langid=1&itemid=12702 (Accessed 20 September 2015).

Chapter 7

1   https://www.collinsdictionary.com/dictionary/english-thesaurus/indifference?show CookiePolicy=true (Accessed 26 March 2019).

2   Here, and in the following section, I am drawing heavily upon Cotter (2017a: 51–5).

3   See Cotter (2017a: 52–4) for extended introductions to these individuals.

4   This is, as Knott, Poole and Taira argue, a relatively recent development, as back in the early 1980s 'atheism and secularism … were not seen as a threat or enemy of the Churches' (2013: 169).

5   See discourses on *Living* in Chapter 4.

6   See also Gilroy (2004), Knott (2015), Watson (2006),Wessendorf (2014a, b), Wise and Velayutham (2014) and others.

7   See BBC News Online (2014).

8   See Baumann (1996) for more on 'dominant' versus 'demotic' discourses.

9   And we must remember that my sampling technique involved finding informants who were invested in the Southside in some way.

References

Academy of Social Sciences. (2016), 'No Religion Steadily Becoming Norm in UK Society, Says Leading Academic'. *Campaign for Social Science* (blog). 22 July. https://campaignforsocialscience.org.uk/news/no-religion-steadily-becoming-norm-uk-society-says-academic/.

Adams, D. (1982), *Life, the Universe and Everything*. London: Pan Books.

Alexander, N. G. (2019), *Race in a Godless World: Atheism, Race, and Civilization 1850–1914*. Manchester: Manchester University Press.

Amarasingam, A. (2010), 'To Err in Their Ways: The Attribution Biases of the New Atheists', *Studies in Religion/Sciences Religieuses* 39 (4): 573–88.

Ambasciano, L. (2018), *An Unnatural History of Religions: Academia, Post-Truth, and the Quest for Scientific Knowledge*. London: Bloomsbury.

Amin, A. (2006), 'Collective Culture and Urban Public Space'. *Public Space* (blog). http://www.publicspace.org/en/text-library/eng/b003-collective-culture-and-urban-public-space.

Ammerman, N. T. (2007), 'Introduction: Observing Religious Modern Lives', in N. T. Ammerman (ed.), *Everyday Religion: Observing Modern Religious Lives*, 3–19. Oxford: Oxford University Press.

Anderson, R. D., M. Lynch and N. Phillipson (2003), *The University of Edinburgh: An Illustrated History*. Edinburgh: Edinburgh University Press.

Anttonen, V. (2000), 'Sacred', in W. Braun and R. T. McCutcheon (eds), *Guide to the Study of Religion*, 271–82. London: Cassell.

Arnal, W. E., and R. T. McCutcheon (2012), 'Introduction: On the Persistence of Imagining Religion', in W. E. Arnal and R. T. McCutcheon, *The Sacred Is the Profane: The Political Nature of 'Religion'*, 1–16. Oxford: Oxford University Press.

Arweck, E., and E. Nesbitt (2010), 'Plurality at Close Quarters: Mixed-Faith Families in the UK', *Journal of Religion in Europe* 3: 155–82.

Asad, T. (1993), *Genealogies of Religion: Discipline and Reasons of Power in Christianity and Islam*. Baltimore and London: Johns Hopkins University Press.

Asad, T. (2002), 'The Construction of Religion as an Anthropological Category', in M. Lambeck (ed.), *A Reader in the Anthropology of Religion*, 114–32. Oxford: Blackwell.

Asad, T. (2003), *Formations of the Secular: Christianity, Islam, Modernity*. Stanford, CA: Stanford University Press.

Aston, K. (2015), 'Making Nonreligious Matter: Mapping Non-Religious Semiotics, Ceremony and Media in the UK', Unpublished PhD Thesis. London: Goldsmiths, University of London.

Atkinson, R., and J. Flint (2001), 'Accessing Hidden and Hard-to-Reach Populations: Snowball Research Strategies', *Social Research Update* 33. http://sru.soc.surrey.ac.uk/SRU33.pdf.

Bagg, S., and D. Voas (2010), 'The Triumph of Indifference: Irreligion in British Society', in P. Zuckerman (ed.), *Atheism and Secularity – Volume 2: Global Expressions*, 91–111. Santa Barbara: Praeger.

Baggini, J. (2003), *Atheism: A Very Short Introduction*. Oxford: Oxford University Press.

Bailey, E. (1998), *Implicit Religion: An Introduction*. London: Middlesex University Press.

Baird, R. D. (1991), *Category Formation and the History of Religions*. Berlin: Mouton de Gruyter.

Baker, J. O., and B. G. Smith (2009a), 'The Nones: Social Characteristics of the Religiously Unaffiliated', *Social Forces* 87 (3): 1251–63.

Baker, J. O., and B. G. Smith (2009b), 'None Too Simple: Examining Issues of Religious Nonbelief and Nonbelonging in the United States', *Journal for the Scientific Study of Religion* 48 (4): 719–33.

Baker, J. O., and B. G. Smith (2015), *American Secularism: Cultural Contours of Nonreligious Belief Systems*. New York and London: New York University Press.

Banks, M. (2001), *Visual Methods in Social Research*. London: Sage.

Barker, E. (2010), 'The Church without and the God within: Religiosity and/or Spirituality?' in E. Barker (ed.), *The Centrality of Religion in Social Life: Essays in Honour of James A. Beckford*, 187–202. Farnham: Ashgate.

Barth, F. (1998), 'Introduction', in F. Barth (ed.), *Ethnic Groups and Boundaries: The Social Organization of Culture Difference*, 9–38. Long Grove, IL: Waveland Press.

Baumann, G. (1996), *Contesting Culture: Discourses of Identity in Multi-Ethnic London*. Cambridge: Cambridge University Press.

Bayart, J. (2005), *The Illusion of Cultural Identity*. London: Hurst Publishers.

BBC News Online. (2014), 'PM's Christianity Remarks "Divisive"'. *BBC News* (blog). 21 April. http://www.bbc.co.uk/news/uk-27099700.

BBC News Online. (2019), 'Are Arabs Turning Their Backs on Religion?' *BBC News* (blog). 24 June. https://www.bbc.com/news/world-middle-east-48703377.

Beckford, James A. (1999), 'The Politics of Defining Religion in Secular Society: From a Taken for Granted Institution to a Contested Resource', in Jan G. Platvoet and Arie L. Molendijk (eds), *The Pragmatics of Defining Religion: Contexts, Concepts and Contests*, 23–40. Leiden: Brill.

Beckford, J. A. (2003), *Social Theory and Religion*. Cambridge: Cambridge University Press.

Beekers, D., and P. Tamimi Arab (2016), 'Dreams of an Iconic Mosque: Spatial and Temporal Entanglements of a Converted Church in Amsterdam', *Material Religion* 12 (2): 137–64.

Benavides, G. (2003), 'There Is Data for Religion', *Journal of the American Academy of Religion* 71 (4): 895–903.

Bender, C. (2012), 'Practicing Religions', in R. A. Orsi (ed.), *The Cambridge Companion to Religious Studies*, 273–95. New York: Cambridge University Press.

Beredjick, C. (2017), *Queer Disbelief: Why LGBTQ Equality Is an Atheist Issue*. Kindle Edition. Friendly Atheist Press.

Berger, Peter, and Thomas Luckmann (1966). *The Social Construction of Reality: A Treatise in the Sociology of Knowledge*. Garden City: Anchor Books.

Berger, P., ed. (1999), *The Desecularization of the World*. Grand Rapids, MI: W.B. Eerdmans.

Berman, D. (1988), *A History of Atheism in Britain: From Hobbes to Russell*. London: Croom Helm.

Beyer, J. (2009), 'The Land of Sweets'. *Scottish Memories*, April.

Beyer, P. (2015), 'From Atheist to Spiritual but Not Religious: A Punctuated Continuum of Identities Among the Second Generation of Post-1970 Immigrants in Canada', in L. G. Beaman and S. Tomlins (eds), *Atheist Identities – Spaces and Social Contexts*, 137–51. Dordrecht: Springer.

Bird, F., and L. Lamoureux Scholes (2011), 'Research Ethics', in M. Stausberg and S. Engler (eds), *The Routledge Handbook of Research Methods in the Study of Religion*, 81–105. London: Routledge.

Blanes, R. L., and G. Oustinova-Stjepanovic (2015), 'Introduction: Godless People, Doubt, and Atheism', *Social Analysis* 59 (2): 1–19.

Blankholm, J. (2014), 'The Political Advantages of a Polysemous Secular', *Journal for the Scientific Study of Religion* 53 (4): 775–90.

Blankholm, J. (2017), 'The Limits of Religious Indifference', in J. Quack and C. Schuh (eds), *Religious Indifference: New Perspectives from Studies on Secularization and Nonreligion*, 239–58. Dordrecht: Springer.

Blommaert, J. (2011), *Discourse: A Critical Introduction*. Cambridge: Cambridge University Press.

Blommaert, J. (2013), *Ethnography, Superdiversity and Linguistic Landscapes: Chronicles of Complexity*. First Edition. Bristol, Buffalo and Toronto: Multilingual Matters.

Blommaert, J. (2014), 'Lingua Franca Onset in a Superdiverse Neighborhood: Oecumenical Dutch in Antwerp', *Tilburg Papers in Culture Studies* 112 (October): 1–22.

Blommaert, J., J. Collins and S. Slembrouck (2005), 'Polycentricity and Interactional Regimes in "Global Neighborhoods"', *Ethnography* 6: 205–35.

Bluck, R., S. Gilliat-Ray, D. J. Graham, G. Singh, J. Zavos and L. Woodhead (2012), 'Judaism, Sikhism, Islam, Hinduism and Buddhism', in L. Woodhead and R. Catto (eds), *Religion and Change in Modern Britain*, 85–149. London: Routledge.

Bonney, N. (2013a), 'Established Religion, Parliamentary Devolution and New State Religion in the United Kingdom', *Parliamentary Affairs* 66: 425–42.

Bonney, N. (2013b), 'Proportional Prayers: Time for Reflection in the Scottish Parliament', *Parliamentary Affairs* 66: 816–33.

Borowik, I., B. Ančić and R. Tyraľa (2013), 'Central and Eastern Europe', in S. Bullivant and M. Ruse (eds), *The Oxford Handbook of Atheism*, 622–37. New York: Oxford University Press.

Bourdieu, P. (1990), *The Logics of Practice*. Stanford, CA: Stanford University Press.

Bourdieu, P. (1998), *Practical Reason*. Cambridge: Polity Press.

Bowen, D. (2015), 'The Economics of Morality'. *Practical Ethics: Ethics in the News* (blog). 4 March. http://blog.practicalethics.ox.ac.uk/2015/03/the-oxford-uehiro-prize-in-practical-ethics-the-economics-of-morality-by-dillon-bowen/.

Bowler, K. (2013), *Blessed: A History of the American Prosperity Gospel*. Oxford: Oxford University Press.

Bréchon, P. (2017), 'Measuring Religious Indifference in International Sociological Quantitative Surveys (EVS and ISSP)', in J. Quack and C. Schuh (eds), *Religious Indifference: New Perspectives from Studies on Secularization and Nonreligion*, 143–70. Dordrecht: Springer.

Breen, R. L. (2006), 'A Practical Guide to Focus-Group Research', *Journal of Geography in Higher Education* 30 (3): 463–75.

Bremmer, J. N. (2007), 'Atheism in Antiquity', in M. Martin (ed.), *The Cambridge Companion to Atheism*, 11–26. Cambridge: Cambridge University Press.

Brewster, M. E. (2013), 'Atheism, Gender, and Sexuality', in S. Bullivant and M. Ruse (eds), *The Oxford Handbook of Atheism*, 511–24. Oxford: Oxford University Press.

Brierley, P. (1989), *A Century of British Christianity*. London: MARC Europe.

Brierley, P. (2006), *Pulling out of the Nose Dive: A Contemporary Picture of Churchgoing; What the 2005 English Church Census Reveals*. London: Christian Research.

Brighton, S. (2007), 'British Muslims, Multiculturalism and UK Foreign Policy: "Integration" and "Cohesion" in and Beyond the State', *International Affairs (Royal Institute of International Affairs 1944–83)* (1): 1–17.

Brown, C. G. (1992), 'Religion and Secularisation', in T. Dickson and J. H. Treble (eds), *People and Society in Scotland* III: *1914–1990*, 48–79. Edinburgh: John Donald.

Brown, C. G. (2000), *The Death of Christian Britain: Understanding Secularisation, 1800–2000*. Christianity and Society in the Modern World. London: Routledge.

Brown, C. G. (2017), *Becoming Atheist: Humanism and the Secular West*. London: Bloomsbury Academic.

Brown, C. G, and G. Lynch (2012), 'Cultural Perspectives', in L. Woodhead and R. Catto (eds), *Religion and Change in Modern Britain*, 329–51. London: Routledge.

Brown, S. J. (2010), 'Beliefs and Religions', in T. Griffiths and G. Morton (eds), *A History of Everyday Life in Scotland, 1800 to 1900*, 116–46. Edinburgh: Edinburgh University Press.

Brown, W., J. Dobbernack, T. Modood, G. Newey, A. F. March, L. Tønder and R. Forst (2015), 'What Is Important in Theorizing Tolerance Today?' *Contemporary Political Theory* 14 (2): 159–96.

Bruce, S. (1995), *Religion in Modern Britain*. Oxford: Oxford University Press.

Bruce, S. (1996), *Religion in the Modern World: From Cathedrals to Cults*. Oxford: Oxford University Press.

Bruce, S. (2002), *God Is Dead: Secularisation in the West*. Oxford: Blackwell.

Bruce, S. (2009), 'The Importance of Social Science in the Study of Religion', *Fieldwork in Religion* 4 (1): 7–28.

Bruce, S. (2011), *Secularization: In Defence of an Unfashionable Theory*. Oxford: Oxford University Press.

Bruce, S. (2013), 'Post-Secularity and Religion in Britain: An Empirical Assessment', *Journal of Contemporary Religion* 28 (3): 369–84.

Bruce, S. (2014a), *Scottish Gods: Religion in Modern Scotland 1900–2012*. First Edition. Edinburgh: Edinburgh University Press.

Bruce, S. (2014b), 'Late Secularization and Religion as Alien', *Open Theology* 1 (1): 13–23.

Bruce, S., T. Glendinning, I. Paterson and M. Rosie (2004), *Sectarianism in Scotland*. Edinburgh: Edinburgh University Press.

Bryant, A. N. (2006), 'Exploring Religious Pluralism in Higher Education: Non-Majority Religious Perspectives Among Entering First-Year College Students', *Religion & Education* 33 (1): 1–25.

Buckley, M. J. (1987), *At the Origins of Modern Atheism*. New Haven: Yale University Press.

Budd, S. (1977), *Varieties of Unbelief: Atheists and Agnostics in English Society 1850–1960*. London: Heinemann.

Bullivant, S. (2008), 'Introducing Irreligious Experiences', *Implicit Religion* 11 (1): 7–24.

Bullivant, S. (2012), 'Not so Indifferent After All? Self-Conscious Atheism and the Secularisation Thesis', *Approaching Religion* 2 (1): 100–6.

Bullivant, S. (2013), 'Defining "Atheism"', in S. Bullivant and M. Ruse (eds), *The Oxford Handbook of Atheism*, 11–21. New York: Oxford University Press.

Bullivant, S. (2016), 'Catholic Disaffiliation in Britain: A Quantitative Overview', *Journal of Contemporary Religion* 31 (2): 181–97.

Bullivant, S. (2017), 'The "No Religion" Population of Britain: Recent Data from the British Social Attitudes Survey (2015) and the European Social Survey (2014)'. 3. Catholic Research Forum Reports. London: St Mary's University, Twickenham. https://www.stmarys.ac.uk/research/centres/benedict-xvi/no-religion-population.aspx.

Bullivant, S., and L. Lee (2012), 'Interdisciplinary Studies of Non-Religion and Secularity: The State of the Union', *Journal of Contemporary Religion* 27 (1): 19–27.

Bullivant, S., M. Farias, J. Lanman and L. Lee (2019), *Understanding Unbelief: Atheists and Aghostics Around the World*. London: St Mary's University, Twickenham.

Bullock, J. (2017), 'The Sociology of the Sunday Assembly: "Belonging Without Believing" in a Post-Christian Context', Unpublished PhD Thesis. London: Kingston University.

Burchardt, M. (2017), 'Is Religious Indiffernce Bad for Secularism? Lessons from Canada', in J. Quack and C. Schuh (eds), *Religious Indifference: New Perspectives from Studies on Secularization and Nonreligion*, 83–99. Dordrecht: Springer.

Burnett, T. (2012), 'What Is Scientism?' *AAAS* (blog). 2012. http://www.aaas.org/page/
    what-scientism.
Burr, V. (1995), *An Introduction to Social Constructionism*. London: Routledge.
Cady, L., and T. Fessenden (2013), 'Gendering the Divide: Relgion, the Secular, and the
    Politics of Sexual Difference', in L. Cady and T. Fessenden (eds), *Religion, the Secular,
    and the Politics of Sexual Difference*, 3–24. New York: Columbia University Press.
Cameron, C. (2019), *Black Freethinkers: A History of African American Secularism*.
    Evanston, IL: Northwestern University Press.
Campbell, C. (1971), *Toward a Sociology of Irreligion*. London: Macmillan.
Caporale, R., and A. Grumelli, eds (1971), *The Culture of Unbelief: Studies and
    Proceedings from the First International Symposium on Belief Held at Rome, March
    22–27, 1969*. Berkeley: University of California Press.
Casanova, J. (2009), 'Immigration and the New Religious Pluralism: European
    Union-United States Comparison', in G. Brahm Levey and T. Modood (eds),
    Secularism, Religion and Multicultural Citizenship, 139–63. Cambridge: Cambridge
    University Press.
Catto, R. (2017), 'Interfaith Dialogue and the Challenge of Indifference: Reflections
    from Fieldwork in the City of Peace and Reconciliation', in J. Quack and C. Schuh
    (eds), *Religious Indifference: New Perspectives from Studies on Secularization and
    Nonreligion*, 65–82. Dordrecht: Springer.
Catto, R., and J. Eccles (2013), '(Dis)Believing and Belonging: Investigating the
    Narratives of Young British Atheists', *Temenos* 49 (1): 37–63.
Cavanaugh, W. T. (2009), *The Myth of Religious Violence: Secular Ideology and the Roots
    of Modern Conflict*. New York: Oxford University Press.
Certeau, M. de. (1984), *The Practice of Everyday Life*. S. F. Rendall (trans.). Berkeley:
    University of California Press.
Cheruvallil-Contractor, S., T. Hooley, N. Moore, K. Purdam and P. Weller (2013),
    'Researching the Non-Religious: Methods and Methodological Issues, Challenges
    and Controversies', in A. Day, G. Vincett and C. R. Cotter (eds), *Social Identities
    Between the Sacred and the Secular*, 173–89. Farnham: Ashgate.
Chimienti, M., and I. van Liempt (2015), 'Super-Diversity and the Art of Living in
    Ethnically Concentrated Urban Areas', *Identities* 22 (1): 19–35.
Cimino, R., and C. Smith (2007), 'Secular Humanism and Atheism Beyond Progressive
    Secularism', *Sociology of Religion* 68 (4): 407–24.
Cimino, R., and C. Smith (2010), 'The New Atheism and the Empowerment of
    American Freethinkers', in A. Amarasingam (ed.), *Religion and the New Atheism:
    A Critical Appraisal*, 139–56. Leiden and Boston: Brill.
Cimino, R., and C. Smith (2015), 'Secularist Rituals in the US: Solidarity and
    Legitimization', in L. G. Beaman and S. Tomlins (eds), *Atheist Identities – Spaces and
    Social Contexts*, 87–100. Dordrecht: Springer.
City of Edinburgh Council (1996), *Peoples of Edinburgh: Methodology and Evaluation*.
    Edinburgh: City of Edinburgh Council.

Clements, B. (2012), 'Research Note: The Sources of Public Feelings Towards Religious Groups in Britain: The Role of Social Factors, Religious Characteristics, and Political Attitudes', *Journal of Contemporary Religion* 27 (3): 419–31.

Clements, B. (2015), *Religion and Public Opinion in Britain*. Basingstoke: Palgrave Macmillan.

Coleman, T. J. III, C. F. Silver and J. M. Holcombe (2013), 'Focusing on Horizontal Transcendence: Much More Than "Non-Belief"', *Essays in the Philosophy of Humanism* 21 (2): 1–18.

Commission on Integration and Cohesion. (2007), 'Our Shared Future: Final Report of the Commission on Integration and Cohesion'. Commission on Integration and Cohesion. http://resources.cohesioninstitute.org.uk/Publications/Documents/Document/Default.aspx?recordId=18.

Commission on Religious Education. (2018), *Religion and Worldviews: The Way Forward*. London: Religious Education Council of England and Wales. https://www.commissiononre.org.uk/wp-content/uploads/2018/09/Final-Report-of-the-Commission-on-RE.pdf.

Conrad, N. G. (2018), 'An Argument for Unbelief: A Discussion About Terminology', *Secularism and Nonreligion* 7 (11): 1–8.

Copeman, J., and J. Quack (2015), 'Godless People and Dead Bodies: Materiality and the Morality of Atheist Materialism', *Social Analysis* 59 (2): 40–61.

Copson, A. (2015), 'What Is Humanism?' in A. Copson and A. C. Grayling (eds), *The Wiley Blackwell Handbook of Humanism*, 1–33. Chichester: John Wiley & Sons, Ltd.

Copson, A. (2019), 'Opinion: It's Time We Made Humanist Marriages Available to All'. *The Independent*. 11 March. https://www.independent.co.uk/voices/humanist-wedding-marriage-divorce-england-wales-scotland-a8817851.html.

Cornwell, E. Y., and L. J. Waite (2009), 'Social Disconnectedness, Perceived Isolation, and Health Among Older Adults', *Journal of Health and Social Behavior* 50 (1): 31–48.

Costa, N. da. (2017), 'Creencia e Increencia Desde Las Vivencias Cotidianas. Una Mirada Desde Uruguay', *Estudos de Religi˜ao* 31 (3): 33–53.

Cotter, C. R. (2011a), 'Consciousness Raising: The Critique, Agenda, and Inherent Precariousness of Contemporary Anglophone Atheism', *International Journal for the Study of New Religions* 2 (1): 77–103.

Cotter, C. R. (2011b), 'Toward a Typology of "Nonreligion": A Qualitative Analysis of Everyday Narratives of Scottish University Students'. Unpublished MSc by Research Dissertation, Edinburgh: University of Edinburgh. http://www.academia.edu/1329691/Toward_a_Typology_of_Nonreligion_A_Qualitative_Analysis_of_Everyday_Narratives_of_Scottish_University_Students.

Cotter, C. R. (2012), 'Secular Sacreds and the Sacred Secular'. *The Religious Studies Project*. November. http://www.religiousstudiesproject.com/2012/11/07/christopher-r-cotter-secular-sacreds/.

Cotter, C. R. (2015), 'Without God yet Not Without Nuance: A Qualitative Study of Atheism and Non-Religion Among Scottish University Students', in L. G. Beaman and S. Tomlins (eds), *Atheist Identities – Spaces and Social Contexts*, 171–94. Dordrecht: Springer.

Cotter, C. R. (2016), 'Religion-Related Discourse: A Critical Approach to Non-Religion in Edinburgh's Southside'. Unpublished PhD Thesis. Lancaster: Lancaster University. http://eprints.lancs.ac.uk/85489/.

Cotter, C. R. (2017a), 'A Discursive Approach to "Religious Indifference": Critical Reflections from Edinburgh's Southside', in J. Quack and C. Schuh (eds), *Religious Indifference: New Perspectives from Studies on Secularization and Nonreligion*, 43–63. Dordrecht: Springer.

Cotter, C. R. (2017b), 'New Atheism, Open-Mindedness, and Critical Thinking', in C. R. Cotter, P. Quadrio and J. Tuckett (eds), *New Atheism: Critical Perspectives and Contemporary Debates*, 33–50. Dordrecht: Springer.

Cotter, C. R. (2017c), 'You're Greek? Well … I'm (Northern) Irish, Kind'a', in R. T. McCutcheon (ed.), *Fabricating Identities*, 34–41. Sheffield: Equinox.

Cotter, C. R., and D. G. Robertson, eds. (2016a), *After World Religions: Reconstructing Religious Studies*. London: Routledge.

Cotter, C. R., and D. G. Robertson (2016b), 'Introduction: The World Religions Paradigm in Contemporary Religious Studies', in C. R. Cotter and D. G. Robertson (eds), *After World Religions: Reconstructing Religious Studies*, 1–20. Abingdon and New York: Routledge.

Cotter, C. R., and I. Alderman (2018), 'What if We Stopped Fanning the Flames?' *Sinai and Synapses* (blog). 18 October. https://sinaiandsynapses.org/multimedia-archive/what-if-we-stopped-fanning-the-flames/.

Cotter, C. R., R. Aechtner and J. Quack (2012), *Non-Religiosity, Identity, and Ritual Panel Session*. Hungarian Culture Foundation, Budapest, Hungary: NSRN. http://nsrn.net/1523-2/.

Cotter, C. R., P. Quadrio and J. Tuckett (2017), 'Introduction', in C. R. Cotter, P. Quadrio and J. Tuckett (eds) *New Atheism: Critical Perspectives and Contemporary Debates*, 1–13. Dordrecht: Springer.

Cotter, C. R., G. Davie, J. A. Beckford, S. Chattoo, M. Lövheim, M. A. Vásquez and A. Day (2016), 'An Author Meets Her Critics: Around Abby Day's Believing in Belonging', *Religion and Society: Advances in Research* 7: 97–115.

Cox, D., and R. P. Jones (2017), 'America's Changing Religious Identity'. *PRRI* (blog). 9 June. https://www.prri.org/research/american-religious-landscape-christian-religiously-unaffiliated/.

Cox, J. L. (2006), *A Guide to the Phenomenology of Religion: Key Figures, Formative Influences and Subsequent Debates*. London: Continuum.

Cox, J. L. (2016), 'The Study of Religion and Non-Religion in the Emerging Field of Non-Religion Studies: Its Significance for Interpreting Australian Aboriginal Religions', in J. L. Cox and A. Possamai (eds), *Religion and Non-Religion Among Australian Aboriginal Peoples*, 25–43. London and New York: Routledge.

Cox, J. L., and A. Possamai (2016a), 'Introduction: The Australian Census, Religious Diversity and the Religious Nones Among Indigenous Australians', in J. L. Cox and A. Possamai (eds), *Religion and Non-Religion Among Australian Aboriginal Peoples*, 3–23. London and New York: Routledge.

Cox, J. L., and A. Possamai, eds (2016b), *Religion and Non-Religion Among Australian Aboriginal Peoples*. London and New York: Routledge.

Cox, J. L., and S. Sutcliffe (2006), 'Religious Studies in Scotland: A Persistent Tension with Divinity', *Religion* 20: 1–28.

Cragun, R. T. (2015), 'Who Are the "New Atheists"?' in L. G. Beaman and S. Tomlins (eds), *Atheist Identities – Spaces and Social Contexts*, 195–211. Dordrecht: Springer

Cragun, R. T., and J. H. Hammer (2011), '"One Person's Apostate Is Another Person's Convert": What Terminology Tells Us About Pro-Religious Hegemony in the Sociology of Religion', *Humanity and Society* 35: 159–75.

Cragun, R. T., and J. E. Sumerau (2017), 'No One Expects a Transgender Jew: Religious, Sexual and Gendered Intersections in the Evaluation of Religious and Nonreligious Others', *Secularism and Nonreligion* 6 (1): 1–16.

Cragun, R. T., B. A. Kosmin, A. Keysar, J. H. Hammer and M. Nielsen (2012), 'On the Receiving End: Discrimination Toward the Non-Religious in the United States', *Journal of Contemporary Religion* 27 (1): 105–27.

Crystal, D., ed. (1990), 'Humanism', in *The Cambridge Encyclopaedia*. Cambridge: Cambridge University Press.

Dahl, V., E. Amnå, S. Banaji, M. Landberg, J. Šerek, N. Ribeiro, M. Beilmann, V. Pavlopoulos and B. Zani (2018), 'Apathy or Alienation? Political Passivity Among Youths Across Eight European Union Countries', *European Journal of Developmental Psychology* 15 (3): 284–301.

Daiches, D. (2001), *Two Worlds: An Edinburgh Jewish Childhood and Promised Lands: A Portrait of My Father*. Edinburgh: Canongate Classics.

Dalferth, I. U. (2010), 'Post-Secular Society: Christianity and the Dialectics of the Secular', *Journal of the American Academy of Religion* 78 (2): 317–45.

Dalton, D. R., J. C. Wimbush and C. M. Daily (1994), 'Using the Unmatched Count Technique (Uct) to Estimate Base Rates for Sensitive Behavior', *Personnel Psychology* 47 (4): 817–29.

Dassonneville, R., and M. Hooghe (2018), 'Indifference and Alienation: Diverging Dimensions of Electoral Dealignment in Europe', *Acta Politica* 53 (1): 1–23.

Davie, G. (1994), *Religion in Britain Since 1945: Believing Without Belonging*. Oxford: Blackwell.

Davie, G. (2000a), 'Religion in Modern Britain: Changing Sociological Assumptions', *Sociology* 34 (1): 113–28.

Davie, G. (2000b), *Religion in Modern Europe: A Memory Mutates*. Oxford: Oxford University Press.

Davie, G. (2007), 'Vicarious Religion: A Methodological Challenge', in N. T. Ammerman (ed.), *Everyday Religion: Observing Modern Religious Lives*, 21–36. Oxford and New York: Oxford University Press.

Davie, G. (2008), 'From Believing Without Belonging to Vicarious Religion: Understanding the Patterns of Religion in Modern Europe', in D. V. A. Olson and D. Pollack (eds), *Role of Religion in Modern Societies*, 165–76. New York: Routledge.

Davie, G. (2010), 'Resacralization', in B. S. Turner (ed.), *The New Blackwell Companion to the Sociology of Religion*, 160–77. Chichester: Wiley-Blackwell.

Davie, G. (2014), 'Managing Pluralism: The European Case', *Society* 51 (6): 613–22.

Davie, G. (2015), *Religion in Britain: A Persistent Paradox*. Second Revised Edition. Hoboken: Wiley-Blackwell.

Davie, G., and L. Woodhead (2009), 'Secularism and Secularization', in L. Woodhead, H. Kawanami and C. Partridge (eds), *Religions in the Modern World: Traditions and Transformations*, Second Edition, 524–34. London: Routledge.

Davie, G., L. Woodhead and R. Catto (2016), 'Secularism and Secularization', in L. Woodhead, H. Kawanami and C. Partridge (eds), *Religion in the Modern World: Traditions and Transformations*, Third Edition, 551–70. New York: Routledge.

Dawkins, R. (2007), *The God Delusion*. London: Black Swan.

Day, A. (2009), 'Researching Belief Without Asking Religious Questions', *Fieldwork in Religion* 4 (1): 86–104.

Day, A. (2010), 'Propositions and Performativity: Relocating Belief to the Social', *Culture and Religion* 11 (1): 9–30.

Day, A. (2011), *Believing in Belonging: Belief and Social Identity in the Modern World*. Oxford: Oxford University Press.

Day, A., and L. Lee (2014), 'Making Sense of Surveys and Censuses: Issues in Religious Self-Identification', *Religion* 44 (3): 345–56.

Demerath, N. J., III. (1969), 'Irreligion, A-Religion, and the Rise of the Religion-Less Church: Two Case Studies in Organisational Convergence', *Sociological Analysis* 30 (4): 191–203.

Demerath, N. J., III, and V. Thiessen (1966), 'On Spitting Against the Wind: Organizational Precariousness and American Irreligion', *American Journal of Sociology* 71 (6): 674–87.

Dennett, D. C. (2007), *Breaking the Spell: Religion as a Natural Phenomenon*. London: Penguin.

Derkx, P. (2015), 'The Future of Humanism', in A. Copson and A. C. Grayling (eds), *The Wiley Blackwell Handbook of Humanism*, 426–39. Chichester: John Wiley & Sons, Ltd.

Dijk, T. A. van, ed. (2007), *Discourse Studies*. 5 vols. London: Sage.

Douglas, M. (1966), *Purity and Danger: An Analysis of the Concepts of Pollution and Taboo*. New York: Routledge & Kegan Paul PLC.

Drachmann, A. B. (1922), *Atheism in Pagan Antiquity*. Chicago: Ares Publishers.

Dutton, E. (2008), *Meeting Jesus at University: Rites of Passage and Student Evangelicals*. Aldershot: Ashgate.

Eccles, J., and R. Catto (2015), 'Espousing Apostasy and Feminism? Older and Younger British Female Apostates Compared', *Secularism and Nonreligion* 4 (1): 1–12.

Edgell, P., J. Frost, and E. Stewart (2017), 'From Existential to Social Understandings of Risk: Examining Gender Differences in Nonreligion', *Social Currents* 4 (6): 556–74.

Edgell, P., J. Gerteis, and D. Hartmann (2006), 'Atheists as "Other": Moral Boundaries and Cultural Membership in American Society', *American Sociological Review* 71 (2): 211–34.

Edinburgh Evening News. (2008), '106 Years of City Living for Southsider'. *Edinburgh Evening News*. 26 January. http://www.scotsman.com/news/106-years-of-city-living-for-southsider-1-1242572.

Edinburgh Evening News. (2015), 'New "Skin" for Ugly Edinburgh University Tower'. *Edinburgh Evening News*. 26 June. http://www.edinburghnews.scotsman.com/news/new-skin-for-ugly-edinburgh-university-tower-1-3813596.

Edwards, M. (2013), 'The First Millennium', in S. Bullivant and M. Ruse (eds), *The Oxford Handbook of Atheism*, 152–63. New York: Oxford University Press.

Elgot, J. (2014), 'Half of Brits Say Religion Does More Harm Than Good, and Atheists Can Be Just as Moral'. *Huffington Post*. 4 November. http://www.huffingtonpost.co.uk/2014/11/03/religion-beyond-belief_n_6094442.html.

Eller, J. D. (2010), 'What Is Atheism?' in P. Zuckerman (ed.), *Atheism and Secularity – Volume 1: Issues, Concepts and Definitions*, 1–18. Santa Barbara: Praeger.

Engelke, M. (2011), 'The Anthropology of After Religion'. Paper presented to *Atheism and Anthropology: Researching Atheism and Self-Searching Belief and Experience Workshop*. University College London.

Engelke, M. (2014), 'Christianity and the Anthropology of Secular Humanism', *Current Anthropology* 55 (S10): S292–301.

Engelke, M. (2015a), 'Humanist Ceremonies: The Case of Non-Religious Funerals in England', in A. Copson and A. C. Grayling (eds), *The Wiley Blackwell Handbook of Humanism*, 216–33. Chichester: John Wiley & Sons, Ltd.

Engelke, M. (2015b), 'On Atheism and Non-Religion: An Afterword', *Social Analysis* 59 (2): 135–45.

Engelke, M. (2015c), 'The Coffin Question: Death and Materiality in Humanist Funerals', *Material Religion* 11 (1): 26–48.

Engler, S. (2011a), 'Grounded Theory', in M. Stausberg and S. Engler (eds), *The Routledge Handbook of Research Methods in the Study of Religion*, 256–74. London: Routledge.

Engler, S. (2011b), '"Religion," "the Secular" and the Critical Study of Religion', *Studies in Religion/Sciences Religieuses* 40 (4): 419–42.

Enkvist, V., and P. Nilson (2016), 'The Hidden Return of Religion: Problematising Religion in Law and Law in Religion in the Swedish Regulation of Faith Communities', in A. Lind, M. Lövheim and U. Zackariasson (eds), *Reconsidering Religion, Law, and Democracy: New Challenges for Society and Research*, 93–108. Lund: Nordic Academic Press.

Eriksen, T. H. (2015), 'Rebuilding the Ship at Sea: Super-Diversity, Person and Conduct in Eastern Oslo', *Global Networks* 15 (1): 1–20.

Evangelical Focus (2019), '80% of Wedding Ceremonies in Spain Are Not Religious'.
Evangelical Focus. 11 April. http://evangelicalfocus.com/europe/4366/80_of_
wedding_ceremonies_in_Spain_are_not_religious.

Fairclough, N. (2003), *Analysing Discourse: Textual Analysis for Social Research*.
London: Routledge.

Fairclough, N. (2005), 'Critical Discourse Analysis', *Marges Linguistiques* 9: 79–94.

Fairclough, N., and R. Wodak (1997), 'Critical Discourse Analysis', in T. A. van Dijk
(ed.), *Discourse Studies. A Multidisciplinary Introduction*, 258–84. London: Sage.

Fairclough, N., J. Mulderrig and R. Wodak (2011), 'Critical Discourse Analysis', in T. A.
van Dijk (ed.), *Discourse Studies. A Multidisciplinary Introduction*, Second Edition,
357–78. London: Sage.

Fenton, C. (2002), 'A Century of Change in George Square (1876–1976)', *Book of the Old
Edinburgh Club* 5: 35–81.

Fergusson, D. (2009), *Faith and Its Critics*. Oxford: Oxford University Press.

Fincher, R. (2003), 'Planning for Cities of Diversity, Difference and Encounter',
Australian Planner 40 (1): 55–8.

Finger, A. (2017), 'Four Horsemen (and a Horsewoman): What Gender Is New
Atheism?' in C. R. Cotter, P. Quadrio and J. Tuckett (eds), *New Atheism: Critical
Perspectives and Contemporary Debates*, 155–70. Dordrecht: Springer.

Fitzgerald, T. (2000a), 'Russell T. McCutcheon's Manufacturing Religion', *Culture and
Religion* 1 (1): 99–104.

Fitzgerald, T. (2000b), *The Ideology of Religious Studies*. New York and Oxford: Oxford
University Press.

Fitzgerald, T. (2003), 'Religion and the Secular in Japan: Problems in History, Social
Anthropology and the Study of Religion'. *Electronic Journal of Contemporary
Japanese Studies*. July. http://www.japanesestudies.org.uk/discussionpapers/
Fitzgerald.html.

Fitzgerald, T. (2007a), *Discourse on Civility and Barbarity: A Critical History of Religion
and Related Categories*. New York and Oxford: Oxford University Press.

Fitzgerald, T., ed. (2007b), *Religion and the Secular: Historical and Colonial Formations*.
London and Oakville CT: Equinox.

Fitzgerald, T. (2011), *Religion and Politics in International Relations*. London:
Continuum.

Fitzgerald, T. (2015a), 'Negative Liberty, Liberal Faith Postulates, and World Disorder',
in T. Stack, N. Goldenberg and T. Fitzgerald (eds), *Religion as a Category of
Governance and Sovereignty*, 248–79. Leiden and Boston: Brill.

Fitzgerald, T. (2015b), 'Critical Religion and Critical Research on Religion: Religion and
Politics as Modern Fictions', *Critical Research on Religion* 3 (3): 303–19.

Flynn, T., and T. J. Coleman III (2014), 'Secular Humanism'. *The Religious Studies Project*
(blog). 27 January. https://www.religiousstudiesproject.com/podcast/tom-flynn-on-
secular-humanism/.

Foucault, M. (1973), *The Order of Things*. London: Routledge.

Foucault, M. (1979), *Discipline and Punish: The Birth of the Prison*. New York: Vintage Books.

Foucault, M. (1984), 'What Is Enlightenment?' in P. Rabinow (ed.), *The Foucault Reader*. London: Penguin.

Foucault, M. (1989), *The Archaeology of Knowledge*. World of Man. London: Routledge.

Foucault, M. (1998), *The History of Sexuality, Volume 1: The Will to Knowledge*. London: Penguin.

Francis, M. D. M. (2015), 'Why the "Sacred" Is a Better Resource than "Religion" for Understanding Terrorism', *Terrorism and Political Violence* 28 (5): 1–16.

Frazier, J. (2013), 'Hinduism', in S. Bullivant and M. Ruse (eds), *The Oxford Handbook of Atheism*, 367–79. New York: Oxford University Press.

Frost, J. (2017), 'Rejecting Rejection Identities: Negotiating Positive Non-Religiosity at the Sunday Assembly', in R. T. Cragun, C. Manning and L. L. Fazzino (eds), *Organized Secularism in the United States: New Directions in Research*, 171–90. Boston: De Gruyter.

Gale, R. (2004), 'The Multicultural City and the Politics of Religious Architecture: Urban Planning, Mosques and Meaning-Making in Birmingham, UK', *Built Environment* 30 (1): 30–44.

Gane, N. (2002), *Max Weber and Postmodern Theory: Rationalization Versus Re-Enchantment*. Basingstoke: Palgrave.

Ganiel, G., and P. Jones (2012), 'Religion, Politics and Law', in L. Woodhead and R. Catto (eds), *Religion and Change in Modern Britain*, 299–321. London: Routledge.

Garling, S. (2013), 'Approaching Religion Through Linguistics: Methodological Thoughts on a Linguistic Analysis of "religion" in Political Communication', *Approaching Religion* 3 (1): 16–24.

Geertz, C. (1968), 'Religion as a Cultural System', in D. R. Cutler (ed.), *The Religious Situation*, 639–88. Boston: Beacon Press.

Gergen, K. J. (1999), *An Invitation to Social Construction*. London: Sage.

Gervais, W. M. (2013), 'In Godlessness We Distrust: Using Social Psychology to Solve the Puzzle of Anti-Atheist Prejudice', *Social and Personality Psychology Compass* 7 (6): 366–77.

Gervais, W. M., and M. B. Najle (2018), 'How Many Atheists Are There?' *Social Psychological and Personality Science* 9 (1): 3–10.

Gholami, R. (2015), *Secularism and Identity: Non-Islamiosity in the Iranian Diaspora*. London: Routledge.

Gilroy, P. (2004), *After Empire: Melancholia or Convivial Culture?* Oxford: Routledge.

Goldenberg, N. (2018), 'Forget About Defining "It": Reflections on Thinking Differently in Religious Studies', in B. Stoddard (ed.), *Method Today: Redescribing Approaches to the Study of Religion*, 79–95. Sheffield: Equinox.

Gore, R., L. Galen, P. Zuckerman, D. Pollock and F. L. Shults (2019), 'Good Without God? Connecting Religiosity, Affiliation And Pro-Sociality Using World Values Survey Data and Agent-Based Simulation'. http://scholar.google.co.uk/scholar_

url?url=https://osf.io/preprints/socarxiv/jnpe9/download&hl=en&sa=X&d=888409 3425451073504&scisig=AAGBfm0imi5DxFMpPySTb98A6ouflOITbQ&nossl.

Gould, S. J. (1998), *Leonardo's Mountain of Clams and the Diet of Worms*. New York: Harmony Books.

Granholm, K. (2013), 'Esoteric Currents as Discursive Complexes', *Religion* 43 (1): 46–69.

Gray, J. G. (1962a), 'Buccleuch Pend', in J. G. Gray (ed.), *The South Side Story: An Anthology of the South Side of Edinburgh*, 73–4. Glasgow: W. F. Knox & Co.

Gray, J. G. (1962b), 'Introduction', in J. G. Gray (ed.), *The South Side Story: An Anthology of the South Side of Edinburgh*, 5–6. Glasgow: W. F. Knox & Co.

Gray, J. G., ed. (1962c), *The South Side Story: An Anthology of the South Side of Edinburgh*. Glasgow: W. F. Knox & Co.

Gray, W. F. (1962a), 'A Old Jewish Cemetery', in J. G. Gray (ed.), *The South Side Story: An Anthology of the South Side of Edinburgh*, 35–6. Glasgow: W. F. Knox & Co.

Gray, W. F. (1962b), 'Convent of St. Catherine of Siena', in J. G. Gray (ed.), *The South Side Story: An Anthology of the South Side of Edinburgh*, 29–30. Glasgow: W. F. Knox & Co.

Gray, W. F. (1962c), 'Sciennes Hill House', in J. G. Gray (ed.), *The South Side Story: An Anthology of the South Side of Edinburgh*, 13–14. Glasgow: W. F. Knox & Co.

Gray, W. F. (1962d), 'The Archer's Hall', in J. G. Gray (ed.), *The South Side Story: An Anthology of the South Side of Edinburgh*, 45–47. Glasgow: W. F. Knox & Co.

Greene, R. A. (2011), 'Religious Belief Is Human Nature, Huge New Study Claims'. *CNN Website*. 12 May. http://religion.blogs.cnn.com/2011/05/12/religious-belief-is-human-nature-huge-new-study-claims/.

Guenther, K. M. (2019), 'Secular Sexism: The Persistence of Gender Inequality in the US New Atheist Movement', *Women's Studies International Forum* 72: 47–55.

Guest, M., E. Olson and J. Wolffe (2012), 'Christianity: A Loss of Monopoly', in L. Woodhead and R. Catto (eds), *Religion and Change in Modern Britain*, 57–78. London: Routledge.

Gunning, J., and R. Jackson (2011), 'What's so "Religious" About "Religious Terrorism"?' *Critical Studies on Terrorism* 4 (3): 369–88.

Guthrie, S. E. (1995), *Faces in the Clouds: A New Theory of Religion*. New York: Oxford University Press.

Habgood, J. (2000), *Varieties of Unbelief*. London: Darton, Longman and Todd.

Hadaway, C. K., and W. C. Roof (1979), 'Those Who Stay Religious "Nones" and Those Who Don't: A Research Note', *Journal for the Scientific Study of Religion* 18 (2): 194–200.

Hall, D. D., ed. (1997), *Lived Religion in America: Toward a History of Practice*. Princeton, NJ: Princeton University Press.

Harris, S. (2007), *Letter to a Christian Nation: A Challenge to Faith*. London: Bantam Press.

Harrison, P., ed. (2010), *The Cambridge Companion to Science and Religion*. Cambridge: Cambridge University Press.

Harskamp, A. van. (2008), 'Existential Insecurity and New Religiosity: An Essay on Some Religion-Making Characteristics of Modernity', *Social Compass* 55 (1): 9–19.

Hassall, C., and I. Bushfield (2014), 'Increasing Diversity in Emerging Non-Religious Communities', *Secularism and Nonreligion* 3 (December).

Hedges, P. (2016), 'The Deconstruction of Religion: So What?' *The Religious Studies Project* (blog). 22 September. http://www.religiousstudiesproject.com/2016/09/22/the-deconstruction-of-religion-so-what/.

Herald Scotland. (2017), 'Atheism Booming in Scotland as Number of Those Without Religion Rises'. *HeraldScotland*. 17 September. http://www.heraldscotland.com/news/15540508.Atheism_booming_in_Scotland_as_number_of_those_without_religion_rises/.

Hervieu-Léger, D. (2000), *Religion as a Chain of Memory*. New Brunswick: Rutgers University Press.

Hewstone, M., N. Tausch, J. Hughes and E. Cairns (2007), 'Prejudice, Intergroup Contact and Identity: Do Neighbourhoods Matter?' in M. Wetherell, M. Lafleche and R. Berkeley (eds), *Identity, Ethnic Diversity and Community Cohesion*. Los Angeles: Sage.

Hingley, L. (2011), 'Photographer as Researcher in the Project "Under Gods: Stories from Soho Road"', *Visual Studies* 26 (3): 260–9.

Hitchens, C. (2008), *God Is Not Great: How Religion Poisons Everything*. London: Atlantic Books.

Hjelm, T. (2011), 'Discourse Analysis', in M. Stausberg and S. Engler (eds), *The Routledge Handbook of Research Methods in the Study of Religion*, 134–50. London: Routledge.

Hjelm, T. (2014a), *Social Constructionisms*. Basingstoke: Palgrave Macmillan.

Hjelm, T. (2014b), 'Understanding the New Visibility of Religion', *Journal of Religion in Europe* 7 (3–4): 203–22.

Hoesly, D. (2015), '"Need a Minister? How About Your Brother?": The Universal Life Church Between Religion and Non-Religion', *Secularism and Nonreligion* 4 (12): 1–13.

Hood, R. W., Jr., and Z. Chen (2013), 'Conversion and Deconversion', in S. Bullivant and M. Ruse (eds), *The Oxford Handbook of Atheism*, 538–49. New York: Oxford University Press.

Hopkins, P. E. (2007), 'Positionalities and Knowledge: Negotiating Ethics in Practice', *ACME: An International E-Journal for Critical Geographies* 6 (3): 386–94.

Horii, M. (2018), *The Category of 'Religion' in Contemporary Japan – Shūkyō and Temple Buddhism*. New York: Palgrave Macmillan.

Hormel, L. M. (2010), 'Atheism and Secularity in the Former Soviet Union', in P. Zuckerman (ed.), *Atheism and Secularity – Volume 2: Global Expressions*, 45–71. Santa Barbara: Praeger.

Hughes, A. W. (2015), *Islam and the Tyranny of Authenticity: An Inquiry into Disciplinary Apologetics and Self-Deception*. Sheffield: Equinox.

Humanists UK. (2019), 'Number of Non-Religious People in Britain Jumps by
    46%, New Figures Show'. *Humanists UK* (blog). 9 April. https://humanism.org.
    uk/2019/04/09/number-of-non-religious-people-in-britain-jumps-by-46-new-
    figures-show/.
Huntington, S. P. (2011), *The Clash of Civilizations and the Remaking of World Order*.
    New York: Simon & Schuster.
Hutchinson, S. (2011), *Moral Combat: Black Atheists, Gender Politics, and the Values
    Wars*. Kindle Edition. Los Angeles: Infidel Books.
Huxley, T. H. (1893), *Essays upon Some Controverted Questions*. New York: D. Appleton
    and Co.
Huxley, T. H. (1899), *Agnosticism and Christianity*. https://mathcs.clarku.edu/huxley/
    CE5/Agn-X.html.
Hwang, K. (2013), 'Atheism, Health and Well-Being', in S. Bullivant and M. Ruse (eds),
    The Oxford Handbook of Atheism, 525–36. Oxford: Oxford University Press.
Hyman, G. (2007), 'Atheism in Modern History', in M. Martin (ed.), *The Cambridge
    Companion to Atheism*, 27–46. Cambridge: Cambridge University Press.
Jackson, R. (2016), *Inclusive Study of Religions and World Views in Schools: Signposts
    Form the Council of Europe*. Strasbourg: Council of Europe Publishing.
Jäger, S., and F. Maier (2009), 'Theoretical and Methodological Aspects of Foucauldian
    Critical Discourse Analysis and Dispositive Analysis', in R. Wodak and M. Meyer
    (eds), *Methods of Critical Discourse Analysis*, 34–61. Thousand Oaks, CA: Sage.
James, A. (2013), *Assholes: A Theory*. London: Nicholas Brealey Publishing.
James, W. (1985), *The Varieties of Religious Experience*. Cambridge, MA: Harvard
    University Press.
Jantzen, G. (1998), *Becoming Divine: Towards a Feminist Philosophy of Religion*.
    Manchester: Manchester University Press.
Jenkins, J. (2019), ''Nones' Now as Big as Evangelicals, Catholics in the US'. *Religion
    News Service* (blog). 21 March. https://religionnews.com/2019/03/21/nones-now-as-
    big-as-evangelicals-catholics-in-the-us/.
Jenkins, T. (1999), *Religion in English Everyday Life: An Ethnographic Approach*. New
    York and Oxford: Berghahn Books.
Johnson, A. (2013), 'An Apology for the New Atheism', *International Journal of
    Philosophy of Religion* 73: 5–28.
Johnson, P. (2015), 'Feminism and Humanism', in A. Copson and A. C. Grayling (eds),
    The Wiley Blackwell Handbook of Humanism, 305–24. Chichester: John Wiley &
    Sons, Ltd.
Jong, J. (2015), 'On (Not) Defining (Non)Religion', *Science, Religion and Culture* 2 (3):
    15–24.
Josephson, J. A. (2012), *The Invention of Religion in Japan*. Chicago: University of
    Chicago Press.
Josephson-Storm, J. Ã. (2017), *The Myth of Disenchantment: Magic, Modernity, and the
    Birth of the Human Sciences*. Chicago: Chicago University Press.

Kaplan, B. L. (2007), *Divided by Faith: Religious Conflict and the Practice of Toleration in Early Modern Europe*. Cambridge, MA: Harvard University Press.

Kasselstrand, I. (2018), '"We Still Wanted That Sense of Occasion": Traditions and Meaning-Making in Scottish Humanist Marriage Ceremonies', *Scottish Affairs* 27 (3): 273–93.

King, R. (1999), *Orientalism and Religion: Post-Colonial Theory, India and the 'Mystic East'*. London and New York: Routledge.

Klug, P. (2017), 'Varieties of Nonreligion: Why Some People Criticize Religion, While Others Just Don't Care', in J. Quack and C. Schuh (eds), *Religious Indifference: New Perspectives from Studies on Secularization and Nonreligion*, 219–37. Dordrecht: Springer.

Knott, K. (1998), 'Issues in the Study of Religions and Locality', *Method & Theory in the Study of Religion* 3 (10): 279–90.

Knott, K. (2005), *The Location of Religion: A Spatial Analysis*. London and Oakville CT: Equinox.

Knott, K. (2008), 'Inside, Outside and the Space In-Between: Territories and Boundaries in the Study of Religion', *Temenos: Nordic Journal of Comparative Religion* 44 (1): 41–66.

Knott, K. (2009), 'From Locality to Location and Back Again: A Spatial Journey in the Study of Religion', *Religion* 39 (2): 154–60.

Knott, K. (2013), 'The Secular Sacred: In-between or Both/And?' in A. Day, G. Vincett and C. R. Cotter (eds), *Social Identities Between the Sacred and the Secular*, 201–21. Farnham: Ashgate.

Knott, K. (2014), 'Interrogating the Secular: A Spatial Approach', in R. van den Breemer, J. Casanova and T. Wyller (eds), *Secular and Sacred? The Scandinavian Case of Religion in Human* Rights, *Law and Public Space*, 34–55. Göttingen: Vandenhoeck and Ruprecht.

Knott, K. (2015), 'Walls and Other Unremarkable Boundaries in South London: Impenetrable Infrastructure or Portals of Time, Space and Cultural Difference?' *New Diversities* 17 (2): 15–34.

Knott, K., E. Poole and T. Taira (2013), *Media Portrayals of Religion and the Secular Sacred: Representation and Change*. Farnham: Ashgate.

Knott, K., V. Krech and B. Meyer (2016), 'Iconic Religion in Urban Space', *Material Religion* 12 (2): 123–36.

Knott, K., E. Poole and T. Taira (n.d), 'Notes on Discourse Analysis'.

Kolysh, S. (2017), 'Straight Gods, White Devils: Exploring Paths to Non-Religion in the Lives of Black LGBTQ People', *Secularism and Nonreligion* 6 (2): 1–13.

Kong, L. (1993), 'Ideological Hegemony and the Political Symbolism of Religious Buildings in Singapore', *Society and Space* 11: 23–45.

Kurczewska, J. (2008), 'Local Civil Societies in Poland at the Turn of XX and XXI Centuries: A Diagnosis', in S. Eliaeson (ed.), *Building Civil Society and Democracy in New Europe*, 130–58. Newcastle: Cambridge Scholars Publishing.

Landau, L. B., and I. Freemantle (2010), 'Tactical Cosmopolitanism and Idioms of Belonging: Insertion and Self-Exclusion in Johannesburg', *Journal of Ethnic & Migration Studies* 36 (3): 375–90.

Law, S. (2013), 'Humanism', in S. Bullivant and M. Ruse (eds), *The Oxford Handbook of Atheism*, 263–77. Oxford: Oxford University Press.

Leach, Sir Edmund. (2004), 'Humanism', in R. L. Gregoy (ed.) *The Oxford Companion to the Mind*. Oxford: Oxford University Press. http://www.oxfordreference.com/view/10.1093/acref/9780198662242.001.0001/acref-9780198662242-e-419.

LeDrew, S. (2016), *The Evolution of Atheism: The Politics of a Modern Movement*. Oxford: Oxford University Press.

Lee, L. (2012a), 'Being Secular: Toward Separate Sociologies of Secularity, Nonreligion and Epistemological Culture'. Unpublished PhD Thesis. Cambridge: University of Cambridge.

Lee, L. (2012b), 'Research Note: Talking about a Revolution: Terminology for the New Field of Non-Religion Studies', *Journal of Contemporary Religion* 27 (1): 129–39.

Lee, L. (2012c), 'Podcast: Lois Lee on Nonreligion'. *The Religious Studies Project* (blog). 8 October. http://www.religiousstudiesproject.com/2012/10/08/podcast-lois-lee-on-non-religion/.

Lee, L. (2013), 'Western Europe', in S. Bullivant and M. Ruse (eds), *The Oxford Handbook of Atheism*, 587–600. New York, NY: Oxford University Press.

Lee, L. (2014), 'Secular or Nonreligious? Investigating and Interpreting Generic "Not Religious" Categories and Populations', *Religion* 44 (3): 466–82.

Lee, L. (2015), *Recognizing the Nonreligious: Reimagining the Secular*. Oxford: Oxford University Press.

Lee, L. (2017a), 'Religion, Difference, and Indifference', in J. Quack and C. Schuh (eds), *Religious Indifference: New Perspectives from Studies on Secularization and Nonreligion*, 101–21. Dordrecht: Springer.

Lee, L. (2017b), 'Vehicles of New Atheism: The Atheist Bus Campaign, Non-Religious Representations and Material Culture', in C. R. Cotter, P. A. Quadrio and J. Tuckett (eds), *New Atheism: Critical Perspectives and Contemporary Debates*, 69–86. Dordrecht: Springer.

Lee, L., and C. R. Cotter (2018), 'Podcast: From Non-Religion to Unbelief? A Developing Field'. *The Religious Studies Project* (blog). 26 February. https://www.religiousstudiesproject.com/podcast/from-non-religion-to-unbelief-a-developing-field/.

Lee, L., and S. Bullivant (2016), *The Oxford Dictionary of Atheism* [Online]. Oxford: Oxford University Press.

Leeuwen, B. van. (2010), 'Dealing with Urban Diversity: Promises and Challenges of City Life for Intercultural Citizenship', *Political Theory* 38 (5): 631–57.

Leeuwen, T. van. (2008), *Discourse as Practice: New Tools for Critical Discourse Analysis*. Oxford: Oxford University Press.

Lesley, A. (2019), 'As It Turns Out, Anti-Atheist Stereotypes Aren't True'. World Religion News. 1 June. https://www.worldreligionnews.com/religion-news/turns-anti-atheist-stereotypes-arent-true.

Levey, G. B., and T. Modood, eds. (2008), *Secularism, Religion and Multicultural Citizenship*. Cambridge: Cambridge University Press.

Liang, T. (2010), 'Atheism and Secularity in China', in P. Zuckerman (ed.), *Atheism and Secularity – Volume 2: Global Expressions*, 197–221. Santa Barbara: Praeger.

Lim, C., C. Ann and R. D. Putnam (2010), 'Secular and Liminal: Discovering Heterogeneity Among Religious Nones', *Journal for the Scientific Study of Religion* 49 (4): 596–618.

Lincoln, B. (1992), *Discourse and the Construction of Society: Comparative Studies of Myth, Ritual, and Classification*. New York: Oxford University Press.

Lincoln, B. (1996), 'Theses on Method', *Method and Theory in the Study of Religions* 8: 225–7.

Lincoln, B. (2003), *Holy Terrors: Thinking About Religion After September 11*. Chicago: The University of Chicago Press.

Livezey, L. W. (2000), 'Communities and Enclaves: Where Jews, Christians, Hindus and Muslims Share the Neighbourhood', in L. W. Livezey (ed.), *Public Religion and Urban Transformation: Faith in the City*, 133–61. New York: New York University Press.

Lofton, K. (2014), 'On Teaching Religion. Essays by Jonathan Z. Smith. Edited by Christopher Lehrich', *Journal of the American Academy of Religion* 82 (2): 531–42.

Lopez Jr., D. S. (1998), 'Belief', in M. C. Taylor (ed.), *Critical Terms for Religious Studies*, 21–35. Chicago: University of Chicago Press.

Lundmark, E., and S. LeDrew. (2019), 'Unorganized Atheism and the Secular Movement: Reddit as a Site for Studying "Lived Atheism"', *Social Compass* 66 (1): 112–29.

Mackenzie, G. C. (2018), *The Irony of Reform: Roots of American Political Disenchantment*. London: Routledge.

Mahlamäki, T. (2012), 'Religion and Atheism from a Gender Perspective', *Approaching Religion* 2 (1): 58–65.

Mann, M. (2015), 'Triangle Atheists: Stigma, Identity, and Community Among Atheists in North Carolina's Triangle Region', *Secularism and Nonreligion* 4 (1).

Manning, C. J. (2015), *Losing Our Religion: How Unaffiliated Parents Are Raising Their Children*. New York: New York University Press.

Marten, M. (2014), 'The "No True Scotsman" Fallacy and the Problem of Identity'. *Critical Religion, University of Stirling* (blog). 8 December. http://criticalreligion. org/2014/12/08/the-no-true-scotsman-fallacy-and-the-problem-of-identity/.

Martin, C. (2010), *Masking Hegemony: A Genealogy of Liberalism, Religion and the Private Sphere*. London: Routledge.

Martin, C. (2016), 'Historicism, Reflexivity, and Our Discourses on Theory: Or, Why Lacan Is Not a Garnish'. *The Religious Studies Project* (blog). 21 April. http://www.

religiousstudiesproject.com/2016/04/21/historicism-reflexivity-and-our-discourses-on-theory-or-why-lacan-is-not-a-garnish/.

Martin, C. (2017), *A Critical Introduction to the Study of Religion*. Second Edition. Abingdon and New York: Routledge.

Martin, M. (2007), 'General Introduction', in M. Martin (ed.), *The Cambridge Companion to Atheism*, 1–7. Cambridge: Cambridge University Press.

Masuzawa, T. (2005), *The Invention of World Religions; or, How European Universalism Was Preserved in the Language of Pluralism*. Chicago: University of Chicago Press.

McAnulla, S., S. Kettell and M. Schulzke (2018), *The Politics of New Atheism*. London: Routledge.

McCloud, S. (2017), 'Religions Are Belief Systems', in B. Stoddard and C. Martin (eds), *Stereotyping Religion: Critiquing Clichés*, 11–21. London: Bloomsbury.

McCutcheon, R. T. (1997), *Manufacturing Religion: The Discourse on Sui Generis Religion and the Politics of Nostalgia*. New York and Oxford: Oxford University Press.

McCutcheon, R. T. (2003), *The Discipline of Religion: Structure, Meaning, Rhetoric*. New York: Routledge.

McCutcheon, R. T. (2005), 'Perils of Having One's Cake and Eating It Too', *Religious Studies Review* 31 (1–2): 32–6.

McCutcheon, R. T. (2007), '"They Licked the Platter Clean": On the Co-Dependency of the Religious and the Secular', *Method and Theory in the Study of Religion* 19: 173–99.

McCutcheon, R. T. (2014), *Entanglements: Marking Place in the Field of Religion*. Sheffield: Equinox.

McCutcheon, R. T. (2015), 'The Complete Inverse'. *Culture on the Edge* (blog). 30 August. http://edge.ua.edu/russell-mccutcheon/the-complete-inverse/.

McCutcheon, R. T. (2017a), 'Express Yourself', in R. T. McCutcheon (ed.), *Fabricating Identities*, 139–64. Sheffield: Equinox.

McCutcheon, R. T. (2017b), 'Introduction', in R. T. McCutcheon (ed.), *Fabricating Identities*, 1–9. Sheffield: Equinox.

McGrath, A. (2005), *The Twilight of Atheism: The Rise and Fall of Disbelief in the Modern World*. London: Rider.

McGuire, M. (2008), *Lived Religion: Faith and Practice in Everyday Life*. Oxford: Oxford University Press.

McKearney, P. (2011), 'Heard the One About the Pope? Sadly, Yes'. *The Guardian*, 21 June. http://www.theguardian.com/commentisfree/belief/2011/jun/21/stand-up-comedy-religion.

Meissner, F., and S. Vertovec (2015), 'Comparing Super-Diversity', *Ethnic and Racial Studies* 38 (4): 541–55.

Meulemann, H. (2004), 'Enforced Secularization – Spontaneous Revival? Religious Belief, Unbelief, Uncertainty and Indifference in East and West European Countries 1991–1998', *European Sociological Review* 20 (1): 47–61.

Meyer, B. (2015), 'How to Capture the "Wow": R.R. Marett's Notion of Awe and the Study of Religion', *Journal of the Royal Anthropological Institute* 22 (1): 7–26.

Meyer, B., H. Belting, P. Klassen, C. Pinney and M. Scheer (2014), 'Around Birgit Meyer's "Mediation and the Genesis of Presence: Toward a Material Approach to Religion"', *Religion and Society: Advances in Research* 5: 205–54.

Meyer, M. (2001), 'Between Theory, Method, and Politics: Positioning of the Approaches to CDA', in R. Wodak and M. Meyer (eds), *Methods of Critical Discourse Analysis*, 14–31. London: Sage.

Moberg, M. (2013), 'First-, Second-, and Third-Level Discourse Analytic Approaches in the Study of Religion: Moving from Meta-Theoretical Reflection to Implementation in Practice', *Religion* 43 (1): 4–25.

Modood, T. (2007), *Multiculturalism: A Civic Idea*. Oxford: Polity.

Modood, T. (2014), 'Understanding "Death of Multiculturalism" Discourse Means Understanding Multiculturalism', *Journal of Multicultural Discourses* 9 (3): 201–11.

Modood, T., and S. May (2001), 'Multiculturalism and Education in Britain: An Internally Contested Debate', *International Journal of Educational Research* 35 (3): 305–17.

Mortimer, T., and M. Prideaux (2018), 'Exploring Identities Between the Religious and the Secular through the Attendees of an Ostensibly "Atheist Church"', *Religion* 48 (1): 64–82.

Mumford, L. (2015), 'Living Non-Religious Identity in London', in L. G. Beaman and S. Tomlins (eds), *Atheist Identities – Spaces and Social Contexts*, 153–70. Dordrecht: Springer.

Murphy, A. R., ed. (2011), *The Blackwell Companion to Religion and Violence*. Chichester: Wiley-Blackwell.

Nash, D. (2019), 'Secularist History: Past Perspectives and Future Prospects', *Secularism and Nonreligion* 8 (1): 1–9.

National Records of Scotland. (2012), '2011 Census: First Results on Population Estimates for Scotland – Release 1A'. National Records of Scotland. http://www.scotlandscensus.gov.uk/documents/censusresults/release1a/rel1asb.pdf.

National Records of Scotland. (2013), '2011 Census: Key Results on Population, Ethnicity, Identity, Language, Religion, Health, Housing and Accommodation in Scotland – Release 2A (26 September)'. National Records of Scotland. http://www.scotlandscensus.gov.uk/documents/censusresults/release2a/StatsBulletin2A.pdf.

Neitz, M. Jo. (2011), 'Feminist Methodologies', in M. Stausberg and S. Engler (eds), *The Routledge Handbook of Research Methods in the Study of Religion*, 54–67. London: Routledge.

New Scientist. (2019), 'Most Atheists Believe in the Supernatural, Despite Trusting Science'. New Scientist. 30 May. https://institutions.newscientist.com/article/2204958-most-atheists-believe-in-the-supernatural-despite-trusting-science/.

Nongbri, B. (2013), *Before Religion: A History of a Modern Concept*. New Haven: Yale University Press.

Norman, A. (2011), *Spiritual Tourism: Travel and Religious Practice in Western Society*. London: Continuum.

Norris, P., and R. Inglehart (2004), *Sacred and Secular: Religion and Politics Worldwide*. Cambridge: Cambridge University Press.

Nye, M., and P. Weller (2012), 'Controversies as a Lens on Change', in L. Woodhead and R. Catto (eds), *Religion and Change in Modern Britain*, 34–54. London: Routledge.

Olson, E., P. Hopkins, R. Pain and G. Vincett (2013), 'Retheorizing the Postsecular Present: Embodiment, Spatial Transcendence, and Challenges to Authenticity Among Young Christians in Glasgow, Scotland', *Annals of the Association of American Geographers* 103 (6): 1421–36.

O'Mahony, E. (2014), 'Geographies of Religion and the Secular in Ireland'. *The Religious Studies Project* (blog). 27 October. http://www.religiousstudiesproject. com/2012/10/08/podcast-lois-lee-on-non-religion/.

Orsi, R. (2005), *Between Heaven and Earth: The Religious Worlds People Make and the Scholars Who Study Them*. Princeton, NJ and Oxford: Oxford University Press.

Owen, S. (2011), 'The World Religions Paradigm: Time for a Change', *Arts & Humanities in Higher Education* 10 (3): 253–68.

Owen, S. (2016), 'The Sacred Alternative', in C. R. Cotter and D. G. Robertson (eds), *After World Religions: Reconstructing Religious Studies*, 107–20. Abingdon and New York: Routledge.

Palmer, N., ed. (2007), *Memories of Nicolson Street Church, the Community Centre & the South Side*. Edinburgh: South Side Community Centre.

Paltridge, B. (2006), *Discourse Analysis: An Introduction*. London: Continuum.

Pasquale, F. L. (2007), '"Nonreligious" in the American Northwest', in B. A. Kosmin and A. Keysar (eds), *Secularism and Secularity: Contemporary International Perspectives*. Hartford, 41–58. CI: Institute for the Study of Secularism in Society & Culture.

Pasquale, F. L. (2012), 'The Social Science of Secularity', *Free Inquiry* 33 (2): 17–23.

Paul, G. S. (2010), 'The Evolution of Popular Religiosity and Secularism: How First World Statistics Reveal Why Religion Exists, Why It Has Been Popular, and Why the Most Successful Democracies Are the Most Secular', in P. Zuckerman (ed.), *Atheism and Secularity – Volume 1: Issues, Concepts and Definitions*, 149–207. Santa Barbara: Praeger.

Pew Research Center. (2009), 'A Religious Portrait of African-Americans | Pew Research Center'. 30 January. https://www.pewforum.org/2009/01/30/a-religious-portrait-of-african-americans/.

Pew Research Center. (2015), 'The Future of World Religions: Population Growth Projections, 2010–2050'. 2 April. https://www.pewforum.org/2015/04/02/religious-projections-2010-2050/.

Pinkerton, R. M. (2012), *Kirk o'Field and the Churches of Edinburgh's South Side*. Edinburgh: Roy M. Pinkerton.

Pinkus, J. (1996), 'Foucault'. August. http://www.massey.ac.nz/~alock/theory/foucault. htm.

Poole, E. (2012), 'The Case of Geert Wilders: Multiculturalism, Islam, and Identity in the UK', *Journal of Religion in Europe* 5 (2): 162–91.

Potter, J., and A. Hepburn (2008), 'Discursive Constructionism', in J. A. Holstein and J. F. Gubrium (eds), *Handbook of Constructionist Research*, 275–93. New York: The Guildford Press.

Quack, J. (2012), *Disenchanting India: Organized Rationalism and Criticism of Religion in India*. Oxford: Oxford University Press.

Quack, J. (2013), 'India', in S. Bullivant and M. Ruse (eds), *The Oxford Handbook of Atheism*, 651–64. New York, NY: Oxford University Press.

Quack, J. (2014), 'Outline of a Relational Approach to "Nonreligion"', *Method & Theory in the Study of Religion* 26 (4–5): 439–69.

Quack, J., and C. Schuh (2017a), 'Conceptualising Religious Indifferences in Relation to Religion and Nonreligion', in J. Quack and C. Schuh (eds), *Religious Indifference: New Perspectives from Studies on Secularization and Nonreligion*, 1–23. Dordrecht: Springer.

Quack, J., and C. Schuh, eds. (2017b), *Religious Indifference: New Perspectives from Studies on Secularization and Nonreligion*. Dordrecht: Springer.

Quillen, E. G. (2015a), 'Discourse Analysis and the Definition of Atheism', *Science, Religion and Culture* 2 (3): 25–35.

Quillen, E. G. (2015b), 'Everything Is Fiction: An Experimental Study in the Application of Ethnographic Criticism to Modern Atheist Identity', Unpublished PhD Thesis. Edinburgh: University of Edinburgh.

Quillen, E. G. (2015c), 'Assholes: A Theory of New Atheism'. *Everything Is Fiction* (blog). 20 January. https://everythingisfiction.org/2015/01/20/assholes-a-theory-of-new-atheism/.

Quillen, E. G. (2017), 'The Satirical Sacred: New Atheism, Parody Religion, and the Argument from Fictionalization', in C. R. Cotter, P. Quadrio and J. Tuckett (eds), *New Atheism: Critical Perspectives and Contemporary Debates*, 193–220. Dordrecht: Springer.

Raghavarao, D., and W. T. Federer (1979), 'Block Total Response as an Alternative to the Randomized Response Method in Surveys', *Journal of the Royal Statistical Society. Series B (Methodological)* 41 (1): 40–5.

Ramey, S. W. (2014), 'Textbooks, Assumptions, and Us: Commentary on Jimmy Emanuelsson's "Islam and the Sui-Generis Discourse: Representations of Islam in Textbooks Used in Introductory Courses of Religious Studies in Sweden"', *Method & Theory in the Study of Religion* 26 (1): 108–10.

Ramey, S. W. (2015), 'Introduction: Writing, Riting, and Righting in the Critical Study of Religion', in S. W. Ramey (ed.), *Writing Religion: The Case for the Critical Study of Religion*, Kindle Edition, 1–14. Tuscaloosa: University of Alabama Press.

Ramey, S. W., and M. R. Miller (2013), 'Meaningless Surveys: The Faulty "Mathematics" of the "Nones"'. *The Huffington Post* (blog). 7 November. http://www.huffingtonpost.com/steven-ramey/meaningless-surveys-the-f_b_4225306.html.

Reader, I. (2004), 'Ideology, Academic Inventions and Mystical Anthropology: Responding to Fitzgerald's Errors and Misguided Polemics', *Electronic Journal of Contemporary Japanese Studies*, March. http://www.japanesestudies.org.uk/discussionpapers/Reader.html.

Regnerus, M., C. Smith and M. Fritsch (2003), *Religion in the Lives of American Adolescents: A Review of the Literature*. Chapel Hill: National Study of Youth and Religion. http://youthandreligion.nd.edu/assets/102506/religion_in_the_lives_of_american_adolescents_a_review_of_the_literature.pdf.

Reisigl, M., and R. Wodak (2009), 'The Discourse-Historical Approach', in R. Wodak and M. Meyer (eds), *Methods of Critical Discourse Analysis*, 87–121. London: Sage.

Robertson, D. G. (2016), *UFOs, Conspiracy Theories and the New Age: Millennial Conspiracism*. London: Bloomsbury Academic.

Robertson, D. G. (2017), 'Am I a Religious Studies Scholar?' in R. T. McCutcheon (ed.), *Fabricating Identities*, 13–19. Sheffield: Equinox.

Robinson, L. (2016), 'Separation of Church and Soccer: The Impact of Secularization on Religion-Based Violence in Sports', in J. A. Goulet (ed.), *Religious Diversity Today: Experiencing Religion in the Contemporary World*, Volume 3: Religion Transforming Society and Social Lives, 145–68. Santa Barbara: Praeger.

Roemer, M. K. (2010), 'Atheism and Secularity in Modern Japan', in P. Zuckerman (ed.), *Atheism and Secularity – Volume 2: Global Expressions*, 23–44. Santa Barbara: Praeger.

Rogers, R., E. Malancharuvil-Berkes, M. Mosley, D. Hui and G. O'Garro Joseph (2005), 'Critical Discourse Analysis in Education: A Review of the Literature', *Review of Educational Research* 75 (3): 365–416.

Roxburgh, K. (2012), 'Growth Amidst Decline: Edinburgh's Churches and Scottish Culture', in D. Goodhew (ed.), *Church Growth in Britain: 1980 to the Present*, 209–19. Farnham: Ashgate.

Russell, B. (1997), 'Is There a God?', in J. G. Slater and P. Köllner (eds), *The Collected Papers of Bertrand Russell, Volume 11: Last Philosophical Testament, 1943–68*, 543–8. London: Routledge.

Sagan, C. (1995), *The Demon-Haunted World: Science as a Candle in the Dark*. New York: Ballantine.

Sawer, P. (2018), 'BBC Sticks to Atheist and Humanist Ban on Thought for the Day'. *The Telegraph Online*. 17 November. Infotrac Newsstand. http://link.galegroup.com/apps/doc/A562569925/STND?u=ed_itw&sid=STND&xid=711653d0.

Schäfer, H. (2004), 'The Janus Face of Religion: On the Religious Factor in "New Wars"', *Numen* 51 (4): 407–31.

Schenk, S., M. Burchardt and M. Wohlrab-Sahr (2015), 'Religious Diversity in the Neoliberal Welfare State: Secularity and the Ethos of Egalitarianism in Sweden', *International Sociology* 30 (1): 3–20.

Schielke, S. (2013), 'The Islamic World', in S. Bullivant and M. Ruse (eds), *The Oxford Handbook of Atheism*, 638–59. New York: Oxford University Press.

Schuh, C., M. Burchardt and M. Wohlrab-Sahr (2012), 'Contested Secularities: Religious Minorities and Secular Progressivism in the Netherlands', *Journal of Religion in Europe* 5 (3): 349–83.

Schuh, C., and J. Quack (2017), 'Embedded Indifference and Ways to Research It', in J. Quack and C. Schuh (eds), *Religious Indifference: New Perspectives from Studies on Secularization and Nonreligion*, 259–69. Dordrecht: Springer.

Schwartz, L. (2013), *Infidel Feminism Secularism, Religion and Women's Emancipation, England 1830–1914*. Manchester: Manchester University Press.

Scott, J. W. (2018), *Sex and Secularism*. Princeton: Princeton University Press.

Sedley, D. (2013), 'From the Pre-Socratics to the Hellenistic Age', in S. Bullivant and M. Ruse (eds), *The Oxford Handbook of Atheism*, 139–51. New York: Oxford University Press.

Sharify-Funk, M. (2013), 'Pervasive Anxiety About Islam: A Critical Reading of Contemporary "Clash" Literature', *Religions* 4 (4): 443–68.

Sherkat, D. E., and C. G. Ellison (1999), 'Recent Developments and Current Controversies in the Sociology of Religion', *Annual Review of Sociology* 25: 363–94.

Sherman, R. (2000), *Old Newington, Grange, Liberton & Gilmerton*. Ochiltree: Stenlake Publishing.

Siegers, P. (2017), 'Religious Indifference and Religious Rites of Passage', in J. Quack and C. Schuh (eds), *Religious Indifference: New Perspectives from Studies on Secularization and Nonreligion*, 171–92. Dordrecht: Springer.

Silver, C. F., T. J. Coleman III, R. W. Hood Jr. and J. M. Holcombe (2014), 'The Six Types of Nonbelief: A Qualitative and Quantitative Study of Type and Narrative', *Mental Health, Religion & Culture* 17 (10): 990–1001.

Silver, D. (2006), 'Religion Without Instrumentalization', *European Journal of Sociology/ Archives Européennes de Sociologie* 47 (3): 421–34.

Simmel, G. (1903), 'Die Grossstädte Und Das Geisterleben', in T. Petermann (ed.), *Die Grossstadt. Vorträge Und Aufsätze Zur Städteausstellung*, 185–206. Dresden: Zahn & Jaensch.

Simmons, J. (2018), '"Not That Kind of Atheist": Scepticism as a Lifestyle Movement', *Social Movement Studies* 17 (4): 437–50.

Smith, C. J. (2000), *Historic South Edinburgh*. Edinburgh: John Donald.

Smith, C., M. L. Denton, R. Faris and M. Regnerus (2002), 'Mapping American Adolescent Religious Participation', *Journal for the Scientific Study of Religion* 41 (4): 597–612.

Smith, G. (1989), *Atheism: The Case Against God*. Buffalo: Prometheus.

Smith, J. M. (2017), 'Can the Secular Be the Object of Belief and Belonging? The Sunday Assembly', *Qualitative Sociology* 40 (1): 83–109.

Smith, J. M., and R. T. Cragun (2019), 'Mapping Religion's Other: A Review of the Study of Nonreligion and Secularity', *Journal for the Scientific Study of Religion* 58 (2): 319–35.

Smith, J. Z. (1978), *Map Is Not Territory: Studies in the History of Religion*. Leiden: Brill.

Smith, J. Z. (1982), *Imagining Religion: From Babylon to Jonestown*. Chicago: University of Chicago Press.

Smith, J. Z. (1998), 'Religion, Religions, Religious', in M. C. Taylor (ed.), *Critical Terms for Religious Studies*, 269–84. Chicago: University of Chicago Press.

Smith, J. Z. (2000), 'Classification', in W. Braun and R. T. McCutcheon (eds), *Guide to the Study of Religion*, 35–44. London: Cassell.

Smith, J. Z. (2015), 'God Save This Honorable Court Religion and Civic Discourse', in S. W. Ramey (ed.), *Writing Religion: The Case for the Critical Study of Religion*, Kindle Edition, 17–31. Tuscaloosa: University of Alabama Press.

Smith, N., and C. Katz. (1993), 'Grounding Metaphor: Towards a Spatialized Politics', in M. Keith and S. Pile (eds), *Place and the Politics of Identity*, 67–83. London: Routledge.

Songhorian, S. (2014), 'Empathy and Sympathy: From Description to Prescription', in S. Bonicalzi, L. Caffo and M. Sorgon (eds), *Naturalism and Constructivism in Metaethics*, 51–72. Newcastle: Cambridge Scholars Publishing.

Speed, D., and T. J. Coleman III (2019), 'Nonreligion, Religion, and Public Health'. *The Religious Studies Project* (blog). 22 April. https://www.religiousstudiesproject.com/podcast/nonreligion-religion-and-public-health/.

Stack, T., N. Goldenberg and T. Fitzgerald, eds. (2015), *Religion as a Category of Governance and Sovereignty*. Leiden and Boston: Brill.

Stark, R., and W. S. Bainbridge (1985), *The Future of Religion: Secularization, Revival and Cult Formation*. Berkeley: University of California Press.

Stark, R., and W. S. Bainbridge (1987), *A Theory of Religion*. New York: Peter Lang.

Stark, R., and R. Finke (2000), *Acts of Faith: Explaining the Human Side of Religion*. Berkeley: University of California Press.

Stausberg, M. (2010), 'Distinctions, Differentiations, Ontology, and Non-Humans in Theories of Religion', *Method & Theory in the Study of Religion* 22 (4): 354–74.

Stausberg, M. (2011), 'Free-Listing', in M. Stausberg and S. Engler (eds), *The Routledge Handbook of Research Methods in the Study of Religion*, 245–55. London: Routledge.

Stein, G. (1985), *The Encyclopedia of Unbelief*. Buffalo, NY: Prometheus Books.

Stringer, M. D. (2008), *Contemporary Western Ethnography and Definition of Religion*. London: Continuum.

Stringer, M. D. (2013a), *Discourses of Religious Diversity: Explorations in an Urban Ecology*. Farnham: Ashgate.

Stringer, M. D. (2013b), 'The Sounds of Silence: Searching for the Religious in Everyday Discourse', in A. Day, G. Vincett and C. R. Cotter (eds), *Social Identities Between the Sacred and the Secular*, 161–71. Farnham: Ashgate.

Stringer, M. D. (2014), 'Religion, Ethnicity and National Origins: Exploring the Independence of Variables in a Superdiverse Neighbourhood', *Diskus: The Journal of the British Association for the Study of Religions* 16 (2): 88–100.

Stuckrad, K. von. (2003), 'Discursive Study of Religion: From States of the Mind to Communication and Action', *Method & Theory in the Study of Religion* 15 (3): 255–71.

Stuckrad, K. von. (2005), *Western Esotericism: A Brief History of Secret Knowledge.* Nicholas Goodrick-Clarke (trans.). London: Equinox.

Stuckrad, K. von. (2010a), *Locations of Knowledge in Medieval and Early Modern Europe: Esoteric Discourse and Western Identities.* Leiden and Boston: Brill.

Stuckrad, K. von. (2010b), 'Reflections on the Limits of Reflection: An Invitation to the Discursive Study of Religion', *Method & Theory in the Study of Religion* 22 (2): 156–69.

Stuckrad, K. von. (2013a), 'Discursive Study of Religion: Approaches, Definitions, Implications', *Method & Theory in the Study of Religion* 25 (1): 5–25.

Stuckrad, K. von. (2013b), 'Secular Religion: A Discourse-Historical Approach to Religion in Contemporary Western Europe', *Journal of Contemporary Religion* 28 (1): 1–14.

Sullivan, W. F. (2009), *Prison Religion: Faith-Based Reform and the Constitution.* Princeton: Princeton University Press.

Sutcliffe, S. (2016), 'The Problem of "Religions": Teaching Against the Grain with "New Age Stuff"', in C. R. Cotter, and D. G. Robertson (eds), *After World Religions: Reconstructing Religious Studies*, 23–36. Abingdon and New York: Routledge.

Sutherland, F. (2018), 'Beliefs in Scotland 2018: A Study of Religion and Belief in Scotland'. Edinburgh: Humanist Society Scotland.

Swain, S. A. (2016), 'What's in a Name, a Name Rearranged? Part 1'. *Practicum: Critical Theory, Religion, and Pedagogy* (blog). 20 April. http://practicumreligionblog. blogspot.co.uk/2016/04/whats-in-name-name-rearranged-part-1.html.

Taira, T. (2010), 'Religion as a Discursive Technique: The Politics of Classifying Wicca', *Journal of Contemporary Religion* 25 (3): 379–94.

Taira, T. (2012), 'New Atheism as Identity Politics', in M. Guest and E. Arweck (eds), *Religion and Knowledge: Sociological Perspectives*, 93–109. Farnham: Ashgate.

Taira, T. (2013), 'Making Space for Discursive Study in Religious Studies', *Religion* 43 (1): 26–45.

Tamney, J. B., S. Powell and S. Johnson (1989), 'Innovation Theory and Religious Nones', *Journal for the Scientific Study of Religion* 28 (2): 216–29.

Taves, A. (2018), 'What Is Nonreligion? On the Virtues of a Meaning Systems Framework for Studying Nonreligious and Religious Worldviews in the Context of Everyday Life', *Secularism and Nonreligion* 7 (9): 1–6.

Taves, A., E. Asprem and E. Ihm (2018), 'Psychology, Meaning Making, and the Study of Worldviews: Beyond Religion and Non-Religion', *Psychology of Religion and Spirituality* 10 (3): 207–17.

Taylor, C. (1998), 'Modes of Secularism', in R.Bhargava (ed.), *Secularism and Its Critics: Themes in Politics*, 32–53. New Delhi: Oxford University Press.

Temperman, J., and A. Koltay (2017), *Blasphemy and Freedom of Expression: Comparative, Theoretical and Historical Reflections After the Charlie Hebdo Massacre.* Cambridge: Cambridge University Press.

Thiessen, J., and S. Wilkins-Laflamme (2017), 'Becoming a Religious None: Irreligious Socialization and Disaffiliation', *Journal for the Scientific Study of Religion* 56 (1): 64–82.

Thrower, J. (1979), *Alternative Tradition: A Study of Unbelief in the Ancient World.* Boston: Walter de Gruyter.

Thrower, J. (1980), *Religion and the Rejection of Religion in the Ancient World.* The Hague: Mouton de Gruyter.

Thrower, J. (1983), *Marxist-Leninist 'Scientific Atheism' and the Study of Religion and Atheism in the USSR.* Berlin: Mouton de Gruyter.

Thrower, J. (1990), 'Has Humanism a Religious Dimension?' in A. F. Walls and W. R. Shenk (eds), *Exploring New Religious Movements: Essays in Honor of Harold* W. *Turner.* Elkhart: Mission Focus Publications.

Thrower, J. (2000), *Western Atheism: A Short History.* New York: Prometheus.

Tiefensee, E. (2011), 'Religiöse Indifferenz Als Interdisziplinäre Herausforderung', in G. Pickel and K. Sammet (eds), *Religion Und Religiosität Im Vereinigten Deutschland. Zwanzig Jahre Nach Dem Umbruch*, 79–101. Wiesbaden: VS.

Tomlins, S. (2015), 'A Common Godlessness: A Snapshot of a Canadian University Atheist Club, Why Its Members Joined, and What That Community Means to Them', in L. G. Beaman and S. Tomlins (eds), *Atheist Identities – Spaces and Social Contexts*, 117–36. Dordrecht: Springer.

Tomlins, S., and S. C. Bullivant, eds. (2016), *The Atheist Bus Campaign: Global Manifestations and Responses.* Leiden: Brill.

Towler, R. (1984), *The Need for Certainty: A Sociological Study of Conventional Religion.* London and Boston: Routledge & K. Paul.

Troeltsch, E. (1991), *Protestantisme et Modernité (Protestantism and Modernity), Selected and Translated, M. B. de Launay.* Paris: Gallimard.

Trzebiatowska, M. (2019), '"Atheism Is Not the Problem. The Problem Is Being a Woman." Atheist Women and Reasonable Feminism', *Journal of Gender Studies* 28 (4): 475–87.

Trzebiatowska, M., and S. Bruce (2014), *Why Are Women More Religious than Men?* Oxford: Oxford University Press.

Tuckett, J. D. F., and D. G. Robertson (2014), 'Locating the Locus of Study on "Religion" in Video Games', *Online – Heidelberg Journal of Religions on the Internet* 5 (February): 86–107.

Tweed, T. A. (2008), *Crossing and Dwelling: A Theory of Religion.* Cambridge, MA: Harvard University Press.

Valentine, G., and J. Sadgrove (2013), 'Biographical Narratives of Encounter: The Significance of Mobility and Emplacement in Shaping Attitudes Towards Difference'. *Urban Studies.* September.

Vassenden, A., and M. Andersson (2011), 'Whiteness, Non-Whiteness and "Faith Information Control": Religion Among Young People in Grønland, Oslo', *Ethnic and Racial Studies* 34 (4): 574–93.

Vernon, G. M. (1968), 'The Religious "Nones": A Neglected Category', *Journal for the Scientific Study of Religion* 7 (2): 219–29.

Vertovec, S. (2007), 'Super-Diversity and Its Implications', *Ethnic and Racial Studies* 30 (6): 1024–54.

Vertovec, S., ed. (2015), *Diversities Old and New*. London: Palgrave Macmillan.

Vetter, G. B., and M. Green (1932), 'Personality and Group Factors in the Making of Atheists', *Journal of Abnormal and Social Psychology* 27: 179–94.

Vincett, G., and E. Olson (2012), 'The Religiosity of Young People Growing Up in Poverty', in L. Woodhead and R. Catto (eds), *Religion and Change in Modern Britain*, 196–202. London: Routledge.

Vincett, G., and L. Woodhead (2009), 'Spirituality', in L. Woodhead, H. Kawanami and C. Partridge (eds), *Religions in the Modern World: Traditions and Transformations*, 319–38. London and New York: Routledge.

Vincett, G., E. Olson, P. Hopkins and R. Pain (2012), 'Young People and Performance Christianity in Scotland', *Journal of Contemporary Religion* 27 (2): 275–90.

Voas, D. (2009), 'The Rise and Fall of Fuzzy Fidelity in Europe', *European Sociological Review* 25 (2): 155–68.

Voas, D. (2010), 'Explaining Change over Time in Religious Involvement', in S. Collins-Mayo and P. Dandelion (eds), *Religion and Youth*, 25–32. Surrey: Ashgate.

Voas, D., and A. Crockett (2005), 'Religion in Britain: Neither Believing nor Belonging', *Sociology* 39 (1): 11–28.

Wallis, S. (2014), 'Ticking "No Religion": A Case Study Amongst "Young Nones"', *Diskus: The Journal of the British Association for the Study of Religions* 16 (2): 70–87.

Walsh, F. (2019), 'Less than Half of Irish Weddings Are Catholic'. *The Times*. 11 April. https://www.thetimes.co.uk/article/less-than-half-of-irish-weddings-are-catholic-qmw687xkg.

Walsh, R. F. (2017), 'Religion Is a Private Matter', in B. Stoddard and C. Martin (eds), *Stereotyping Religion: Critiquing Clichés*, 69–81. London: Bloomsbury.

Walters, K. (2010), *Atheism: A Guide for the Perplexed*. London: Continuum.

Warner, R. (2010), *Secularization and Its Discontents*. London: Continuum.

Watson, S. (2006), *City Publics: The (Dis)Enchantments of Urban Encounters*. London: Routledge.

Weber, M. (1949), 'Objectivity in Social Science and Social Policy', in E. A. Shils and H. A. Finch (eds), *The Methodology of the Social Sciences*, 49–112. New York: The Free Press.

Weber, M. (2001), *Protestantische Ethik Und Der Geist Des Kapitalismus*. S. Kalberg (trans.). London: Routledge.

Webster, J. (2013a), *The Anthropology of Protestantism: Faith and Crisis Among Scottish Fishermen*. New York: Palgrave Macmillan.

Webster, J. (2013b), 'The Eschatology of Global Warming in a Scottish Fishing Village', *Cambridge Anthropology* 31 (1): 68–84.

Wells, K., and S. Watson (2005), 'A Politics of Resentment: Shopkeepers in a London Neighbourhood', *Ethnic and Racial Studies* 28 (2): 261–77.

Wessendorf, S. (2014a), 'Researching Social Relations in Super-Diverse Neighbourhoods: Mapping the Field', *IRiS Working Paper Series* 2. http://www. birmingham.ac.uk/Documents/college-social-sciences/social-policy/iris/2014/ working-paper-series/IRiS-WP-2-2014.pdf.

Wessendorf, S. (2014b), *Commonplace Diversity: Social Relations in a Super-Diverse Context*. London: Palgrave Macmillan.

Whylly, S. (2013), 'Japan', in S. Bullivant and M. Ruse (eds), *The Oxford Handbook of Atheism*, 665–79. New York: Oxford University Press.

Wijsen, F. (2013a), 'Editorial: Discourse Analysis in Religious Studies', *Religion* 43 (1): 1–3.

Wijsen, F. (2013b), '"There Are Radical Muslims and Normal Muslims": An Analysis of the Discourse on Islamic Extremism', *Religion* 43 (1): 70–88.

Williams, A. Z. (2011), 'Faith No More'. *New Statesman*. 25 July. http://www. newstatesman.com/religion/2011/07/god-evidence-believe-world.

Williams, M. (2018), 'We No Longer Go to Church but Many Scots Still Have a Belief in Angels and Devils'. *The Herald*. 14 August. https://www.heraldscotland.com/ news/16416433.we-no-longer-go-to-church-but-many-scots-still-have-a-belief-in-angels-and-devils/.

Williams, R. H. (2015), 'Religion and Multiculturalism: A Web of Legal, Institutional, and Cultural Connections', *The Sociological Quarterly* 56 (4): 607–22.

Wilson, B. C. (1998), 'From the Lexical to the Polythetic: A Brief History of the Definition of Religion', in B. C. Wilson and T. A. Indiopulos (eds), *What Is Religion? Origins, Definitions and Explanations*, 141–62. Leiden: Brill.

Wilson, B. S. (1966), *Religion in Secular Society*. Harmondsworth: Penguin Books.

Wise, A., and S. Velayutham (2014), 'Conviviality in Everyday Multiculturalism: Some Brief Comparisons Between Singapore and Sydney', *European Journal of Cultural Studies* 17 (4): 406–30.

Wodak, R. (2011), 'Suppression of the Nazi Past, Coded Languages, and Discourses of Silence: Applying the Discourse-Historical Approach to Post-War Anti-Semitism in Austria', in W. Steinmetz (ed.), *Political Languages in the Age of Extremes*, 351–79. Oxford: Oxford University Press.

Wodak, R., and M. Meyer (2009), 'Critical Discourse Analysis: History, Agenda, Theory and Methodology', in R. Wodak and M. Meyer (eds), *Methods of Critical Discourse Analysis*, 1–33. London: Sage.

Wolf, G. (2006), 'The Church of the Non-Believers'. *Wired*. November. http://www. wired.com/wired/archive/14.11/atheism.html.

Woodhead, L. (2010), 'Epilogue', in S. Collins-Mayo and P. Dandelion (eds), *Religion and Youth*, 239–41. Surrey: Ashgate.

Woodhead, L. (2012a), 'Introduction', in L. Woodhead and R. Catto (eds), *Religion and Change in Modern Britain*, 1–33. London: Routledge.

Woodhead, L. (2012b), 'Strategic and Tactical Religion'. Paper presented at *Sacred Practices of Everyday Life Conference*, 1–15. Edinburgh: Religion and Society. http://www.religionandsociety.org.uk/attachments/files/1337692875_Woodhead-Tactical%20Religion-Edinburgh%20May%202012.pdf.

Woodhead, L. (2016), 'The Rise of "No Religion" in Britain: The Emergence of a New Cultural Majority', *Journal of the British Academy* 4: 245–61.

Wright, A. P. K. (2011), 'Heritage Report: University of Edinburgh, The Royal (Dick) Veterinary College, Summerhall'. http://www.edinburgh.gov.uk.

Yirenkyi, K., and B. K. Takyi (2010), 'Atheism and Secularity in Ghana', in P. Zuckerman (ed.), *Atheism and Secularity – Volume 2: Global Expressions*, edited by Phil Zuckerman, 73–89. Santa Barbara: Praeger.

YouGov. (2016), 'British People More Likely to Believe in Ghosts than a Creator'. 26 March. https://yougov.co.uk/topics/politics/articles-reports/2016/03/26/o-we-of-little-faith.

Zenk, T. (2013), 'New Atheism', in S. Bullivant and M. Ruse (eds), *The Oxford Handbook of Atheism*, 245–60. Oxford: Oxford University Press.

Zuckerman, P. (2007), 'Atheism: Contemporary Numbers and Patterns', in M. Martin (ed.), *The Cambridge Companion to Atheism*, 47–65. Cambridge: Cambridge University Press.

Zuckerman, P. (2010), *Society Without God: What the Least Religious Nations Can Tell Us About Contentment*. New York: New York University Press.

Zuckerman, P. (2011), *Faith No More: Why People Reject Religion*. New York: Oxford University Press.

Zuckerman, P., L. W. Galen and F. L. Pasquale (2016), *The Nonreligious: Understanding Secular People & Societies*. New York: Oxford University Press.

Index

9 781350 095243